Thinking Art:

Beyond Traditional Aesthetics

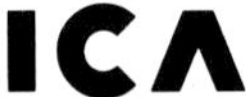

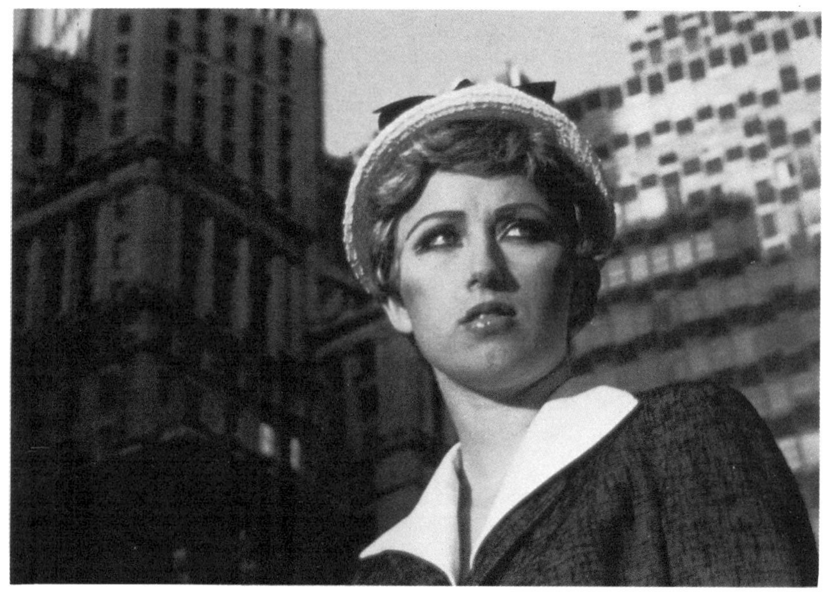

Cindy Sherman. *Untitled Film Still #21*, 1978. Black & white photograph.
(Courtesy Metro Pictures Gallery, NY)

Thinking Art:
Beyond Traditional Aesthetics

Edited by

Andrew Benjamin & Peter Osborne

Philosophical Forum

Institute of Contemporary Arts, London, 1991

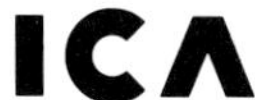

Institute of Contemporary Arts
The Mall, London SW1Y 5AH
Tel: +44 71 930 0493, Fax: +44 71 873 0051
British Library Cataloguing in Publication Data
Thinking art: beyond traditional aesthetics
I. Arts. Philosophy
I. Benjamin, Andrew 1952– II. Osborne, Peter 1958–
III. Institute of Contemporary Arts
700.1
ISBN 0-905263-18-9

Cover: Gerhard Richter. *Woman with Umbrella*, 1964 (detail).
(Courtesy of the artist)

Published with the assistance of the Arts Council of Great Britain.
The Institute of Contemporary Arts is an independent educational charity and while gratefully acknowledging the financial assistance of the Arts Council of Great Britain, Westminster City Council, the London Borough Grants Unit and the British Film Institute, is primarily reliant on its box-office income, membership and donations.

Produced by Graham Whybrow
Cover design by Arefin & Arefin
Printed by Hill & Garwood Printing Ltd.

Arts Council Funded

Contents

Publisher's Note

The ICA Talks programme aims to address a multiplicity of art forms from diverse critical perspectives, creating a space for cultural analysis which is unique outside of academic institutions. The Philosophical Forum was established to explore philosophy's contribution to the understanding of aesthetics and to contribute to new ways of thinking about art. The papers in this volume, originally presented as part of the Forum, reflect both the well-considered, widely varied positions of a number of cultural theoreticians and, to some extent, the spontaneity and open-endedness of live debate. The ICA is a place where practitioners and theorists can meet outside the realms of their particular disciplines and engage with each other and their audience in a way that, at best, enriches the intellectual and creative pursuits of the participants. *Thinking Art* is the first of a new series of documents which will stand as a tribute to the many who have brought their preoccupations to the ICA and helped to sustain a vital arena for the development of new ideas.

Linda Brandon, Director of Talks, ICA

Acknowledgments

The essays in this volume originated as talks presented at the Institute of Contemporary Arts, London, under the auspices of its Philosophical Forum, in the spring and summer of 1990. Linda Brandon and Judith Squires from the ICA Talks Department set up the Forum and organised the series, with Andrew Benjamin and Peter Osborne acting as advisers. Dr Brandt for the Goethe Institute, London, and Sylvain Bourneau for the French Embassy, London, provided financial assistance for the German and French speakers, respectively. Jo Foster typed the manuscript. Cara Kennedy obtained the pictures and the permissions for reproduction. Tony Arefin designed the book. Graham Whybrow acted as production editor in bringing the book to fruition in a remarkably short time after receiving the manuscript. Finally, we would like to thank all those who attended the series from which the papers originated, and contributed to the discussions, for making the book possible. We hope it will be followed by further series of talks and publications on the philosophical dimensions of contemporary cultural debates.

We are grateful to the following artists, galleries and publishers for permission to reproduce the images in the text:

Artists and architects

Greg Bright, Peter Halley, Donald Judd, Mary Kelly, Anselm Kiefer, Gerhard Richter, Massimiliano Fuksas

Galleries

Galerie Fanny Guillon-Laffaille, Paris
Jack Shainman Gallery, New York
Leo Castelli Gallery, New York
Mary Boone Gallery, New York
Metro Pictures, New York
The Pace Gallery, New York
Postmasters Gallery, New York
Sonnabend Gallery, New York
Waddington Galleries, London

Collections, agencies, individuals

Saatchi Collection, London
Museum of Modern Art, New York
Tate Gallery, London
Centre Georges Pompidou, Paris
DACS, London
ARS, New York
ADAGP, Paris
Associated Music Publishers Inc., a division of Music Sales Corporation
Peters Edition Ltd., London
Leslie E Spratt
Zoë Dominic
George Brecht
Pierrette Tal-Coat-Demolon

Every attempt has been made to trace the copyright for reproductions in *Thinking Art*. If there are any omissions, please contact the ICA.

Introduction

In what way, if any, does art need philosophy, or philosophy art? If it was once the role of philosophy to give art its concept, art has long moved beyond the parameters of its traditional aesthetic idea. Modern art constantly transforms the bounds of the 'artistic'. In this respect, it is inherently philosophical in its own right. But this apparent usurpation of the role of philosophy by art itself should not be thought to cut art free from philosophy as a discursive form. In a period in which works of art have taken upon themselves the burden of the definition of their status as 'art', the need for interpretation is both intensified and deepened. Philosophy, which had sought to remain above the critical interpretation of individual works, insofar as it had sought to provide a *universal* concept of aesthetic experience, is compelled to descend to their level to clarify and assess the claims about art that they embody. Philosophy and criticism become inextricably intertwined, and both become bound to art history.

For if, as has been suggested, it is one of the distinctive features of modern art that it makes new claims about art and exemplifies them at the same time – that it is made up of what might be called *originary exemplifications*, examples which bring into existence the ideas they exemplify – understanding these claims will necessarily involve placing them in relation to what has come before. This will not leave the meaning of earlier works untouched. The philosophical interpretation of modern art demands the reinterpretation of traditional forms. The reinterpretation of traditional forms depends upon the critique of traditional aesthetics.

The essays in this volume can all to a greater or lesser extent be described as part of an attempt to think art beyond the bounds of traditional aesthetics. Beyond traditional aesthetics – beyond the aesthetics of tradition – but not thereby necessarily beyond aesthetics. The first three pieces are all concerned with the fate of aesthetics after the critique of its traditional form. Different critical approaches map out, in each case, a different but always problematic future. For Peter Bürger and Howard Caygill it is the impossibility yet necessity of 'art' as an expression of the truth of modernity which is the focus of the analysis. While for Christine Battersby it is the gendering of such traditional terms as 'disinterestedness' and 'genius', and the possibility of a feminist reorientation towards the question of value, which is at stake. All three are agreed in their rejection of the option of simply stepping outside the framework of the concept of art and positing some completely new ('postmodern') approach; in the necessity critically to transform aesthetics, through reflection upon its inherent limits and contradictions.

The next three papers deal in differing ways with the meaning and heritage of abstraction in modernist painting, and the reaction to Greenberg's and Fried's 'formalist' interpretations of abstraction in particular. David Batchelor's discussion focuses on the sense in which abstract art may be said to 'represent', despite the fact that it does not 'depict', and the way in which it is thus able to work upon our expectations, habits and prejudices about the world whilst nonetheless 'abstracting' from it. Peter Osborne considers the return to painting after Conceptualism in the light of three competing perspectives on the meaning of abstraction in modernism, and in the context of current critical debates. The possibility of 'post-conceptual' abstraction, he argues with reference to Gerhard Richter's recent abstract work, turns upon the presence within the work of second-order representational strategies: those capable of registering a self-consciousness of the conditions of representation within representation itself. Margaret

Iversen's piece is concerned with the de-transcendentalising effect of Minimalism in the aftermath of Abstract Expressionism, and its relation to the development of feminist art practice in the late 1970s and early 1980s. The minimalist break, she suggests, was crucial to a particular strand of feminist art, but brought with it limitations of its own.

The essays by Andrew Benjamin and Michael Newman are mainly about the work of individual artists. Benjamin concentrates on five related paintings by Anselm Kiefer and traces the complex interplay of history and memory within them. Kiefer's work, he argues, is directed towards the overcoming of an active forgetting which, in the way in which it poses the problem of representation (the relation of representation to the event re-presented), demands a directly philosophical interpretation. Where Benjamin draws on resources from a way of thinking which numbers Derrida and Lyotard among its representatives, it is to psychoanalytic theory, and Lacan in particular, that Newman turns for the framework of his reading of Cindy Sherman and other recent photowork. Focusing on the interconnected issues of *trompe l'oeil*, the masquerade, and the representation of the feminine, Newman examines the possibilities of 'double mimesis' as a strategy for the allegorical deconstruction or 'undoing' of 'the question of Woman'.

Mimesis (representation through imitation) is also central to Christa Bürger's essay: a re-reading of the aesthetic positions mapped out in Thomas Mann's *Doctor Faustus* in the context of the debate about postmodernism. Here, however, it is Adorno rather than Lacan who is the point of reference. The concept of mimesis lies at the core of Adorno's aesthetics as the ineradicable other of the rational-constructive aspect of artistic production, to which it gives rise. (Expression, one might say, is for Adorno the effect of the mimetic impulse within the mediated whole of the work.) But the precise relation of mimesis to construction and its role in the crisis of modernism remain problematic. Bürger explores these issues by contrasting Adorno's aesthetics with the displaced presentation they are given by Mann in his creation of the fictional composer Adrian Leverkuhn. Whereas for Adorno the idea of 'a breakthrough beyond construction to expression' rescues modernism from the reification it figures, it is understood by Leverkuhn (in a prefiguration of postmodernist versions of the end of art) as a breakthrough beyond 'art' to reality itself. *Doctor Faustus* is thereby posited as a perspective from which to unpick the dialectical structure of Adorno's *Aesthetic Theory* to produce a more ambiguous modernism.

Alastair Williams continues the investigation of the contemporary relevance of Adorno's aesthetics in his examination of the dialectical development of advanced musical language. Once again, it is the relationship between mimesis and construction in late modernism which is at stake. Williams situates his readings of Boulez and Cage within the general terms of Adorno's aesthetic theory, but against the grain of his diagnosis of the impasse of musical modernism. Thus, rather than reducing their work to instances of Adorno's own application of his aesthetics to music, Williams uses the music to breathe fresh life into the philosophical categories, driving them beyond their self-imposed limitations, to produce new interpretive possibilities.

Georgina Born, on the other hand, contests the adequacy of any merely 'aesthetic' theory to the understanding of musical signification. Rather, she suggests, we must view music as 'culture' in the full mediated totality of its multi-textual forms. The argument is supported by a sketch of the contours of musical modernism and concludes with an engagement with Adorno's aesthetics which, whilst recognising it as 'the best start that we have', criticises it for exempting autonomous art from sociological critique.

Sandra Kemp, Jean-Jacques Lecercle and Sylviane Agacinski address the areas of dance, film and architecture, respectively. The dilemma of dance, Kemp argues, is that while in many ways it is closer to life experience than other arts, in its use of the body as a medium, its aesthetic appreciation 'does not reside in any known categories of the understanding'. All the existing models of aesthetic experience, and in particular, text-based ones, are deficient in one way or another. This sense of the inadequacy of linguistically-based models of meaning to the interpretation of movement recurs as the focus of Lecercle's presentation of Deleuze's work on cinema. Deleuze's *Cinema*, he suggests, is more of an occasion to philosophise about the image than a book on cinema as such: a philosophical consideration of a particular kind of image – the moving image – which opens onto a philosophy of the image in general. Its central contention is that 'the cinema is a Bergsonian art', and it is the rehabilitation of the French philosopher Henri Bergson which is at issue. If, as Bergson suggests, language betrays movement, it is in the movement-image that the philosophical inadequacies of language as a model of meaning will be most clearly revealed. As cinema provides philosophy with a model of the image, so philosophy – a philosophy of the image – provides cinema with a deeper self-understanding.

Architecture has been at the forefront of the debate about postmodernism, but there has been little philosophical writing of note about architecture. Agacinski's essay takes up the question of the meaning and possibility of monumentality in modern architecture to ask: 'What does the monument teach us about memory?' Monuments, it argues, are giving, not preserving, gestures. The issue for an aesthetics of architecture is thus not primarily a representational one, but a technical one – in the widest sense of technics as experimentation with the possibilities of matter. For the monument is primarily a memory of itself: a memory of the event of commemoration which, in the unpredictable future of its materiality, always exceeds that event itself.

Aesthetics has been constrained by the limits of what have been taken as paradigmatic instances of 'art'. Yet art has always exceeded universalising aesthetic definitions. If philosophy is to contribute to the deepening of our understanding of art, and art to an increased self-consciousness of the character and limitations of philosophy, each will have to be more open to the other than has hitherto been normal. The essays in this volume, diverse in both subject matter and approach, attest to a growing recognition of the necessity for such openness.

Andrew Benjamin and Peter Osborne
November 1990

Thinking Art:

Beyond Traditional Aesthetics

Aporias of Modern Aesthetics

Peter Bürger

The garden gnome

A garden gnome is no longer a garden gnome. This is the dilemma facing contemporary art that is circumscribed by the unhappy concept of postmodernity. Up to a certain point (let's take 1969, the year of Adorno's death, as a marker) a garden gnome was still a garden gnome. In the '50s Fritz Bürger could sing of the reappearance of this respected horticultural ornament as a sign that German life had returned to normal:

> Throughout the land, wherever you go,
> if you're out for the day or staying at home,
> that lovely little garden gnome
> Praise God – he's back to say hello!

In those days an author didn't need to be any more explicit about what a garden gnome actually meant: it was self-explanatory. But a garden gnome is no longer merely an object used to advertise one's petty-bourgeois taste. It has lost this neat quality of self-evidence now that the ironic appropriation of kitsch has been discovered as a sophisticated and effective means of distancing oneself from the most advanced forms of aesthetic consciousness. These days one cannot help suspecting a garden gnome of being an ironic quotation, which is particularly confusing given that a garden gnome in quotation marks is pretty much indistinguishable from what one might call the real thing. However lovingly you lose yourself in contemplation of these garden midgets, they simply won't give away who (or what) they are.

So what's happened? A border has disappeared that as late as Adorno had the unquestionable status of a metaphysical principle guaranteeing the possibility of art: the border between art and the culture industry and, simultaneously, between art and non-art. If one and the same garden gnome, as a piece of kitsch, signifies the total aesthetic incompetence of its owner, but as quotation testifies to an artistic sensibility so sophisticated as to be perverse, then the basis for Adorno's aesthetic value-judgements has become deeply problematic.

Theorists of the postmodern like Baudrillard have forced similar observations to the polemical conclusion: 'art has today totally penetrated reality. The aestheticisation of the world is complete.'[1] In other words, the border between art and reality has vanished as the two collapse into the universe of the universal simulacrum. It does in fact look as though art is in the process of disintegrating into pure exchange value on the one hand (the great auctions at Christie's and Sotheby's keep announcing new records for the price paid for a single painting) and advertising or design on the other. It would, however, be oversimplifying the issues merely to point out that there is more to art than the sale of Van Gogh's *Sunflowers* or Warhol's *Campbell's Soup Cans*. Instead, let's treat post-structuralist dramatisations of the situation as a theory of the state of contemporary art and put their claims to the test.

Imagine that specialists proved that the *Sunflowers* recently sold at some vertiginous price isn't in fact a Van Gogh. The picture would immediately lose most of its value, although the quality of painting hadn't altered in the slightest. Thus, even as the object of the most insane speculation the picture isn't pure exchange value but is shown to be dependent on the processes of canonisation undertaken by the institution of art in the creation of hierarchies and, moreover, on the assumption that only artistic genius is capable of creating values that no other branch of human activity can come anywhere near.

It is well known that Warhol's *Campbell's Soup Cans* are very similar to Campbell's soup cans. And that's exactly what makes them so confounding. Here we have a mere duplicate with all the rights of an original. The subject has put a line through its ability to express itself in a work of art. But it is precisely through this gesture of self-effacement that it gains an aura which far outshines that of an artistic ego still living off its own powers. At the centre of the institution of art is a subject proving remarkably resilient to its demise.

Here we come up against what I want to call the dialectic of the boundary. Borders such as those between art and non-art, or fiction and reality, do not disappear as easily as the theorists of the postmodern suppose. They exist, instead, constantly under the sign of their own disappearance. Adopting Baudrillard's metaphors, one could say that the border resists all attempts to abolish it. It could in fact be credited with all those spiteful qualities Baudrillard attributes to the object of seduction in *Les Stratégies Fatales*. It is, however, neither the boundary nor the object that is active, but us. Every time the border between art and the everyday is wiped away we react by reinstating it. Paradoxically, the institution that determines what does or doesn't count as a work of art gains in significance to the degree that works of art and everyday objects become indistinguishable.

The dialectic of the boundary points, in its turn, towards a dialectic of the subject. The subject is not the firm basis for action that it appears to be in the discussions of its disappearance. It is rather the precarious form of potential experience. Stuck between the Scylla of a rigid solipsism and the Charybdis of its dissolution in the Other, the subject is the ever fragile mediation between the general and the particular. The literature of modernity testifies to the continuing possibility of the failure of this mediation. To claim, however, that the subject has now finally retired in favour of an immediacy in which all oppositions are blandly dissolved is merely to invert the Enlightenment's discourse of progress and replace self-determination as the end of human history with a state in which all oppositions melt into what Baudrillard calls 'obscenity'. Any such gesture is, of course, still caught within a totalising thought that resists useful insights into the limited purview of theorisations of the present, continuing instead to dream those fantasies of intellectual omnipotence. Even the claim to mediate theory and praxis lives on in such scenarios of impending catastrophe, which ironically hope to promote the very things they describe.

And yet there is a moment of truth in all this talk of the disappearance of art that applies not just to our times but to aesthetic modernity as a whole. It can only be retrieved by the theoretical labour of tracing the aporia that underlies the construction of art in modernity.

The end of art

> The peculiar nature of artistic production and of works of art no longer fills our highest need. We have got beyond venerating works of art as divine and worshipping them... Thought and reflection have spread their wings above fine art... In all these respects, art considered in its highest vocation is a thing of the past.[2]

If aesthetic reflection keeps coming back to Hegel's famous declaration of the end of art, it can hardly be with the intention of reassuring oneself, with Hegel, of the primacy of the concept over aesthetic intuition. Any such argument is immediately contradicted by the fact that the most lively tradition of post-Hegelian thought, which despite all their differences binds Nietzsche, Heidegger and Adorno, decisively rejects Hegel's thesis and places art above the philosophical concept. Since attempts to theorise art in modernity are nevertheless forced to continue glossing Hegel's proposition, one might suppose that it contains more knowledge than can be produced by a reading that stays within the Hegelian system. If we follow up this hunch, we might come across what is genuinely scandalous about Hegelian aesthetics.

Hegel scholars have rightly insisted that the proposition that art has run its course by no means implies that after what Hegel calls the dissolution of romantic art there will be no more art, but that art no longer stands in any necessary relation to truth. Since, however, for Hegel art is essentially defined through its relation to truth, a reading that nevertheless sees the end of art as a termination is correct. When all that remains of the 'sensuous appearance of the *Idea*' is the sensuous appearance – which is what Hegel sees in Dutch genre painting (*AES* I, p. 599) – one is no longer talking about art in the strictly Hegelian sense even if it is still termed art in a weaker sense. Moreover, once one has realised that Hegel's concept of art is thoroughly modern in origin (its precondition being the development of idealist aesthetics from Kant and Schiller through to Schelling), one can begin to grasp the aporia underlying his aesthetics. Hegel's concept, developed systematically, of art as the double unity of the sensible and the intelligible (the Idea in its turn being defined as 'the unity of the concept with its reality' *AES* I, p. 134) only makes sense against a background of the modern experience of alienation. This concept, however, loses its validity for modernity precisely because art is itself dragged into the process of alienation that separates subject and object.

Let's go back over the reasons why Hegel, from the Jena period on, sees 'art in its highest vocation' (that is as the medium through which the truth of an era comes to expression) as a thing of the past. Modernity is the epoch of the great division between subject and object. Their reconciliation is only possible when mediated by the imagination (in religion) or the concept (in philosophy). Art, on the other hand, is characterised by a moment of immediacy:

> For the artist in his production is at the same time a creature of nature, his skill is a *natural* talent; his work is not the pure activity of comprehension which confronts its material entirely and unites itself with it in free thoughts, in pure thinking; on the contrary, the artist, not yet released from his *natural* side is united *directly* with the subject-matter, believes in it, and is identical with it in accordance with his very own self. (*AES* I, p. 604)

Hegel here refers to what Adorno will later call the mimetic moment of artistic production. The artist doesn't treat his subject-matter as an object that he must try to conceptualise but makes himself identical with it. His relation to it is mimetic. But this relation is out of step with modernity because it wants to go back to a time before division instead of trying to overcome it by means of the imagination or the concept.

Attempts to reproduce a Hegelian aesthetics this century have not, as far as I can see, come to terms with the fundamental aporia in Hegel himself who develops a general concept of art while simultaneously denying its application to the modern period. They have, instead, tended to hang on to one or other of the two sides of this contradictory whole.

Joachim Ritter and his pupils relinquish any strong concept of art which, like Hegel's, is committed to truth. Ritter illustrates 'the function of the aesthetic in modern society' – as the subtitle of his essay 'Landscape' puts it – with the example of the naturally beautiful, and by that fact alone ceases to be strictly Hegelian. The ability to represent nature as landscape arises at the same time and to the same degree that it is objectified and consigned to technical use by modern science. Ritter observes that the particular content of each landscape is of only secondary importance when it comes to 'its aesthetic construction' and that aesthetic landscapes, because they are 'essentially without a point of reference', are completely interchangeable. Thus, though he also writes of 'aesthetically mediated truth' in the same context, he cannot actually sustain his use of this concept, defined as it is by its reference to the particular.[3] His pupils have drawn the logical conclusion from this and given up any such concept.[4] Art's task is then limited to compensating for the disenchantment of the world brought about by the modernisation process by encouraging the development of 'the agent of a new enchantment'.[5]

Dieter Henrich, whilst recognising that Hegel's remarks about the art of his time do not correspond to his concept of art, finds too hasty a solution to the aporia by letting 'the limited purview of recent art' guarantee the modernity of the Hegelian thesis. In doing so he robs the aesthetic of the self-destructive tension that arises out of its unwillingness to come to terms with this reduction of its influence over the social totality.[6]

Adorno, on the other hand, hangs onto Hegel's strong definition of art and applies it to the products of aesthetic modernity, without taking into account the fact that this is impossible from the point of view of Hegel's theory. Just as, for Hegel, significant works of art of the past completely express the spirit of their time – *Don Quixote*, for instance, expresses the passage from medieval to modern times in which social conditions have changed so much that the knight's chivalry becomes lunacy [*AES* I, p. 591] – so for Adorno

Beckett's *Endgame* articulates the truth of late capitalist society as it performs the destruction of all the categories of autonomous thought or action normally attributed to the bourgeois subject. In both cases, the individual work is related to a social totality whose essence it fully expresses.

So, either the art of the modern period is no longer the expression of a truth, in which case any transhistorical concept of art must be abandoned leaving us instead with art as a means of compensating for what Max Weber called the world's disenchantment. Or, art remains the medium of truth even in the modern period, thereby controverting the thesis that art has run its course, but equally denying any historical development at the level of the concept. If one tries to keep hold of both sides of Hegel's argument, both a transhistorical concept of art that binds art and truth, and the declaration of art's demise, art becomes impossible with the onset of modernity. For it is then, paradoxically, the expression of a truth it is incapable of expressing. Furthermore, a concept of aesthetic truth grounded in a mimetic practice contradicts modern concepts of truth which always insist on its mediation. Art is the unity of subject and object, of the intellect and the senses and yet that is exactly what it cannot be since alienation is the fundamental condition of modern life. In a word: art in modernity is forever coming up against the conditions of its impossibility.

This Hegelian paradox could in fact be read as a formula for art in modernity, in as much as art becomes at once necessary and impossible. It becomes necessary when the individual, released from the ties of religion, realises that the world he hoped to mould through his own interventions is already firmly in place, and that his project of free action has been reduced to its opposite. He then demands a sphere in which his subjectivity is genuinely able to determine the results of his actions. This sphere is art with its institutionalisation of the concept of symbolic form (or the identity of form and content). The experience underlying the subject's demand for a sphere that allows it to interact with creations that perfectly correlate with the structures of subjectivity is the same one that decrees the impossibility of the creations it desires. For the moment when they did totally correspond to subjectivity, when intellect and senses were perfectly interpenetrating, would of necessity be the moment they were exposed as so many testimonies to their own falsity, flatly contradicting the subject's most basic experiences. Put another way, one could say that, left to his own devices, the bourgeois individual experiences himself as a free agent, though in reality his position is controlled economically by the exigencies of capital accumulation, politically by rivalries between power blocs. The subject that thinks of itself as capable of free action must in reality experience a dependency on processes that are themselves no longer governed by conscious thought. During the Enlightenment, the subject frees itself from a destiny controlled by otherworldly powers only to have human history appear once more as a matter of fate over which it has no control. The modern desire for art arises out of this disjuncture. Because the individual does not realise him- or herself in actions in and for society but only in pursuit of private advantage, he/she experiences society as an external limit to action rather than as something in essence universal. All ends become mere means; the category of the universal or general which previously endowed meaning is then itself stripped of any validity. Even the bourgeois subject, however, is incapable of living without any purpose beyond the simple reproduction of physical existence. Thus, as history withdraws as a possible arena for sensuous experience, so art becomes the site of imaginary self-realisation. The concept of symbolic form reunites the poles torn apart by the individual's real existence. Yet the modern individual knows this reunification of opposites to be illusory. If he/she wants to rescue a truth for him- or herself, he/she must grapple with the separation of subject and object, of ego and the world. Thus alienation necessarily penetrates into the realm of art. The experience of meaning that the subject longed for becomes the never-ending story of the representation of its absence.

Infinite reversals

To theorise how alienation becomes inscribed in art itself one must trace each of the paths adopted by the various attempts at self-realisation. On the one hand, there is the stubborn insistence on the ego's power to shape reality (the course taken by early German Romanticism); on the other, a recognition of the power of the factitious (the course of Realism). Both projects are modern in as much as they are informed by the experience of alienation. Yet this is true to an even greater extent of the movements reacting against Romanticism and Realism in the wake of the failure of the revolutions in 1848, as they highlight the aporias inherent in both the Romantic and the Realistic projects.

The Romantics take modernity's promise of self-realisation at face value. The origin and end of their action is the ego. Pitted against the bourgeois obsession with acquisition and the pursuit of purely material ends, the Romantic ego hopes to experience itself as a freely acting subject. But the object of its activity is of course not the physical world but the world of words. These lie totally at its disposal and it seizes passionately at the sheer endlessness of possible combinations. In this play of concepts, the Romantic subject discovers its own productivity; a productivity that need not crystallise into art but rather remains a form of life. This plan to nourish self-realisation solely from the resources of the ego, or even two interrelated egos, cannot, however, succeed; the Romantic subject is confronted instead with its own groundlessness. Discovering that its limitless power over linguistic combinations is simply the obverse of its impotence in the face of reality, it escapes into the bosom of the church. All that remains is the insight from which it retreated that omnipotence and impotence are indistinguishable in the play of a language that has lost its referent.

For the Realist, on the other hand, language is a tool for the unproblematic representation of reality. Yet this undertaking also threatens to flip into its opposite, in a way the Realist himself, of course, doesn't notice. His belief, inspired by a positivist science, that he could grasp the reality of an era, is in fact only the fantasy of taking possession of a world that is totally transparent. This becomes most obvious in the presentation of characters where we are allowed to see the figures from both inside and out, a device whose artificiality a later generation of modernist writers would thoroughly expose:

> These composite beings, simultaneously internal and external, transparent and opaque, proliferated during the nineteenth century and the first half of the twentieth; they are the children of Realism but themselves bear witness to its perfect unreality.[7]

Literary modernity can be described neither as the sum of its themes and motives, nor as a collection of devices and techniques; it can only be grasped in its entirety as a movement. This movement is twofold. It consists in the subject's constant pursuit of, but constant failure to achieve, self-realisation, and in a search for reality that can only discover its own devices. Art in modernity is thus the site of constant reversals. The omnipotent Romantic ego uses language to discover nothing but its own impotence; the work produced by the Realist with his hunger for reality reveals a textual reality that is the product of literary technique. This double aporia develops as an insight that the subject has into itself and the world but – and this is the decisive point – it can only experience it in the work itself.

Under the sign of modernity the world collapses into the torn halves of subject and object. Yet they re-emerge in art not as a bald opposition but as the incessant mutual inversions of the categories of form and content. In this constant play of form replacing content and content replacing form, meaning can only figure under the threat of its extinction. The author whose naïve trust in the transparency of his medium makes him think he can simply posit meaning (like the Naturalist with his belief in positivist theories of social environment) discovers instead a conspiracy of detail that turns against the overall intention of the work, foregrounding itself as a surreal allegory. Conversely, the attempt to reduce words to the pure materiality of sound-patterns can only show the reader that they still in fact carry meaning.

This play of form and content has its driving force in the discourses that construct the work of art as a work of art. By which I mean not modern art's dependence on explicatory commentary, but something more fundamental: the fact that aesthetic discourse doesn't attach itself to works of art after the fact but is rather that which makes them possible in the first place. We have works of art because we have the institution. If this weren't the case we would only have beautiful objects or fetishes.

Attempts to pinpoint the principles underlying the institution of art can only reveal its peculiar groundlessness. We saw this in the aporetic construction of Hegel's aesthetics, according to which art is simultaneously necessary and impossible in bourgeois society. Necessary because once religious world views have lost their validity people are left looking for a sphere in which they can experience their own actions as meaningful rather than simply expedient. Impossible because the symbolic form which should satisfy the desire for meaning is also shown flatly to contradict the subject's basic experience of alienation; and also because the artist's mimetic approach is incompatible with modern concepts of truth. Art's contradictory relationship to society is not, however, dialectical. Thus there can be no solution or synthesis, only the endless play of displacements in new guises. Yet it is in and through these guises that we experience the world.

Autonomous art has been accompanied by the consciousness of its own inadequacy since its inception. It is only once its autonomy has been institutionalised that it can stake its claim to truth alongside science and ethics, but its consequent status as fiction (what's known as the category of aesthetic appearance) robs it of any claim to validity or real purchase. Thus modern art rebels against its status either by construing itself as political, as in Heine's theory of the end of the artistic epoch, or by declaring that the void that it recognises itself to be is the whole purpose. This is, for instance, the case with Aestheticism, or with Mallarmé's dictum that 'the world was made to culminate in a beautiful book'.[8] Politicisation or messianic over-inflation are the extremes into which modern art must throw itself as soon as it becomes conscious of the constraints dictated by autonomy. And once these positions have been passed through, all that remains is to attack the institution, a task undertaken by the movements of the historical avant-garde in the wake of the shocking experience of the Great War. Their slogan: revolutionise life by liberating the imagination from the strait-jacket of the institution. With violent panache, the surrealists declare themselves to be above the contradictions of modern life and announce the possibility of actions in which chance becomes the objective ally of the subject's desire for self-realisation.

We know that the project was bound to fail. But that doesn't mean that it has disappeared over the horizon of aesthetic experience. On the contrary, since the historical avant-garde, art's self-sublation figures as one of its poles, the other being the self-contained work. Aesthetic experience cannot get beyond the attack on the institution, because its failure seems only to reinforce the institution's boundary. The catastrophic scenarios of postmodernity with their declarations of the imminent end of art have evidently missed out on an aspect of aesthetic experience continually encountered by artists since the historical avant-garde; namely that once you're inside the place called Art there's no getting out again. As if you were King Midas, everything you touch turns to art. Even the blank refusal to produce anything at all is transformed into an aesthetic act. Art, to the outsider, appears as a realm of freedom. To the artist, however, it is a state of constant damnation from which there is no escape. No one has described this aspect of the modern artist's predicament as eloquently as Maurice Blanchot.

What these days goes by the name of post-modernism could more accurately be termed 'post-avant-garde': in other words, an epoch marked by the failure of the historical avant-garde's attack on the artistic institution. Its failure shines a stark light on the position of art in bourgeois society. Art has, so to speak, outlived the realisation of its utopian promise. It now knows what it is. The paradise that the avant-garde wanted to bring down to earth has arrived and is now available to everyone. That's one side of the coin. The other is the survival of a project that is in every respect impossible, but that is still attempted by individuals. It remains a mystery for theory that people should still write and paint. It has, after all, pointed out the aporias that inevitably stymie any such practice. And yet they go on regardless. Some people stake their entire life on it. It seems that the only chance of meaningful action in modernity is whole-hearted engagement with meaninglessness. Consistency is conditional on a readiness to contradict oneself. On the horizon one can discern the figure of Joseph Beuys, who surrendered himself totally to the media but simultaneously worked on esoteric drawings. Art's attempt to assimilate itself to political agitation is the impossible gesture that must be for ever enacted and then retracted. The new life will not come, but it remains an alternative we must continue to suggest.

(translated by Ben Morgan)

Notes

This paper uses the analyses in my *Prosa der Moderne* (Ffm, 1988) as a way into the contemporary debate in aesthetics.

1. J. Baudrillard, 'Towards the vanishing point of art' in F. Roetzer and S. Rogenhofer (eds.), *Kunst machen? Gespraeche und Essays*, Munich, 1990, p. 206; cf. also R. A. Berman who suggests that the postmodern aestheticisation of everyday life can actually be traced back to the historical avant-garde movements ('Konsumgesellschaft. Das Erbe der Avant-garde und die falsche Aufhebung der Aesthetischen Autonomie' in Christa and Peter Bürger (eds.), *Postmoderne: Alltag, Allegorie und Avant-garde*, Ffm, 1987, pp. 56–71, esp. p.68ff.).
2. G. W. F. Hegel, *Aesthetics: Lectures on Fine Art*, trans. T. M. Knox, 2 volumes, Oxford, 1975, pp. 21–22. Hereafter cited in the text as *AES* with volume and page number.
3. J. Ritter, 'Landschaft' in his *Subjektivitaet*, Ffm, 1974, pp. 141–90; cf. esp. p. 157 and p. 183.
4. Cf., for example, W. Oelmueller's contribution to the discussion in his *Kolloquium Kunst und Philosophie 3: das Kunstwerk*, Paderbotn, 1983, p. 204.
5. Cf. O. Marquard, 'Kunst als Kompensation ihres Endes' in W. Oelmueller (ed.), *Kolloquium Kunst und Philosophie 1: Aesthetische Erfahrung*, Paderborn, 1981, p. 161. The concept doesn't actually appear in the two essays by J. Ritter that Marquard cites when presenting his compensation thesis; Ritter does use it, however, to describe the function of the humanities (cf. *Subjektivitaet*, p. 131).
6. D. Henrich, 'Kunst und Kunstphilosophie der Gegenwart' in W. Iser (ed.), *Immanente Aesthetik, Aesthetische Reflexion*, Munich, 1966, pp. 11–32; esp. p. 16 and p. 19.
7. J.-P. Sartre, 'Je – tu – il' in his *Situations IX*, Paris, 1972, p. 294.
8. S. Mallarmé, *Oeuvres completes*, ed. H. Mondor and G. Jean-Hubry, Paris, 1945, p. 872.

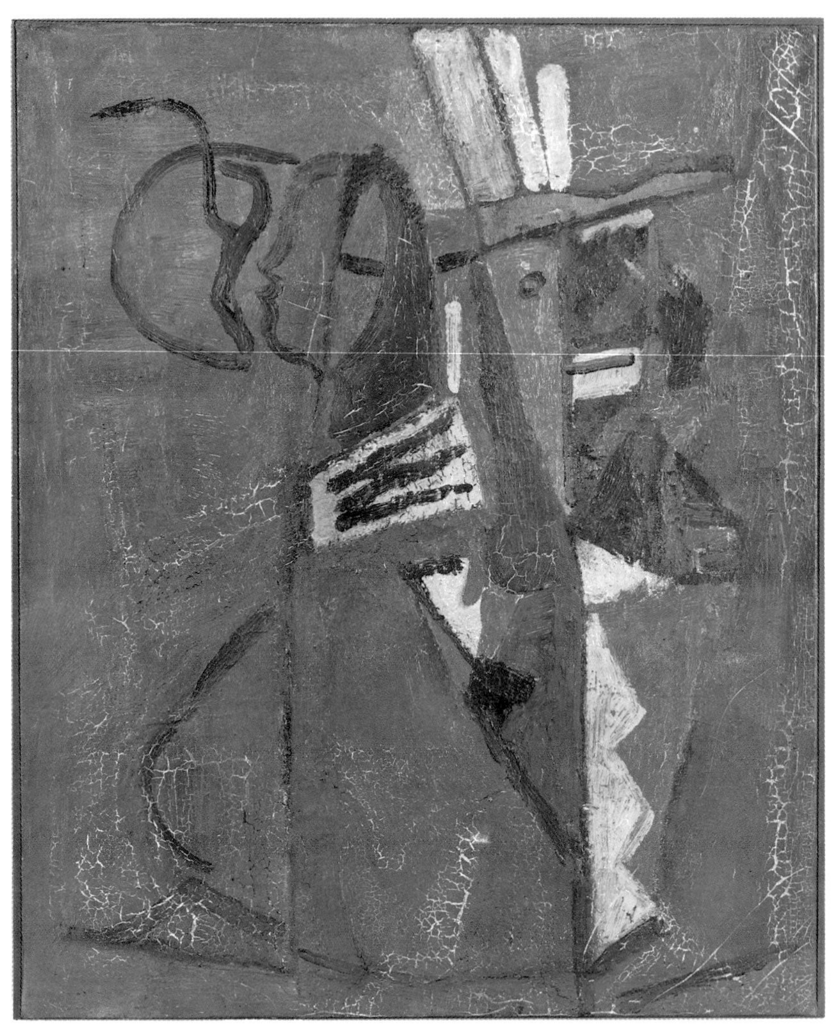

Bram van Velde. *Sans titre, Montrouge*, 1937. Paris, Collection Pompidou. (Copyright DACS 1991)

Aesthetics and the Obligation of Art

Howard Caygill

How to think of art without aesthetic, while recognising that we cannot avoid thinking aesthetically? How to think what might be 'without' or 'beyond' aesthetic, since aesthetic already includes its other, which it calls 'sublime'? And finally, how to meet the *obligation* of art without aesthetic? I will look at two texts and a body of work which address these questions. First is Samuel Beckett's *Three Dialogues* (1949) between 'B' and 'D' on the painters Tal Coat, André Masson, and Bram van Velde, which marked the culmination of a series of writings on the necessity of not-painting. Then follows Heidegger's encounter between aesthetic and Japanese art in his *Dialogue on Language between a Japanese and a Questioner* written in 1953–54. The third is the art of Greg Bright, whose recent work thematises the difficult exit from aesthetic which is at stake in the two texts.

Both texts are wary of Hegel's concession in the Introduction to the *Aesthetics* to 'let the word "Aesthetics" stand; as a mere name it is a matter of indifference to us, and besides it has meanwhile passed over into common speech'.[1] Hegel also shows that it is because aesthetic has become 'well known, but not recognised', that it has become a 'matter of indifference' and thus dangerous. Beckett wearies of aesthetic, but is far from indifferent to it.

For him aesthetic designates a cluster of oppositions which confine art to exchange – art facilitates the traffic between form and matter, freedom and necessity, expression and expressed – art the reconciler, 'But we begin to weary of it, do we not.'[1] Heidegger too is far from indifferent to aesthetic, describing it as a framing (*Gestell*) 'so treacherous, that is to say, so all-embracing, that it can capture all other kinds of experience of art and its nature'.[2]

Yet if it is so embracing, how is it possible to think the obligation of art without it? Perhaps it is not possible, or at least not within the philosophical resources available to us. The most supple of philosophical forms – the dialogue – apparently fails the obligation. Both of these 'reflections' on art without aesthetic are dialogues, but extremely fractured ones, dialogues which refuse dialogue. In Beckett's 'dialogue' on Tal Coat, 'D' reduces 'B' to silence; in the dialogue on Masson 'B' 'exits weeping'; on being accused of absurdity in the third dialogue, 'B' admits guilt, but only 'a fortnight later'. The exchange in Heidegger's dialogue founders in untranslatability, 'muddy sources', mutual incomprehension and interruption. The conversation is haunted by the 'greatest danger' facing a dialogue, which is to smother heterogeneity through the achievement of consensus, a fate to which the dialogue notoriously succumbs. Both writers are aware that the obligation of art cannot be recognised within aesthetic oppositions, but may be met in their negation or excess.

Aesthetic, the mere name, situates art within an economy by making it a messenger between aesthetic oppositions. Against this Beckett dreams 'of an art unresentful of its insuperable indigence and too proud for the farce of giving and receiving' (p. 141). Such an art refuses the terms of trade offered by aesthetic. Heidegger too finds art confined to the metaphysical oppositions of aesthetic, and suggests that if we think of another site – 'We leave it without a name' – we can think of a 'way to give thought to the nature of aesthetics, and direct it back within its boundaries' (p. 42). So instead of being bound by aesthetic we become aware of its metaphysical boundaries, instead of being directed by it, we disturb its directions by intimations of a different, unnamed site.

Both Beckett's and Heidegger's texts are indirect; they point to some

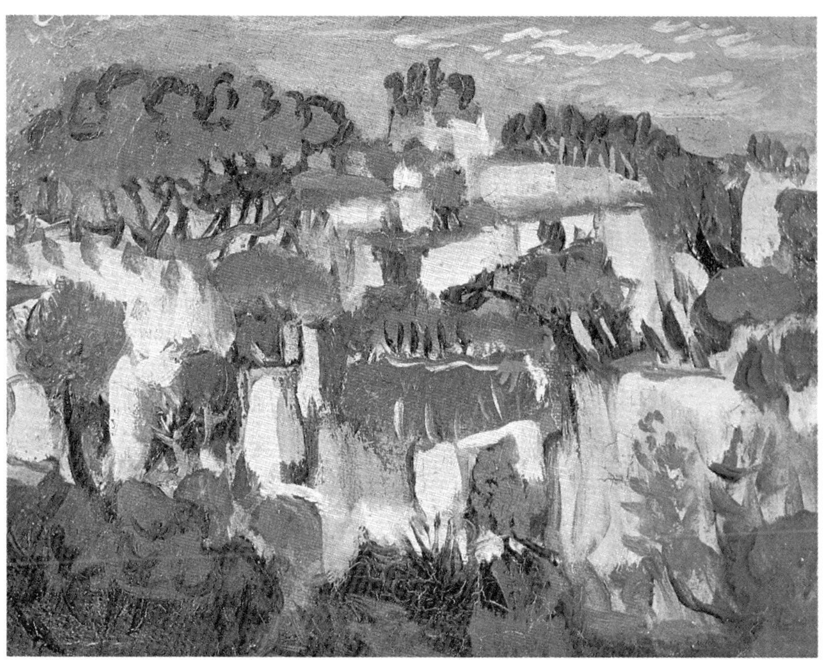

Pierre Tal-Coat. *Paysage du Tholonet*, 1941. Oil on canvas. Neuilly, Collection Maurice Laffaille. (Courtesy Pierrette Tal-Coat-Demolon)

ways in which a thinking of art without aesthetic might go. Their indirection preserves them from the danger of sublimity (although Heidegger's text comes perilously close on occasions). Their dialogues seek a passage from art to thinking which is not bound by the routings or 'translations' established by aesthetic. Beckett's route is through the experience of a painter – Bram van Velde – whose paintings seem at some moments to be unrecuperable by aesthetic: 'For what is this coloured plane, that was not there before. I don't know what it is, having never seen anything like it before. It seems to have nothing to do with art, in any case, if my memories of art are correct (*Prepares to go*)' (p. 145). Heidegger's route is through the Japanese experience of *iki* 'the gracious', an experience which seems to 'fall into the clutches of aesthetic ideation' (p. 43) and yet exceeds the aesthetic framing. In both cases an 'obligation' or 'calling' becomes manifest which is not-aesthetic.

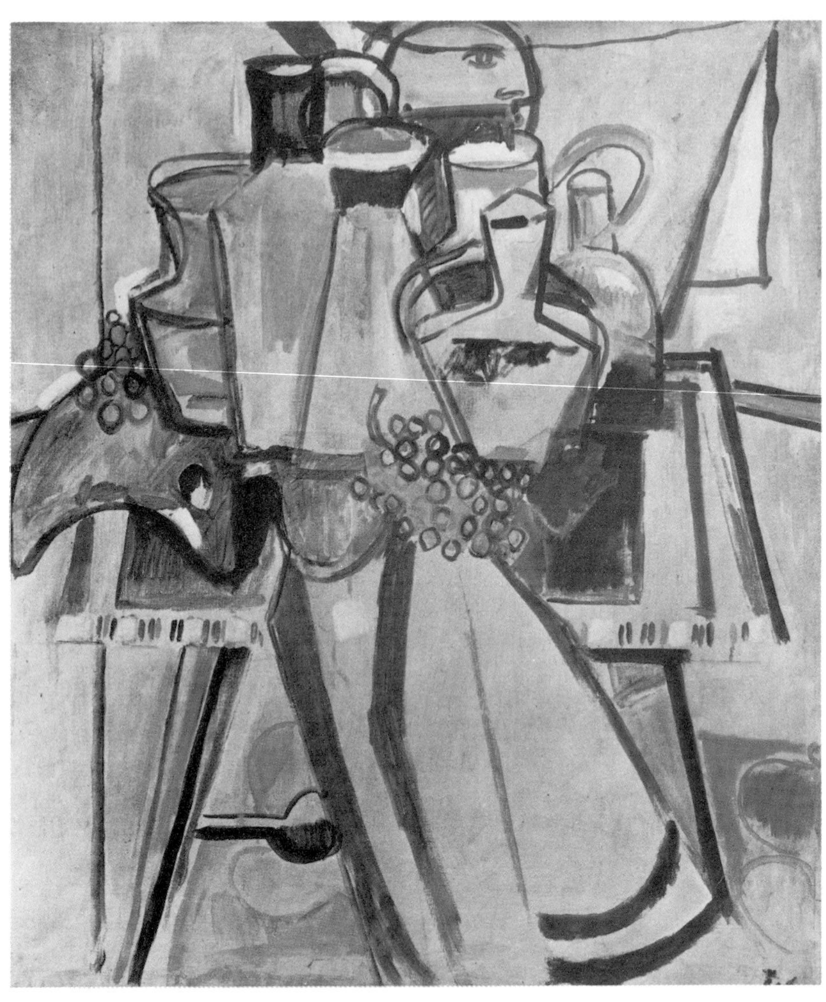

Pierre Tal-Coat. *Sur la Table*, 1944. Oil on canvas. Paris, Private Collection. (Courtesy Pierrette Tal-Coat-Demolon)

In *Painters of the Obstacle*, published a year before the *Three Dialogues*, Beckett describes modern painting as in 'pursuit less of the thing than of its thingness, less of the object than of its condition of being object'.[3] This pursuit takes place across aesthetic dichotomies: Beckett cites substance and accident, subject and object, occasion and representation. Art, as far as he can remember, has always positioned itself within these dichotomies, putting itself either in relation to 'present objects' or to their 'presencing', to use the terms of Heidegger's 'two-fold'. Beckett then describes three ways open for painting: the first two are 'adjustments' of the terms of relation, while the third is a refusal of relation. The refusal nevertheless acknowledges the 'obstacle' or aporetic character of the relation in the obligation to paint.

First there is 'the way back to the old assumption, through the winter of its refutations, the way of the repentant' (p. 167). Then there is the way 'which is not a way, but a last attempt to live within the conquered territory'. While these adjustments strive to maintain the relation to present objects or to their presencing, the third is 'an art of acceptance, seeing in the absence of relation and the absence of object a new relation and a new object'. But this 'new' relation and object is unthinkable except in rigorously aporetic, and unpaintable, terms:

> An endless unveiling, veil behind veil, plane after plane of imperfect transparencies, light and space themselves, veils an unveiling towards the unveilable, the nothing, the thing again. And burial in the unique, in a place of impenetrable nearnesses, cell painted on the stone of cell, art of incarceration.

This is the place described at the beginning of *The Unnameable* as 'aporia pure and simple'; the painting it describes is one which has no place, does not take place, will not be placed. There is only the obligation to speak, to go on, to paint.

In the *Three Dialogues*, the three ways – the first two possessions or occupations of way and place and the third refusal to take place – are named Tal Coat, André Masson, and Bram van Velde. All three are 'in difficulty' (aporia) but only the third is 'in search of difficulty rather than in its clutch'. Speaking of Tal Coat 'D' praises this painting in aesthetic terms – in

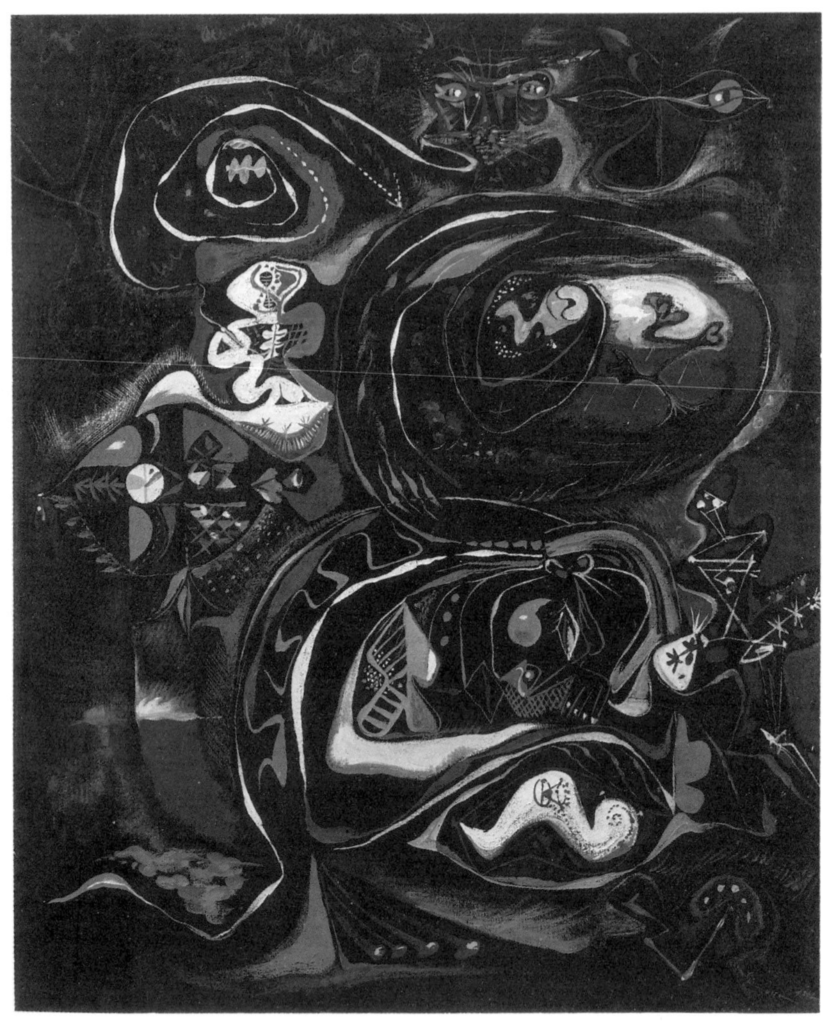

André Masson. *Meditation on an Oak Leaf*, 1942. Tempera, pastel and sand on canvas, 40" x 33". New York, Collection, The Museum of Modern Art. (Copyright DACS 1991)

'ordering' and 'mastering', 'transmitting' and 'discovering' sensation the painter explores the condition of painting. But 'B' refuses to allow a qualitative distinction between painting present things – that is, 'surveying the world with the eyes of building contractors' and painting their presencing. The latter is only an enlargement of the relation of subject to object. 'D's aesthetic appeal to Tal Coat's 'disinterested' expression is met by 'B's not-aesthetic appeal to 'the expression that there is nothing to express, nothing with which to express, nothing from which to express, no power to express, no desire to express, together with the obligation to express' (p. 139). But having proposed this obligation without aesthetic, 'B' is silenced by his interlocutor.

In the second dialogue, the sublimity of Masson's 'painting the void' defended by 'D' – for him Tal Coat is beautiful, Masson sublime, a performance of aesthetic and its contained other – is exposed by 'B' as another bid for mastery and possession of the object. The helplessness before the void is only admitted as 'spice to the "exploit" it jeopardised'. 'His so extremely intelligent remarks on space breathe the same possessiveness as the notebooks of Leonardo who, when he speaks of *disfazione*, knows that for him not one fragment will be lost' (p. 141). Once again 'D' responds violently, insisting on the aesthetic reconciliation between things and their ideal, between the 'things of time that pass and hurry us away, [and] a time that endures and gives increase'. In the face of this appeal to the profit-motive, 'B' exits weeping.

The third dialogue turns to an art which does not wish to 'give increase', does not wish to profit the viewer. Bram van Velde 'cannot paint, since he is obliged to paint' (p. 142). But this obligation is not aesthetic; the artist is bereft of such aesthetic resources as subject, object, and relation, he has 'nothing to paint, nothing to paint with'. In Heidegger's terms there is no message nor any means to send it, yet there is obligation. The obligation to paint cannot be thought in terms of a traffic between aesthetic dichotomies such as subject/object, material/ideal, expression/expressed. This painting is no longer invested in aesthetic: 'Van Velde is the first whose painting is bereft, rid if you prefer, of occasion in every shape and form, ideal as well as material and the first whose hands have not been tied by the certitude that expression is an impossible act' (p. 143). His painting points to an 'art of a new order', one which is not confined to the privileged oppositions of aesthetic. However, this order is unnameable, even though Beckett suffers the temptation to return it to aesthetic: 'I know that all that is required now, in order even to bring this horrible matter to an acceptable conclusion, is to make of this submission, this admission, this fidelity to failure, a new occasion, a new term of relation, and of the act which, unable to act, obliged to act, he makes, an expressive act, even if only of itself, of its impossibility, of its obligation' (p. 145). 'B' refuses this reincorporation, and being accused of having 'forgotten something' warmly remembers that he is, or has been, mistaken: 'Yes, yes, I am mistaken, I am mistaken.'

Heidegger's attempt to think the obligation of art without aesthetic, without investment in its dichotomies, follows an analogous route to Beckett's. Beckett pursues a *via negativa* – a way of negation – which thinks the obligation of art through the negation of aesthetic; Heidegger follows the *via eminentia* – the way of excess – which thinks the obligation through showing its excess over the terms of aesthetic. This excess is marked by the Japanese term *iki*. The *Dialogue on Language* revolves around the attempt by Shuzo Kuki, one of Heidegger's early Japanese students, to produce an 'aesthetic interpretation of *iki*' in his *Iki no kozo* (*The Structure of Iki*). I will restrict my comments to the one issue of *iki*'s excess over its aesthetic framing, even though there are so many issues in this text – such as memory, photography, film, translation, and grammatology – that deserve closer study.

The 'Japanese' begins by answering the 'Questioner's' concern that 'the name "aesthetics" and what it names grow out of European thinking, out of philosophy. Consequently, aesthetic consideration must ultimately remain alien to East Asian thinking' (p. 2). For the 'Japanese' aesthetic 'offers the concepts' to grasp *iki*, concepts which seem necessary to him 'because since the encounter with European thinking, there has come to light a certain incapacity in our language'. This 'incapacity' (*Unvermoegen*) is the absence in the Japanese language of 'the delimiting power to represent objects related in an unequivocal order above and below each other'. Rather than seeing this as an essential 'lack' (*Mangel*) within the Japanese language, the questioner suggests that aesthetic invents a lack in Japanese thinking, which it then offers to remedy on its own terms.

The questioner thinks that aesthetic is an inappropriate frame for thinking Japanese art, and the dialogue is informed by a sense of obligation not to translate *iki* in aesthetic terms. Nevertheless the pivotal distinction in aesthetics since Baumgarten between '...the *aistheton*, what can be perceived by the senses ... [and] the *noeton* the nonsensuous' is translated by the Japanese words *iro* – colour – and *ku* – emptiness, the open, the sky: 'we say: without *Iro*, no *Ku*'. According to aesthetics, art is the reconciliation of the ideal and the sensuous; it is where subject and object can meet apparently without domination. It offers a harmonious settlement of the opposition of the sensuous and non-sensuous, a settlement which receives its apotheosis in Schiller's *Aesthetic Education*. Now *iki* the gracious, could be thought in these terms, as a manifestation of the ideal, but the dialogue tries 'to detach *iki*, which we just translated with "grace" from aesthetics, that is to say from the subject-object relation. I do not mean gracious in the sense of a stimulus that enchants... Q: that is not in the sense of what stimulates, of impressions, of *aisthesis* – but? J: Rather in the opposite direction; but I am aware that with this indication I still remain entangled in aesthetics' (p. 44). The exit from such 'entanglement' is not by way of privileging the opposite term of the relation, sensuous over ideal, object over subject, this would be sublime and so remain within aesthetic. The way out, if such it can be thought, is through the excess over the terms represented by 'grace' or *charis* (the gift) – the obligation or giving that does not obey the economy of aesthetic – Heidegger calls it 'appropriation'.

In the closing pages of the dialogue, the 'Japanese' returns to the point 'where I named to you the Japanese words allegedly corresponding to the distinction between *aestheton* and *noeton*: *iro* and *Ku*. *Iro* means more than colour and whatever can be perceived by the senses. *Ku*, the open, the sky's emptiness, means more than the supra-sensible' (p. 45). The Questioner asks 'You could not say in what the "more" consists.' The Japanese can't state the excess, but he can point to the direction 'in which they [*iro/ku*] hint'. This is towards an 'obligation' which is not contained within the limits of aesthetic, a promise and an entrusting which is excessive. As with Beckett,

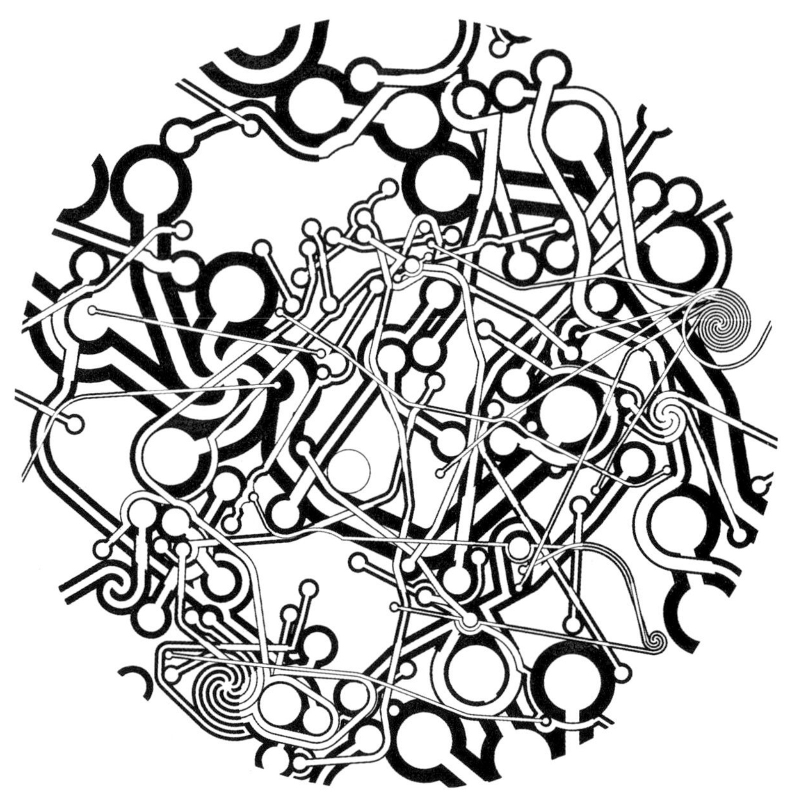

Greg Bright. *Ghost-Telepoint III*, 1984, ink on paper. (Courtesy of the artist)

this obligation is unstatable and should not be reduced to aesthetic terms.

Both writers suggest that the beyond-aesthetic cannot be spoken, although it can be not-spoken through negation or through excess. These moments are crucial for the critique of aesthetic, since by pointing beyond it they recognise its limits. Once these limits are recognised it becomes possible to frame them further, to show their historical formation, their exclusions, their reductions, their privileges. This then gradually opens a new space not only for art and the thinking of art, but also for other practices such as 'politics' which in its modern form is deeply implicated in aesthetic oppositions.

The search for this space has shaped Greg Bright's career in art. His attempts to exit from painting are repeatedly frustrated by an obligation to return to it. His paintings and sculptures present neither things nor 'thingness', but inscribe a route which, refusing to pass through aesthetic oppositions, nevertheless marks the recognition of an obligation. These works offer ways which are both excessive and negative. From the disciplined abandon of the early earthworks at Pilton (1971) to the abandoned discipline of *Ghost Telepoint III* (1984), a work emerges which under the form of the route can sustain Beckett's recursive vision of an 'art of incarceration' – a work bereft but obliged.

More recently Bright has begun to draw out the politics implied in art's obligatory resistance to aesthetic. The 'revolutionary memory' proposed in the 'Meta-Suite' for painting, music, and text (1987–1990) modulates the experience of the ways of negation and excess into an aporetic Hegelianism which recollects art while destroying aesthetic. The metaphysical oppositions of aesthetic identified by Heidegger – sensible/ideal, subject/object, freedom/necessity – along with figure/ground, appear in this work as ruins, as the issue of a violence met with violence. Here the limits of aesthetic are recognised through art, and the presentation of aesthetic's destruction manifests an obligation to art which is none other than the promise of the law.

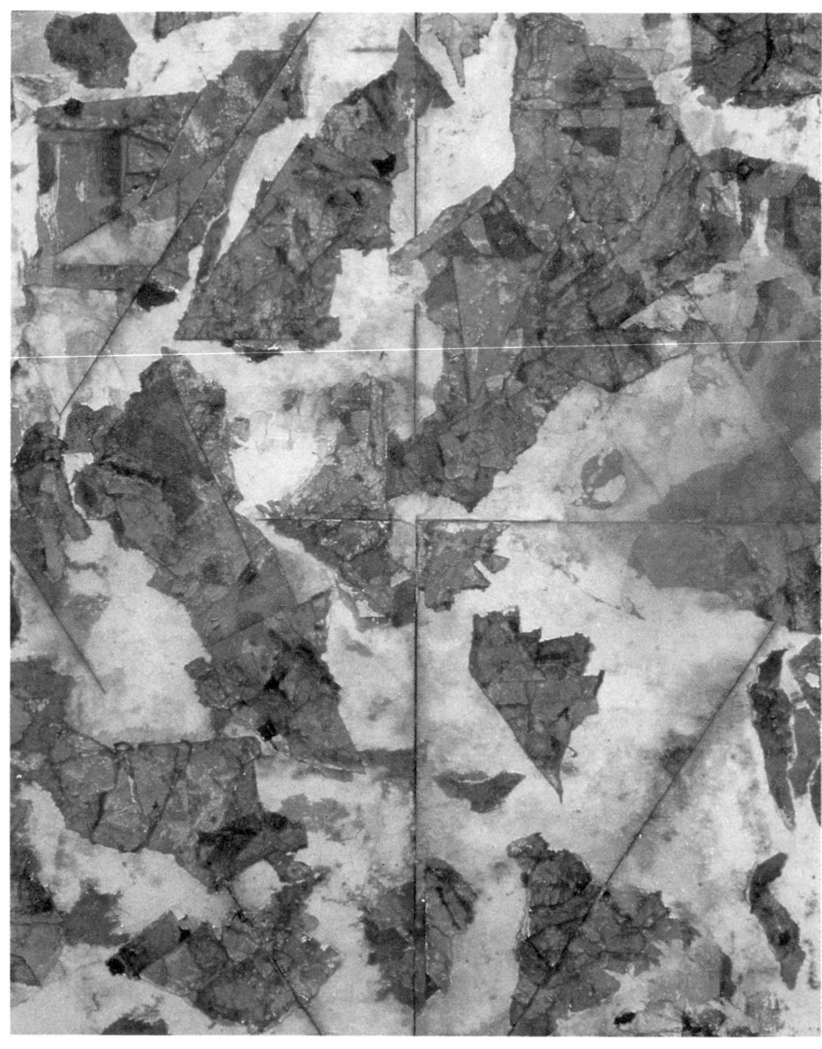

Greg Bright. *The Dominion of the Law*, 1989, central panel of 5 in Painting Suite No. 1, 1988, belonging to Meta-Suite No. 1, 1987–90, gouache on paper. (Courtesy of the artist)

Notes

1. 'Three Dialogues', in *Disjecta*, London, 1983, p. 144.

2. *On the Way to Language*, trans. P. D. Hertz, New York, 1971, p. 43.

3. French text, *Disjecta*, p. 136; Beckett's partial translation in cat. *Bram van Velde*, Musée Nationale d'Art Moderne, Centre Georges Pompidou, Paris, 1989, p. 166.

Situating the Aesthetic: a Feminist Defence

Christine Battersby

For many philosophers writing in the analytic tradition, David Hume, the eighteenth-century Scot, was the father of philosophy. Analogies have been made between his gently ironic account of the psychological origins of metaphysical 'ideas' and Ludwig Wittgenstein's more playful (more modern) scepticism towards metaphysical language and metaphysical problems. But Hume – at least the narrowed-down, tidied-up Hume of the analytic philosophers – was at his least exciting when writing about matters of taste. For this Hume believed that all knowledge derives from experience, and then reduced all questions about a 'standard of taste' to questions about a consensus: in effect, advocating a kind of opinion poll of properly educated connoisseurs with sensibilities fine enough (but not *over*-refined) to be able to respond accurately and adequately to qualities inherent in the object or art-work assessed. Hume compared aesthetic taste to wine-tasting: 'good' and 'bad', 'beautiful' and 'sublime' qualities in objects were discriminated by a highly-trained élite who articulated the preferences of the common man.

Given such an account of aesthetic taste, the radical move into an attack on such a notion is obvious. For who are these connoisseurs?

What are their class allegiances? And to what sex and race do they belong? Rejecting notions of objectivity along with those of impartiality, analytic philosophers on the British left have tended to stress that the notion of an aesthetic quality is itself an ideological construct. At its most extreme, this position is transmuted into one that insists that the very category of 'art' is itself oppressive of the working classes. Wittgensteinian notions of language-games and 'forms of life' have been used to buttress reductive claims which are greatly at odds with Wittgenstein's own comments on aesthetic worth.

Wittgenstein countered twentieth-century (German) notions of 'culture'; but without fundamentally disrupting the language of cultural and aesthetic value. By contrast, the British analytic philosopher, Roger Taylor, used Wittgensteinian conceptual analysis to argue that it is a mistake:

> to say, as has been said in the history of aesthetics, that one's society's art is only the art of the upper classes, and that real art is something else... Art is nothing over and above what has been socially established as art. What is called art in our society is art regardless of what future societies call art and, therefore, the supposition ... that our society might have got the art-list wrong assumes, wrongly, that there is something to get right or wrong. The only mistake that can be made is one of not knowing the conventions of the society (i.e. not knowing what society calls art).[1]

In this passage from *Art, An Enemy of the People* (1978), Taylor is implicitly attacking Marx's own notion of aesthetic worth. For Marx (along with most continental Marxists) believed that aesthetic taste can itself be subject to revolution; that there is more to artistic appreciation than the consensus of a majority or an élite; that, indeed, revolutionising attitudes to art can itself be an important instrument of social change. For Marx all art was very far from always being an 'enemy of the people'. Taylor distances himself from Marxism. But his polemic is significant, for it demonstrates neatly how the empiricist and analytic approach that is characteristic of British philosophy can so easily reduce all questions of artistic value to ones about the sociology of taste. More-Marxist-than-Marx, all notions of artistic progress are analogously flattened into a polemic about the need to sweep away the very category of art itself.

It seems to me that philosophers working within this British tradition must bear part of the responsibility for the fact that in English-speaking cultures the question of what might or might not be a part of a radical aesthetic has been rather a side issue in leftist politics. Thus, in post-war Britain philosophical aesthetics increasingly became an area left open to the traditionalists: to right-wing thinkers, such as Roger Scruton, or to those who saw themselves as apolitical – but who did nothing to disturb the political *status quo*.[2] Terry Eagleton's recent book, *The Ideology of the Aesthetic*, reveals that such a position is, at last, changing. In ways that often irritate – but which are nevertheless important as indicators of a social trend – Eagleton has attempted to reposition his own left-wing attitudes towards 'the aesthetic' against a background of aesthetic theory that has reached down to the present from Kant, through German idealism, through Hegel, through Marx and the Frankfurt School.[3]

Given Eagleton's efforts, it might perhaps be considered otiose to spend time criticising Taylor's rather dated form of reductive aesthetics ... except for the fact that some of the most sophisticated and influential feminist theorists of the arts can still sound as crude as Taylor when the subject of aesthetic value comes into play. In this paper I will defend the traditional subject matter of aesthetics against those Marxist and socialist feminists who think that they need to take a position 'beyond' or counter to feminist aesthetics. But my defence of aesthetics will be undertaken with a radical end in view. For I believe that feminists need to work towards a fundamental revaluing of all aesthetic values. And I thus advocate a *revision* of notions of aesthetic worth that is at odds with the *excision* of such categories advocated, for example, by Griselda Pollock.

Pollock's importance to feminist art theory (including my own) can hardly be overstated. She makes theoretical distinctions far in advance of those of Taylor, and would scorn his use of Wittgensteinian techniques of linguistic analysis. Nevertheless, in her essay on feminist art histories and Marxism in *Vision and Difference*, Pollock adopts a stance towards 'Literary appreciation and art-history-as-appreciation' as dismissive as Taylor's attitude to art itself. For her the concern 'with quality – i.e. positive and negative evaluations of artefacts' – condemns both these disciplines out of hand. Pointing out that art by women has historically been assessed as poor-quality art, Pollock remarks:

> ... feminists are easily tempted to respond by trying to assert that women's art is just as good as men's; it has merely to be judged by yet another set of criteria. But this only creates an alternative method of appreciation – another way of consuming art. They attribute to women's art other qualities, claiming that it expresses a feminine essence, or interpret it by saying it tends to a central 'core' type of imagery derived from the form of the female genitals and from female bodily experience. All too familiar formal psychologistic or stylistic criteria are marshalled to estimate women's art. The effect is to leave intact that very notion of evaluating art, and of course the normative standards by which it is done...
>
> I am arguing that feminist art history has to reject all this evaluative criticism and stop merely juggling the aesthetic criteria for appreciating art. Instead it should concentrate on historical forms of explanation of women's artistic *production*.[4]

Although feminists have evaluated art-works and whole art-genres from either moral, prudential or straightforwardly political perspectives, within feminist art and literary history there has been no sustained attempt to develop a feminist theory of aesthetic value. Indeed, the whole topic has been neglected ... apart from a certain seepage from French theoreticians whose projects are often equated with 'feminist aesthetics'. This conflation is (rightly) one of the targets of Rita Felski's attack in *Beyond Feminist Aesthetics*, since the most influential of these writers (Kristeva and Cixous) are concerned with describing a *féminin* attitude which has more to do with culturally constructed notions of 'the feminine' than with being either female or feminist.[5] Thus Cixous notes that, in the past, it was more likely to be male authors than female authors whose works fall into the approved category of the *féminin*.[6]

Luce Irigaray, whose work can be more sensibly read as working towards a feminist aesthetics, has been less influential. Too easily heard as a philosophical essentialist, her project of speaking *as a woman* has to be understood in terms of her rejection of such philosophical 'masters' as Plato, Kant, Freud and Derrida.[7] But in English-language cultures – cut off from the philosophical traditions out of which Irigaray emerges – the notion that an aesthetic evaluation might be feminist (and not be simply a sociological report or a moral or political judgement) is found somewhat baffling. Thus in the above-quoted passage Pollock presents the feminist aesthetician with a false dichotomy: she must *either* eschew all aesthetic value judgements, *or* lapse into essentialism and formalism.

But why must any feminist revaluation of the notion of aesthetic value treat female bodies and experience in a biologistic way and/or adopt the old values of patriarchal art? Why does Felski (illegitimately) entitle her (legitimate) attack on essentialist and formalistic tendencies in feminist literary criticism *Beyond Feminist Aesthetics*? Why has 'aesthetics' become a dirty word to those on the left in English-language cultures? Radical responses appear to have been based on non-radical readings of the history of philosophy. There are other ways of understanding that history which will help us begin to disentangle those elements of past aesthetics which need to be preserved, and those which must be either abandoned or transformed for the purposes of a feminist aesthetics.

In its original (eighteenth-century) meaning, the subject-matter of aesthetics was the 'science of the senses'. The word 'aesthetics' comes to us from the German theorists (particularly Baumgarten and – most influentially – Immanuel Kant), rather than from empiricists like Hume who did not believe a 'science of taste' was possible. The German inventors of this branch of philosophy were concerned to discover how it might be possible to reach universal conclusions (valid for all persons) on the basis of individual, immediate (= passive and unconceptualised) sense experience. I think the hostility that feminists (and Marxists) often feel towards the notion of aesthetic evaluation comes, in part, from a confusion of 'aesthetics' with 'aestheticism'. But it is only contingently – via the Kantian system – that aesthetics became allied with an aestheticist attitude towards the world.

As Kant explains in the *Critique of Judgement* (1790), a purely aesthetic judgement has eight characteristics. Firstly, it is made up from feelings of pleasure and pain. Secondly, it is immediate. In other words, although it is possible to rationalise aesthetic judgements after the fact, the judgements themselves are not based on a reasoning process. Thirdly, such a judgement is particular; it involves an individual experiencing subject responding to a unique object. Fourthly, the judgement is non-conceptual. Aesthetic response is said to be imaginative, and not based on the understanding of rules. Fifthly, aesthetic judgements are subjective – despite the fact that they also appear to have universal validity, and to apply not only to oneself, but to all experiencing human subjects.

According to Kant – and this is the sixth point – this universality is possible because the purely aesthetic response abstracts from the merely contingent features of the experience (from that which is historically variable and accidental). The purely aesthetic response transcends all emotion and all 'charm' or 'attraction' exerted by the object on the observer. Indeed, in its purest form even the existence of the object was seen as irrelevant to the aesthetic attitude. There could be no question of taking into account the object's use-value or its material value. Kant calls this transcendent attitude 'disinterested'.[8]

The seventh point is that for Kant it is the 'formal' features of the object that provide the focus of the aesthetic attitude. And, as always in Kant, form – that which makes a thing what it is and not something else – is explicated in terms of the space-time characteristics of the world. These characteristics are not straightforwardly 'out there', but are read onto the world by man's productive imagination. Finally, as an eighth point, it should be pointed out that for Kant the purest kind of aesthetic response – the pleasure in the 'beautiful' – is based on a 'disinterested' appreciation of the harmony that is implicit in the form of an object. It is a response to that which makes an object a whole and not simply a multiplicity of parts. But since form is itself a product of the human imagination, what man is in effect taking pleasure in is the mind's power over nature.

I should add as an important addendum to this that Kant also registers that there are other less pure forms of aesthetic pleasure. His key example is that of the 'sublime', which involves a response to the terrifying (to gaunt mountains, thunder, storm-ridden seas, earthquakes, etc.). Here the pleasure comes from the overcoming of threat and of pain: of registering that the world is constructed by the imagination as an unknowable infinity which, at any moment, threatens to overwhelm the ego and reveal to the self its limits. But since the sublime involves registering this threat and transcending this threat, the enjoyment of the sublime is itself also an enjoyment of power over nature.

From a feminist point of view there are many aspects of Kant's analysis that require criticism, since the ties that Kant makes between aesthetic pleasure and power are gendered through and through.[9] But it is, I believe, his notion of a 'disinterested' withdrawal from all material and use-value that has done most to bring the notion of the aesthetic into disrepute. For, during the nineteenth century, the aesthetic movement developed this notion of Kant's to an extreme. The aesthetic was equated with a particular attitude of mind: with a blanking out of moral, social and political considerations ... and with an indifference to bodily dictates and needs. But disinterest is not integral to the notion of the aesthetic in its original meaning of a 'science of taste', and is a mode of artistic evaluation that feminists can and must revise and resist. For it by no means follows that to deny that aesthetic judgements are disinterested is to deny that there are no evaluative standards that can be developed to discriminate between adequate and inadequate responses to art-works ... or good and bad art-works.

Aesthetic evaluation comes in many forms. There is, for example, the type of evaluation that I analysed in *Gender and Genius*: that of deciding which artists deserve to be counted 'great', 'important' or even 'geniuses'. I argued there that present-day women artists will suffer unless we recognise how gendered the standards are that are used to determine which artists are 'great', and unless feminists develop some alternative standards for aesthetic discrimination. Since these ideas have been developed much more fully elsewhere, I want here to focus on other, more pervasive, modes of aesthetic evaluation, starting with the evaluative element that is built into the *description* of particular qualities of an art-work. Thus, claims about an art-work's 'authenticity', 'originality', 'delicacy', 'forcefulness' or 'subtlety' are not purely 'factual' statements that can be straightforwardly verified or falsified. All these terms fuse factual and descriptive elements in ways that make interpretation – and even apparently neutral descriptions – evaluative through and through.

There is, of course, *some* descriptive element in the use of a word like 'authentic'. To say that a blues song is authentic is not simply to say that one approves of it or that other people approve of it. 'Authenticity' is not just a quality in a musical composition that can be heard in an immediate way by a listener with suitably trained ears – although it is of course true that this is a judgement that is often made fairly instantaneously. 'Authenticity' involves situating the musical composition or performance in terms of a variety of *traditions* which are themselves evaluated as expressions of uncontrived emotion and/or character. We are dealing here with a highly complex value judgement of an aesthetic type which involves reference to standards; and I would thus reject Kant's notion that aesthetic judgements must be 'immediate', must abstract from all sensual appeal, and concentrate (in an utterly 'disinterested' way) on the 'form' of an object.

Since I accept neither 'immediacy' nor 'disinterestedness' as integral aspects of aesthetic judgement, it might be felt that I have moved so far away from traditional notions of 'aesthetic value' as to make my own position anti-aesthetical. But I would resist such a conclusion. Indeed, I would wish to go so far as to say that there is no way of escaping the necessity of judging aesthetically, and that there is no value-neutral critical space from which feminists can speak. Even to give priority to political, ethical or utilitarian value judgements over aesthetic judgements is, in effect, to opt for a particular variety of aesthetic value.

For me aesthetic evaluation takes place in the context of certain evoked *traditions* which bring along with them *standards* for discriminating particular qualities and features of art objects. I certainly would not want to move back to a form of pre-Kantian empiricism in which judgements of taste are simply represented as passive responses to pre-given 'objective' qualities which cause either like or dislike ... and in which the only role for the artistic critic would be to either discover or refine the social consensus. This is because to evaluate a painting favourably is not simply to say that one likes it, that others like it, or that an élite of critics like it. An evaluation is not a report (either about external properties or about the state of mind of the observer). There is no contradiction in English in saying, 'I think Bacon is a great painter of the nude, but I can't stand him.'

To evaluate is not to describe what one *does* like or think, but what one *ought* to like or think. It is to set up an ideal observer as a standard of comparison; against which one's own (and others') likes and dislikes are to be judged. Sociologists of taste who seek to establish an equivalence between aesthetic judgements and records of social consensus have to refuse this crucial distinction between the ideal and the real. Hence Pierre Bourdieu's complaint that Kant's *Critique of Judgement* remains grammatically locked 'in the register of *Sollen*, "ought"'.[10] In his *Distinction: A Social Critique of the Judgement of Taste* (1979), Bourdieu uses questionnaire techniques in an attempt to reduce Kantian aesthetic preferences to factual claims about the attitudes and judgements of the French high-bourgeoisie.

Aesthetic judgements are not expressions of like or dislike by actual, historical individuals. They are expressions of approval or disapproval by *ideal* individuals by reference to standards derived from *traditions* (which are not simply there as 'historical givens', but which have to be constructed by the observers). Feminist art and literary critics have shown that there are traditions of female art that run alongside (and between) the dominant traditions of art selected by the high-bourgeoisie. These matrilineal lines of influence and pattern need to be made visible, so that productions by women can be made more comprehensible and be better assessed by 'ideal observers' who judge the art-work in viewing conditions that are as-near-as-possible ideal, and in terms of a range of knowledge, experience, sensitivity and emotion that are appropriate for the art-work under observation. It is against these norms that all one's responses to the art-work have to be judged.

I am not claiming that these ideal observers actually exist, nor that for all art there is only one ideal observer (with only one range of experience, of sensitivity, of emotions and knowledge). It seems highly implausible to suppose that the ideal observer of a building by Le Corbusier would require the same qualities of mind and of knowledge as the ideal observer of a portrait by Angelica Kauffman. Whether each art-work has only *one* ideal observer (i.e. whether aesthetic evaluations are universals) is a matter for debate. Personally, I would want to say that there is more than one valid response to each art-work (which is not to say, of course, that all responses are equally valid). But, as a feminist, I would also want to say that my ideal observers are not 'gentlemanly connoisseurs'. Instead, my own ideal posits observers with experiences and life-histories that have led them to empathise with art produced at the margins, and in opposition to the prevailing rhetorics of exclusion. An engagement with feminist theory and practice might produce such an openness of response; but so, too, might poverty or an involvement with the issues of 'black' and 'third-world' peoples.

There is also no reason whatsoever why an 'ideal' observer should be theorised in a Kantian fashion as transcending or lacking emotion or sexual appetite – or as solely rational. To make such moves would be to downgrade matter, emotionality and the 'feminine' in ways that require a feminist analysis and a feminist critique. But neither, I would wish to insist, can a feminist aesthetics be simply equated with a reversal of the old hierarchies that placed (masculine) form and rationality over (feminine) emotion and matter. I haven't time to provide a full critique of such notions here; I would simply point to the arguments in *Gender and Genius* where I show that, in the field of aesthetics, 'feminine' characteristics were long ago appropriated by male artists in ways that disadvantaged female artists in the history of culture.

I can't close this paper, however, without mentioning a further way in which evaluation creeps into the most apparently value-neutral descriptions of art; and that is via the notion of an 'Artist'. Gombrich opened his best-seller, *The Story of Art*, by suggesting that there is really no such thing as 'Art', only a series of artists. Against him I argue that there is really no such thing as an artist, only a series of art-works that critics hold together via the notion of an *oeuvre*. Not everything that is produced by those working in the arts gets counted into an oeuvre. Sketches for paintings sometimes count; but graffiti, doodles and marginalia are usually excluded. And so is the entire output of some individuals whose work is explained in terms of certain already-established traditions: 'Schools', 'Circles',

'Tendencies' or 'Movements' or 'Genres'. For the concept of an *oeuvre* is itself an evaluative category which looks to the notion of an individual's life, development and maturation to explicate the phenomenon of *unity through change*.

It is this notion of unity through change which we need to focus on to understand this difficult notion of an *oeuvre*. For an artist to have an *oeuvre* implies that there is some shape to his life, and that there are historical, geographical and social explications that can explain why this individual remains the same individual despite the myriad changes, pieces and contradictions which mark his or her work. An artist who is not credited with an *oeuvre* is one whose art-works have been treated in isolation (not as fragments of a fully individual, psychically rich self), or whose art-works have been treated as the product of non-individual collectives. It is not that an *oeuvre* is not located in terms of tradition, but that the *oeuvre* is considered as non-reducible to the traditions which the artist adapted or employed. Indeed, the great artist is precisely the one who is seen to mark the tradition in ways that determine the boundary between the old and the new. In Kant's famous phrase: 'The genius gives the rule to art.'

There have been sex-differential erasures from the history of the arts. The *oeuvres* of women artists and authors have disintegrated, since they have been seen to lack form: that which shapes matter, binds the accidents together into a unity, and makes a thing what it is and not something else. Women's works have been scattered and dispersed to a much greater extent than those of (white) males. The concept '*oeuvre*' has been used in gender-discriminatory ways. Nor is this simply because of the material disadvantages under which women produced their art. Inherent in the notion of an *oeuvre* – and hence built into the notion of an 'artist' – is a value judgement: a notion of a significant, important or (at least) interesting expression of a fully-human self. But since our ways of judging human maturation take the male personality as both norm and ideal, women have had to struggle to get their art-works interpreted in such generous ways.

As a philosopher I will not be happy until feminist critics register the centrality of aesthetic value judgements at every level of discussion and response to cultural production. For I see it as an urgent task to work out ways of theorising aesthetic value so as to benefit women in the arts. But as a feminist I will not be happy until philosophers recognise the deep level at which aesthetic value judgements are gendered. Amongst the humanities subjects in Britain philosophy has been perhaps the slowest to open itself up to feminist transformations; and of the various fields of feminist philosophy in other English-language cultures, feminist aesthetics is amongst the least developed. But feminist philosophers have an important role to play in exposing the many ways in which gender issues disturb and pervert what in our culture gets categorised as 'Art' and who gets seen as 'an Artist'.

My own task then as both a philosopher and a feminist is to reform our notion of 'aesthetic value' in such a way as to benefit women. And that means that I am fundamentally opposed to Roger Taylor's idea that all art is an enemy of the people; to Griselda Pollock's claim that feminists must reject all forms of aesthetic value; and to any suggestion that the way ahead lies 'beyond' feminist aesthetics. As both a feminist and a philosopher I am, therefore, not ashamed to situate myself in a tradition of theorising the arts that reaches back to Immanuel Kant. Indeed, I believe that this is what must be done if we are to discover how feminists can (collectively) transform our notion of aesthetic value.

Obviously, this is a large task; and it is not one that any one person can do alone – especially since we lack most of the basic historical scholarship that would reveal gender bias in the history of our aesthetic vocabulary. Terms like 'universal', 'rational', 'abstract', 'form', 'structure', 'matter', 'organic', 'natural', 'functional', 'imaginative', 'beautiful', 'sublime' are commonly used in art criticism; but all require a feminist analysis of the type that I have elsewhere supplied for 'genius'. And so do such apparently innocuous terms as '*oeuvre*'. I am therefore glad to have had a chance to signal the scale of the tasks ahead. Feminist aesthetics must fracture the ideal of one universal, historically-timeless canon of 'great art' discoverable by any 'disinterested' observer ... and must also resist the rhetoric of one universally constant, unchanging 'feminine essence' governing art by women. But holding these resistances in tandem is not contradictory. To assert both these things together does not mean that we must conclude that feminist aesthetics cannot exist.

Notes

1. Roger L. Taylor, *Art, An Enemy of the People* (Hassocks, Sussex: Harvester, 1978), pp. 49–50.
2. Roger Scruton's *Art and Imagination: A Study in the Philosophy of Mind* (London: Methuen, 1974) ends with the phrase 'ethics and aesthetics are one'. But the space that Scruton thus makes for a political dimension in aesthetics is not left-wing.
3. Terry Eagleton's *The Ideology of the Aesthetic* (Oxford: Blackwell, 1990) is uneven in detail and conception. The book does, however, have merits – particularly in signalling a new openness to the aesthetic (that comes not just from Eagleton, but from the prestigious list of professional philosophers consulted by Eagleton, and acknowledged in his introduction).
4. Griselda Pollock, *Vision and Difference: Femininity, Feminism and Histories of Art* (London: Routledge, 1988), pp. 26–27.
5. Rita Felski, *Beyond Feminist Aesthetics: Feminist Literature and Social Change* (London: Hutchinson Radius, 1989).
6. Hélène Cixous, *Writing Differences: Readings from the Seminar of Hélène Cixous*, ed. Susan Sellers (Open University Press, 1988), p. 25. For more on this topic see my *Gender and Genius: Towards a Feminist Aesthetics* (London: The Women's Press, 1989; Indiana University Press, 1990).
7. Diana Fuss, *Essentially Speaking: Feminism, Nature and Difference* (London: Routledge, 1990) usefully defends Irigaray from such a reading. Fuss and Whitford (whose *Luce Irigaray: Philosophy in the Feminine* and *Irigaray Reader* will be appearing shortly) have persuaded me that I should have placed more emphasis in *Gender and Genius* on the differences between Irigaray's position and those of Cixous and Kristeva.
8. This is where Kant's mature position in the *Critique of Judgement* (1790) diverges from that of his early essay 'Observations on the Feeling of the Beautiful and Sublime' (1764). In the early work all beauty has a fundamental grounding in attraction (especially sexual attraction), and women are the paradigm examples of the beautiful. In the late work women are still positioned as beautiful. But the link is much more problematical, since an appreciation of them as sexual objects has to transcend all charm and sexual appeal.
9. *Gender and Genius* begins this task. But there I concentrated primarily on the continuities, rather than on the differences, between Kant's early and late positions: i.e. that in both women are excluded from the production and pleasures of the sublime.
10. Pierre Bourdieu, *Distinction: A Social Critique of the Judgement of Taste* (1979), trans. Richard Nice (London: Routledge, 1986), p. 488.

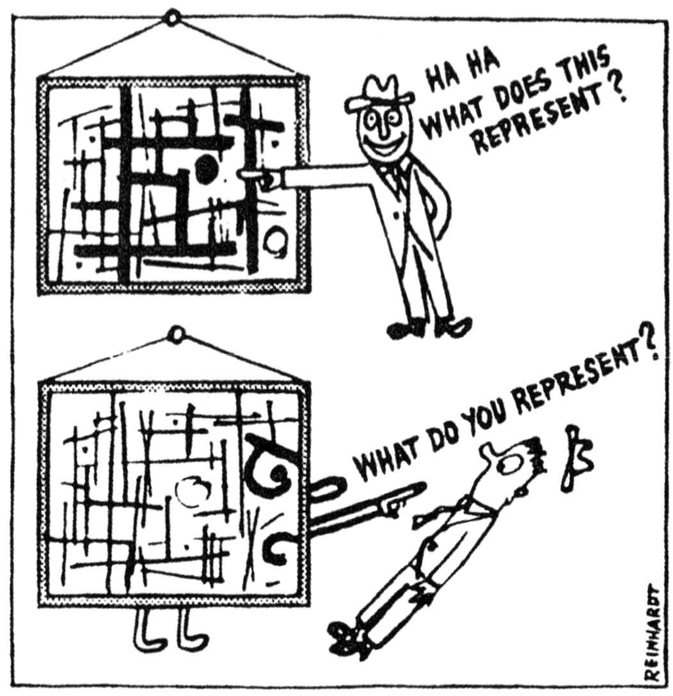

Figure. 1. Ad Reinhardt. *What does this represent…*, 1948.
Reproduced in *Art Comics and Satires* by Tom Hess. (Copyright Anna Reinhardt)

Abstraction, Modernism, Representation

David Batchelor

Abstraction and modernism

There is a small two-part cartoon by the American artist Ad Reinhardt which was probably drawn in the late 1940s. In the upper part a man in a suit and a hat is shown pointing at an abstract painting made up of several lines and a few blobs. He looks straight out of the picture and smiles broadly as he says 'Ha. Ha. What does this represent?' (fig. 1). In the lower part of the cartoon the lines and blobs in the painting have been drawn together to form a furrowed brow, a glaring eye and an angry mouth. The picture has grown two feet, a nose and an arm which points accusingly back at the man. He, in turn, is knocked off his heels as the painting demands 'What do you represent?'[1]

The overall point of the cartoon seems obvious enough: it mocks a certain kind of ignorance of and resistance to an art which doesn't appear to represent anything because it doesn't deal in the currency of resemblance. It could be a kind of snob's humour at the expense of the insensitive and graceless philistines who pass for the general public. It could be, but it probably isn't. Reinhardt's series of 'Art Cartoons', from which this is taken, didn't deal with such generalisations. Rather his subjects were drawn from, and his attention was directed at, the institutions, the rhetoric, the fashions and the figures – in short, the culture – of high art. If the person in the cartoon has any species identity, he is likely to be an inhabitant of that world, not that inhabitant's imaginary other.

It is also, of course, a cartoon about the potential of art. It asserts a belief in the capacity of art to enable reflection *upon* the prevailing conventions, habits and prejudices of a culture, rather than to be a mute reflection *of* that dominant culture. The man in the hat clearly didn't expect such reflexivity from art, and we're left with the impression he probably didn't want it much either.

The point of introducing this cartoon is simply that, some forty or more years on, it remains remarkably vivid. Abstract art continues to get a bad press in some quarters, and to present a number of problems to its interpreters – some logical, some political, some moral. Not all these problems are peculiar to abstract art, but it can be argued that abstract art tends to intensify some of the difficulties present in the interpretation of any art. For a start, abstract art has always been accorded a special place in the history of modernism, if not as its ultimate goal, then at least as its highest achievement. But with modernism in crisis and under attack from a range of positions over a number of years, where does that leave abstract art? Can we talk of non-modernist abstraction? Or of post-modernist abstraction? Or is abstract art so intimately tied to the interests and ideology of modernism that it must be treated merely as its symptom, a symptom which must vanish as soon as the disease which produced it is cured?

Before such issues can be properly discussed there are a series of prior questions to be considered. What, for example, was the status of abstract art within modernism? And how was it treated? In the same way as non-abstract art, or differently? Is all late modernist art invariably abstract? And so on. Greenberg, at least, was quite clear and categorical on most of these issues.[2] What differentiated modernist from non- or pre-modernist art for him had little or nothing to do with its iconic or non-iconic status. Rather, modernist art tended to develop and to work within a different type of picture-space, one which did away with chiaroscuro and perspective in favour of a more 'optical' space and 'all-over' composition of line and/or planes of flat colour. Thus there was as much scope for a non-modernist abstraction (in the work of Victor Vasarelly for example) as there was for non-abstract modernism (in the work of, say, Matisse or Leger). And furthermore, as far as criticism was concerned, there was no requirement to treat the two types of art in different ways or to evaluate them according to different scales. For Greenberg iconicity was just one aspect among several in painting (such as line, colour, paint quality, etc.), the presence or absence of which 'has no more to do with value in painting or sculpture than presence or absence of a libretto has to do with value in music'.[3]

The latter parts of this argument, that aesthetic value is autonomous, and independent of any moral value which may be derived from the iconic aspects of the work, are of course familiar and visible in a range of modernist critical writing from the early twentieth century. They are also evident in the theoretical writing associated with the Symbolist group from the last two decades of the nineteenth century, that is to say, several years before the advent of fully abstract art. Taking a lead from Baudelaire's theory of 'correspondence', Albert Aurier, Maurice Denis and others were able to argue that not only value but meaning in art was embodied in colour, line, shape and composition.

Abstraction and the crisis of modernism

The significant and vociferous critique of modernism which has been expressed from, among other areas, the social history of art has had a lot to say about Greenberg's and others' tendency both to devalue the iconic aspects of early modernist painting and entirely to pass over the wider ramifications of the culture of high art, its institutional ratification, and so forth. T. J. Clark's seminal studies on Courbet and Manet have suggested the relevance of such issues both to questions of meaning in art and to judgements of value, as had the work of Meyer Shapiro before him. But, in this country at least, very little subsequent work from this arena has had anything to say about abstract art in particular or even twentieth-century art in general. The social historical gaze has tended to remain fixed on, or fixated by, late nineteenth-century painting, or, more specifically, the culture of late nineteenth-century art. Some of the reasons for this are fairly clear.

Such work often provides a wealth of iconic detail of the kind which allows a fairly untroubled transition from talking about specific works of art to more general discussions of culture, gender, race, and (last of all these days) class. As often as not paintings are reduced to 'images', and art to a mere symptom. An obvious problem with abstract art in this context is its lack of a convenient iconic bridge between the work of art and the world it inhabits.

For better or worse modernism has provided a reasonably succinct historical and technical frame of reference for the discussion of abstract art, and some clear criteria for determining the issue of relevance in that discussion. Both Greenberg's and Michael Fried's so-called formalism may be understood, in part, as a product of a rigorous scepticism concerning both the substance of claims made about the meaning or 'content' of works of art, and the value of such claims in matters of criticism. As Greenberg put it in an essay from 1967:

> I, who am considered an arch-'formalist' used to indulge in that kind of talk about 'content' myself. If I do not do so any longer it is because it came to me, dismayingly, some years ago that I could assert the opposite of whatever it was I did say about 'content' and not get found out; that I could say almost anything I pleased about 'content' and sound plausible.[4]

The point for Greenberg was not that art had no content, but that its content was precisely that which was 'indefinable, unparaphraseable, undiscussable... The unspecifiability of its "content" is what constitutes art as art'.[5] Thus Greenberg presented his 'formalism' as a product of the recognition of limitations – without which criticism would become arbitrary, unconnected to its object.

But what, for Greenberg, may have been an attempt to face up to some fundamental difficulties in interpretation, for others, has become evidence of a wilful closure against inquiry. Much writing in the social and cultural history of art has tended, often, to see in 'formalist' art and criticism only the reflection of a particular cultural content, and to see its own task as one of revealing the real agenda, the machinations of power, hidden behind the modernists' conspiracy of silence. It is approximately in these terms that what little discussion there has been of post-war abstract art has taken place. Most recently, Anna Chave has published a substantial volume on Mark Rothko and a long article on Minimal art.[6] Chave's methods for dealing with abstract art, for bringing it into the orbit of social history, combine the familiar and the exotic. In one respect her method amounts to a curious inversion of the modernist treatment of abstract art. That is, whereas it could be argued that modernism, in marginalising the iconic aspects of picturing, has tended to reduce all art to the condition of the abstract, Chave has reduced abstract art to the condition of resemblance-based representation by treating it as cryptically iconic. This iconifying of the abstract is based in not much more than a combination of literalness and selectiveness in the matter of the artists' expressed interest and intentions, deconstructive redundancy, and a certain amount of screw-up-your-eyes-until-you-can-see-it methodology. Thus she is able to read a selection of work by Flavin, Andre, Noland and others as highly schematised *depictions* – of phalluses, military emblems, and so on (figs. 2 and 3). Once established, this hidden iconography becomes the main platform upon which the principal assertion of the essay is built, the assertion that 'The blank face of Minimalism may come into focus as the face of capital, the face of authority, the face of the father'.[7]

Figure 2 (left). Kenneth Noland. *Chevron 4*, 1964. Collection Krefeld Museum, West Germany. (Copyright DACS 1991). Figure 3. Dan Flavin. *The Diagonal of May 25, 1963 (to Robert Rosenblum)*, 1963. Cool white fluourescent light, 96" x 3³/4", Edition of 3. (Copyright 1991 Dan Flavin/ARS, NY.) (Courtesy Leo Castelli Gallery)

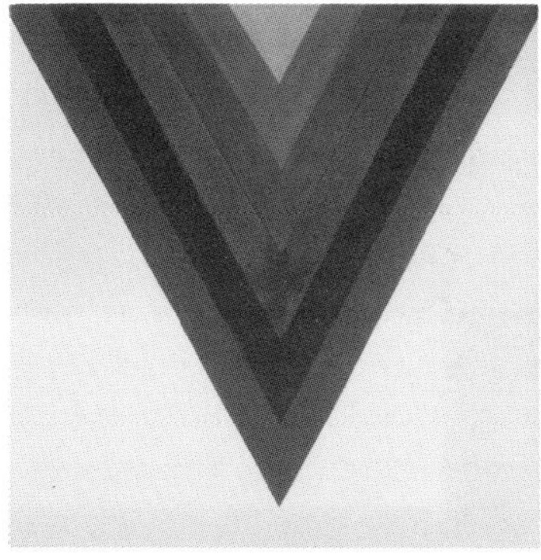

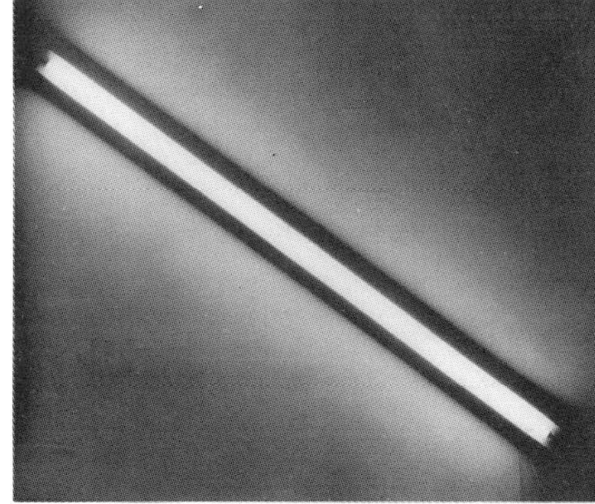

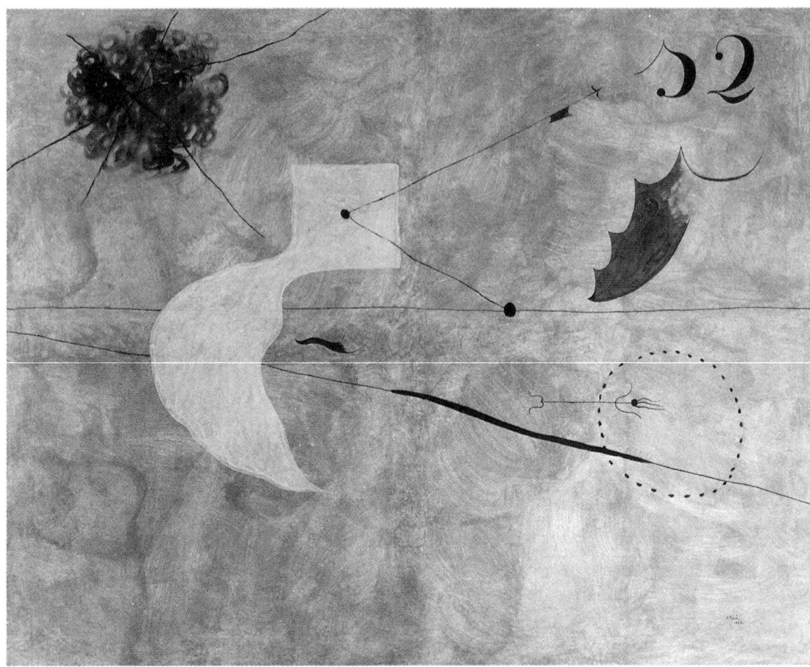

Figure 4: Joan Miro. *La Sieste*, 1925. Paris, Collection Pompidou Centre. (Copyright ADAGP, Paris and DACS, London)

Little space is allowed for any semantic complexity here. Even if we accept these distinctly dodgy claims made for the depicted content of the works, scant attention is given to, or space allowed for, those features of representation which are bound heavily to modify any 'literal' meanings. Artistic representation is littered with examples of quotation, irony, parody, hyperbole, and many other less literary forms of displacement and *making strange*. To pass over such possibilities is to indulge in a form of wilful aspect-blindness. To pass over all the counter examples, the stack of work which cannot so easily be made to fit the phallocentric bill – a Louis 'floral' for instance – just seems like a case of selecting the evidence to fit the theory.

There is of course a whole range of modern art (including work by Kandinsky, Miro, Stuart Davis and others) which *has* exploited the device of abstracting from a naturalistic source (through editing, schematisation, reduction, distortion, substitution, etc.) to the point where that source is largely unrecognisable, and unrecoverable without the aid of some clues or a key (fig. 4). But it is something of the order of a category mistake to treat all abstract art as if it were of this sort. The American artist Peter Halley has made a career out of doing just this, both in his own paintings and in his interpretations of earlier examples of abstract art (fig. 5). In effect he has reduced the issue to a version of that children's game where an apparently abstract composition of a few lines and circles is revealed to be not a camel in front of a pyramid, or a bear up a tree, but a Foucault behind a panopticon, or a Baudrillard up a conduit.[8]

Abstraction and representation

Nevertheless, both Chave and Halley have sought to tackle an issue which is often, and strategically, excluded in modernism, the issue of how abstract art functions as representation, and what particular works of abstract art can be said to represent or mean. This remains a difficult area. One reason for

Figure 5: Peter Halley. *Two Cells with Circulating Conduit*, 1986. 64" x 104". Private collection. (Courtesy of the artist)

this has to do, I think, with a tendency to confuse representation with depiction, or to assume that the former is necessarily dependent upon or derived from the latter. At least, both Chave and Halley seem to work according to the principle that in order to treat works of abstract art as representations they first have to be shown to depict some *thing*. I can see no reason for this other than it being a hangover from the convention for dealing with non-abstract pictures: step 1, what does x depict; step 2, what does x represent, etc. An interesting mirror image of this assumption is supplied by the sculptor Don Judd who insists that insofar as nothing is depicted in his sculptures – as he does not use one material (say, stone) to represent another (say, flesh) – his work therefore does not represent anything.[9] (fig. 6)

Figure 6 (left). Donald Judd. *Untitled,* IDJ 88–4ABCDEF Aluminium AG Menkiten, 1988. (Courtesy Waddington Galleries and the artist). Figure 7 (right). Frank Stella. *Six Mile Bottom*, 1960. London, Collection Tate Gallery. (Copyright 1991 Frank Stella/ARS, NY.)

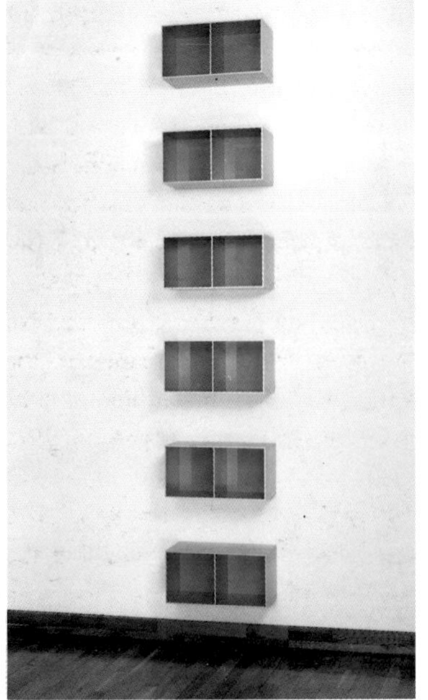

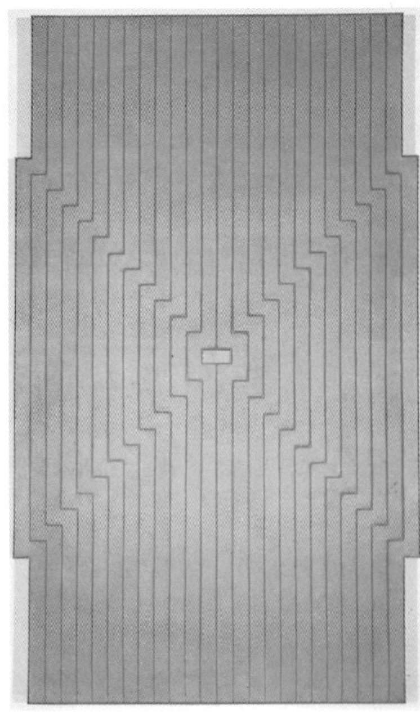

Both these examples treat representation as depiction dependant, and base their (entirely opposed) claims about abstract art on this assumption. But, leaving aside the point that the relation between depiction and representation is, at least, highly unstable, clearly there are ways in which abstract art can be dealt with as representation without having to resort to iconification.[10] For example, it seems more helpful to think of works of art (abstract or otherwise) as representing not through the depiction of things but through the indication, or intimation, or more or less complex relations of likeness. Foremost among these is the relationship that is indicated in any work of art between the work and other existing examples or types of art. An early Mondrian or Malevich establishes a relationship with Cubist painting; an early Pollock or Rothko with Surrealism; an early Stella or Lichtenstein or Rauschenberg or Johns with Abstract Expressionism; and so forth (fig. 7). This process is essential: if an artist fails to establish such a relationship in his or her work, that work will tend to be regarded simply as irrelevant to the discourse of modern art. It will, as they say, fail to signify. But that relationship, that likeness, is itself not simple or unmediated. It is subject to complication and development in a variety of possible ways and for a variety of possible reasons. For a work to express some kind of critical or qualified relationship with its antecedents it will require some feature which may be read as indicative of such a qualification. Rauschenberg, for example, 'doubled' an apparently spontaneous abstract expressionist painting and he famously erased another. Stella crowded out the expressionistic aspects of abstract painting, eliminated the 'impulsive' gesture by reducing the autographic aspects of the work to a series of predetermined patterns more or less deduced from the shape of the stretcher. In each of these cases the work's qualified relationship with its antecedent is indicated through a modification of technique, is embodied in such a technical modification.

Such qualifications are rarely made simply for the sake of novelty. They are markers, usually, of some kind of unease with or apprehension about the perceived aims or meanings of that prior work, and thus also markers of an endeavour to bring into the work different ways of reflecting on the world. This is probably at the heart of much ambitious art: the aim not just to

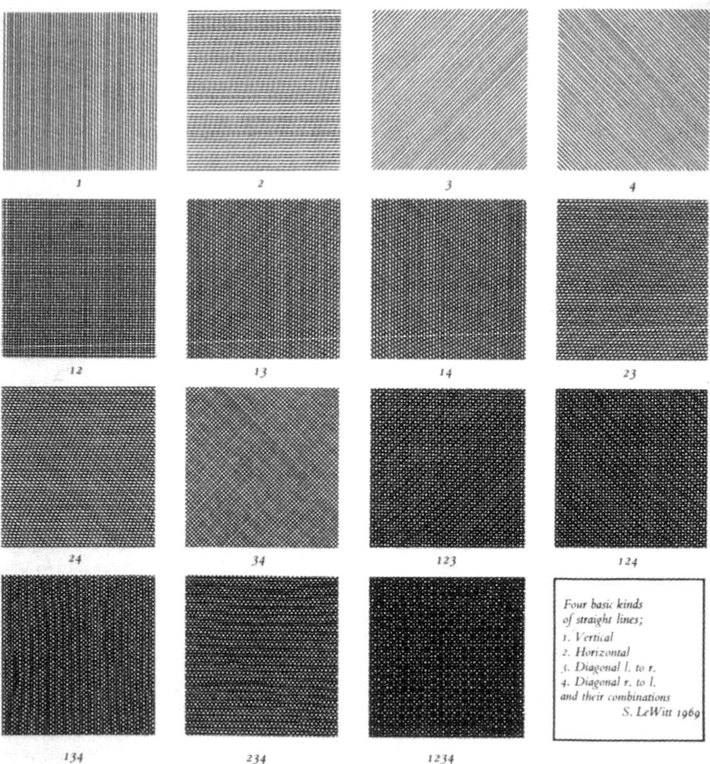

Figure 8. Sol LeWitt. *Four Basic Kinds of Straight Lines and All Their Combinations in 15 Parts*, 1969. (Copyright 1991 Sol LeWitt/ARS, NY)

depict novel things in the world, but to represent the world in unaccustomed ways.[11] This is evident in the work of Courbet, Cubism, Constructivism and Conceptual art, as well as in much work which doesn't alliterate so easily. The details of any particular examples will differ: at different moments different types of ideas have been brought to bear in the work of dismantling what had become merely conventionalised styles, merely routine or fixed relations of likeness. But whether these ideas are derived from Plato or Hegel, Marx or Freud, Nietzsche or Beckett or whoever, they are only likely to have any substance if they can be said to exist in the work, to be embodied in the expressive resources of art (as opposed to being stipulated about the work at some stage or other). And there is no reason to assume that this work of likening must be carried by one aspect of a picture more than another. All its thematised features are by definition enlisted in this work – its size, scale, surface, composition, colour, etc., as well as any iconic features it may contain.[12]

In this sense it may be argued that a Mondrian or a Rothko or a LeWitt is an image of *something*, but not an image of some *thing*. It seems safer to think of the work as representing, or attempting to express, a kind of conception or understanding of a world, to be *like* that world in an abstract way.[13] Such likeness is of course not inherent in a particular colour, material, type of brushwork, or whatever. Rather it acquires its meaning by being placed in a relationship of difference with related antecedent works. Thus, for example, the elimination of painterliness and the employment of ruled line and geometric composition (in conjunction with certain materials, size, scale, etc.) would have connoted something quite different in a LeWitt of the 1960s from, say, a Mondrian of the 1920s (figs. 8 and 9). It is the recognition of this kind of relativity in pictorial representation which departs from Symbolist-based and idealist accounts which have tended to treat the meaning of colour, line, shape and form either as fixed properties and/or as only accessible to, only within the grasp of, a rare few exalted sensibilities.

If representation is regarded more as a matter of calling attention to relations of likeness, of, as it were, pointing in certain directions rather than stating a finite set of things, then many of the difficulties embedded in depiction based accounts of art, abstract or otherwise, begin to fall away. Donald Davidson has talked about metaphors in such a fashion. The work of likening that is enacted in a metaphor, he stresses, cannot be paraphrased or reduced to a finite list of predicates without remainder: a metaphor does not work by having 'a special meaning, a specific cognitive content'. Rather 'metaphor and simile ... are devices that serve to alert us to aspects of the world by inviting us to make comparisons'.[14] This is not to say that pictures are metaphors in any direct sense; it is more that metaphors are picture-like in the way they work. At the same time, however, Davidson's discussion of the content of metaphors bears more than a passing resemblance to

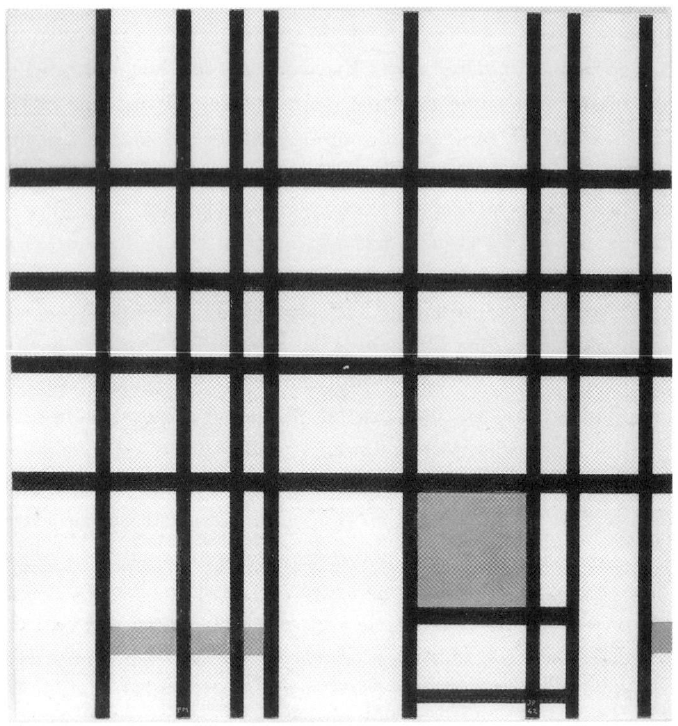

Figure 9. Piet Mondrian. *Composition with Red, Yellow, and Blue*, 1935. London, Collection Tate Gallery. (Copyright DACS 1991)

Greenberg's comments about the content of works of art. In the same essay Greenberg talked of the 'precious freedom' which came from art, 'the freedom to be surprised, taken aback, have your expectations confounded...'[15]

A picture may or may not *succeed* in alerting its viewer to an unaccustomed way of seeing the world, in confounding expectations, in the same way that a joke may or may not succeed in making its audience laugh. And in either case this may be due to some lack in the work or in its recipient. But this is a very different matter from the claim or assumption that pictures *cannot* work on our expectations, habits and prejudices; cannot say as much about us as we say about them.

Notes

1. See Ad Reinhardt, *Art Comics and Satires*, Truman Gallery, NY, 1976.

2. Clement Greenberg, 'Abstract, representational and so forth', 1954, reprinted in *Art & Culture*, Thames & Hudson, London, 1973, pp. 133–38.

3. *Ibid.*, p. 133.

4. Clement Greenberg, 'Complaints of an art critic', *Artforum*, Vol. IV, No. 2, October 1967, pp. 38–39. Reprinted in *Modernism, Criticism, Realism*, ed. C. Harrison and F. Orten, Harper & Row, London, 1984, pp. 3–8.

5. *Ibid.*, p. 39.

6. Anna Chave, *Mark Rothko: Subjects in Abstraction*, Harvard, 1989; 'Minimalism and the rhetoric of power', *Arts Magazine*, January 1990, pp. 44–63.

7. Chave, 'Minimalism and the rhetoric of power', p. 51.

8. Peter Halley, *Collected Essays: 1981-87*, Bischofsberger, Zurich, 1988. See also my 'A man in a sombrero frying an egg', *Artscribe*, No. 76, Summer 1989, pp. 93–95 for further discussion.

9. See, for example, 'A small kind of order: Donald Judd interviewed by David Batchelor', *Artscribe*, No. 78, November-December 1989, pp. 62–67.

10. For a discussion on the distinction between the iconic and the non-iconic, see, for example, Flint Schier, *Deeper into Pictures*, Cambridge, 1986, pp. 43–44.

11. Such conceptions are at the heart of modernist conceptions of value. In its most succinct form see Greenberg's critique of Surrealist painting in *The Collected Essays and Criticism*, Vol. 1, 1939–1944, Chicago, 1986, pp. 225–31.

12. See, for example, Rosalind Krauss, 'LeWitt in Progress', *The Originality of the Avant Garde and Other Modernist Myths*, Cambridge, Mass., 1985, pp. 244–58, for a good case study.

13. See W. J. T. Mitchel, *Iconology*, Chicago, 1986, chapter 1, for an extended discussion of 'likeness in non-iconic imagery'.

14. Donald Davidson, 'What metaphors mean', in *On Metaphor*, ed. Sheldon Sacks, Chicago and London, 1979, pp. 29–45.

15. Greenberg, 'Complaints of an art critic', *op. cit.*, p. 39.

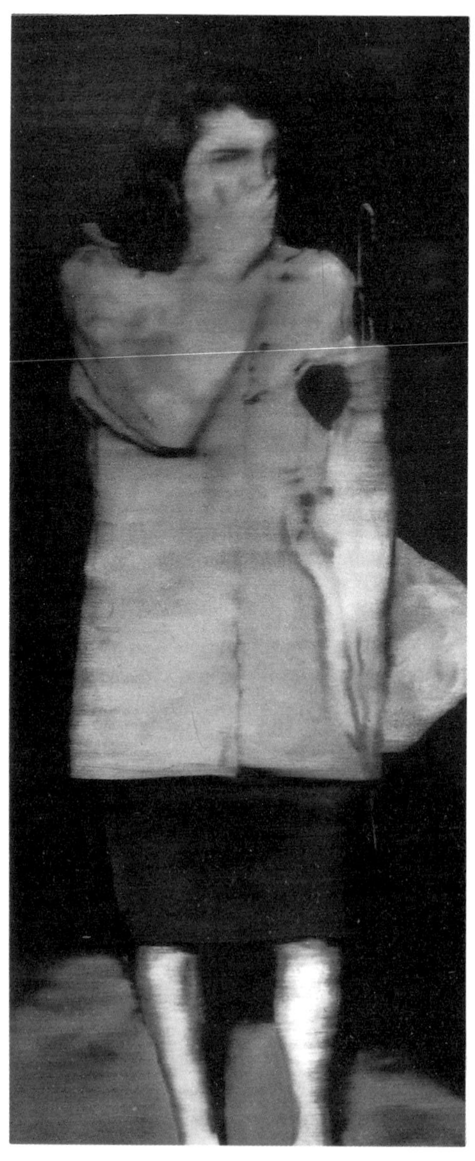

Gerhard Richter. *Woman with Umbrella*, 1964. (Courtesy of the artist)

Modernism, Abstraction, and the Return to Painting

Peter Osborne

However much they may disagree about other things, critics are in broad agreement about at least three features of the current situation in the visual arts:

> 1. 'Art exists today in a state of pluralism: no style or even mode of art is dominant';[1]
> 2. This pluralism is the result of the progressive breakdown or self-destruction of the previously hegemonic modernist project, enacted in painting and sculpture during the 1960s and early 1970s by minimalist and conceptual art in a radicalisation of the project of abstraction, in conjunction with the parallel but nonetheless very different departure of Pop;
> 3. This situation involves the legitimation (or at least the absence of a convincing delegitimation) of a 'return' to painting, and to figurative and expressive painting in particular, in one form or another.

That there is agreement about very little else follows from the idea of pluralism. For it is the absence of a hegemonic critical discourse, rather than the mere fact of a multiplicity of forms and styles, that makes this multiplicity a 'plurality' in any critically significant sense of the term. 'Pluralism', in other words, is as much a description of the state of criticism as of art practice; the sign of a crisis for a certain kind of criticism as much as a marker for some new creative diversity. The extent to which this crisis is immanent to totalising models of critical practice, rather than (more simply) the result of a change in institutional conditions,[2] remains contentious; as do all judgements of its liberating or reactionary nature. Yet there can be no denying that the last twenty years have seen major changes in the art institutions of Western capitalist states; or that these changes have powerfully facilitated both the erosion of the traditional function of criticism as the mediating agency of art's place in the market and the dissemination of 'pluralism' as an aesthetic and political value. The new pluralism and the return to painting which it involves are located in a quite different context from the late modernist art of the 1960s and early 1970s, in reaction to which they are generally understood.

It is, of course, with reference to this context – theorised in terms of the abolition of the division between 'high art' and 'mass culture' in a new form of cultural commodification – that the idea of postmodernism as a new 'cultural dominant' has been most forcefully propounded.[3] But it would be a mistake to reduce the complex transformation of cultural forms that has taken place over the last three decades to a *homogenisation* of cultural space. The increased influence of the commodity-form within the productive and distributive circuits of the art market should not blind us to its specificity as a market; any more than its character as 'art' need blind us to its social form. It is with reference to a certain kind of purportedly 'postmodernist' painting that some of the oldest myths about individual creativity are currently being recycled in a more intensely commodified form. The critical task of comprehending (judging the meaning) of the latest artistic phenomena, with reference to the increasingly problematic status of 'art', remains. How we are to orientate ourselves towards them – what interpretive framework we are to adopt – will depend upon our understanding of the nature and fate of the modernism they have replaced.[4]

Superficially, we are presented with two main responses to the apparent, but perhaps prematurely announced, death of modernism in the visual arts: *relief and celebration* at the demise of a repressive and authoritarian artistic purism, whose canon of prohibitions robbed art of its pleasure, intelligibility and democratic function, driving it into the trap of conceptualism where it was forced to deny its own essential nature in order to survive, and could live on only through intellectual gimmicry (a position for which the label of 'postmodernism' is often used to cover an essentially anti-modernist agenda);[5] and *anger, mourning and a sense of loss* at the apparent betrayal of modernism's critical legacy and the failure to replace it with any convincing or historically sensitive alternative account of art's role, direction or legitimate procedures in the new 'post' modernist phase. Neither response is adequate, though each expresses a real concern. The difficulty lies in thinking the two together through the construction of a perspective capable of comprehending the continuity of current developments with their past as well as their difference. The central issues at stake with respect to painting would seem to be the role and consequences of *abstraction* and the nature, and especially the politics, of *expression*.

Historically, three alternative perspectives on these issues present themselves, each of which corresponds to a particular moment in the development of modern art. The first is what might be called the Kandinsky/Malevich/Mondrian tradition of the *spiritual* self-understanding of abstraction, associated with the first phase of abstract painting in Europe from 1910 onwards. This tradition feeds into Surrealism, but in a rather complex way. It also informs the way in which a number of American painters in the post-war years understood their work – in particular Newman and Rothko: Rosenberg's 'theological sector' of Abstract Expressionism – although the form of their transcendentalism was significantly different, and generally much vaguer in its theoretical content. Pollock and others did, of course, make use of the Surrealists' concept of the unconscious, albeit in a Jungian rather than a Freudian sense, but this seems to have contributed little more than the general notion of the archetype. However, this was not the interpretive framework adopted by the most influential critical sponsor of this work: namely Clement Greenberg.

This is my second perspective: the Greenbergian tradition of understanding abstraction as the consequence and means of a self-limiting, self-critical *purism* which reduces the task of modern art to the 'pure' one of exploring the emotional content of the physical properties of traditional artistic media. It is this tradition which was given a phenomenological turn by Michael Fried's emphasis on opticality in his famous 'Art and Objecthood' essay from 1967. It corresponds to the period of American abstract painting from the early 1940s through to the colourfield paintings and 'post-painterly abstraction' of the early 1960s. It is closely connected to the development of minimalism, but disavows the minimalists' renunciation of expressive qualities through a radical paring down of artistic means to what Greenberg saw as a standardised and 'unartistic' formulaism. It entered into crisis in the mid-1960s.

My third approach has certain affinities with this second, purist tradition but must be distinguished from it in principle. It is the German tradition of Frankfurt critical theory represented pre-eminently by the philosopher, musicologist and cultural critic Theodor Adorno. Its primary distinguishing feature is its determination to transcend a merely art-historical or 'internalist' perspective on artistic development in the direction of a totalising (but de-totalised) socio-historical account which integrates its understanding of the social determinations of artistic practice into its understanding of 'aesthetic' or artistic categories. It is at once more sociological and more philosophical than Greenberg's approach, understanding abstraction neither in terms of transcendent spiritual values (Kandinsky/Malevich/Mondrian), nor in terms of a purity of artistic means (Greenberg), but as both a reflection of the form of social experience in developed capitalist societies and a specific artistic strategy to express such experience (alienation) through its distance from and dissonance with established aesthetic norms. The continuing historical value and modality of abstraction is thus here to be judged not in terms of some 'purification' of the arts, but in terms of its on-going vitality as a critical strategy through which to express the alienated forms of modern life and to combat the neutralisation of artistic autonomy by the appropriation of its forms by the culture industry. Adorno's work spans the period from the European avant-garde of the 1930s to the array of minimalist, conceptual and anti-art movements of the 1960s. It is from its ability to reconstruct the immanent artistic logic and dilemmas of this development that it derives its enduring strength.

Each approach encompasses a multitude of possible emphases and inflections (especially the first one), but they do offer broadly competing interpretive perspectives. It has been through a mediated return to the first (the spiritual one), and the criticism, neglect or downgrading of the other two, that those who have sought a legitimating ancestry for recent painterly practices have, in the main, turned.[6] I will now say a little more about the understanding within each of the relationship of abstraction to expression.

Kandinsky/Malevich/Mondrian: spiritual abstraction

This is the tradition which enacts the basic movement within early twentieth-century modernism from an emphasis on expression to one on abstraction. Its understanding of abstraction is heavily reliant on a neo-Platonic metaphysical realism about spiritual values, derived in the main (although not exclusively) from Theosophical texts, but it begins with an equally strong sense of the act of painting as the expression of spiritual values. This becomes progressively weaker as the tradition develops in the direction of a formal-constructive, geometrical abstraction within which it is not so much the expressive qualities of the act of painting which is important (indeed, these are radically downgraded and suppressed as 'naturalistic') as the direct expression of spiritual values as painterly values in geometrical forms. The idea of expression is not eliminated, but it is transcendentally transformed. This is a tradition, in other words, at least in Malevich and Mondrian (Kandinsky remains connected to the quasi-naturalistic spiritualism of early expressionism), in which the subject (the artist), although entrusted with the materialisation of a spiritual task – the discovery and expression of spiritual values by 'pure painterly values' – becomes so transcendentalised as to more or less disappear from the process in any embodied or socially significant sense. The material subjectivity of the painter becomes the mere *cipher* for a cosmic transcendentalism.[7]

Malevich's and Mondrian's painting is 'non-objective' only in the sense that it is non-*naturalistic*. It expresses, although it does not depict, a spiritual but phenomenologically present reality – a reality the intuition of which has, at the time, associated with the coming of a new age. Abstraction prefiguratively expresses an ideal transcendence, through but not *in* the act of painting.

There are, of course, both *mystical* and more directly *social-utopian* variations of emphasis within this spiritual problematic. It was the latter which quickly won out in post-Revolutionary Russia in the move to the more technically-based geometricism and practical, social-utilitarian utopianism of constructivism. Lissitzky even went so far as to declare Suprematism the next historical stage after communism: 'AFTER THE OLD TESTAMENT THERE CAME THE NEW – AFTER THE NEW THE COMMUNIST – AND AFTER THE COMMUNIST THERE FOLLOWS FINALLY THE TESTAMENT OF SUPREMATISM.'[8] It is with the closure of this moment, this political horizon (and the rather different fate of *actual*, historical communism) that the more mystical (and mystificatory) element of the spiritual interpretation has returned to an increasingly central position in the art world. In the meantime, however, what might be called the 'absolutist' tradition of *identifying* aesthetic modernity with abstraction was continued, outside its original theoretical and social context of spiritualist metaphysics and socio technological utopianism, in a very different way, in the formal purism of Greenberg's modernism.

Greenberg: for abstraction, against expression

Greenberg may be read as beginning where Constructivism left off in its de-transcendentalisation of Suprematism, with two crucial differences. If Constructivism replaced Suprematism's cosmic transcendentalism with the revolutionary utilitarianism of the historical avant-garde, whilst preserving and extending its formal developments, Greenberg performed a more strictly art-historical retrieval of the movement towards abstraction, under the very different social and political conditions of war-time American capitalism. And he did so, not with regard to Suprematism, but with reference to the progress of post-cubist French abstraction and the old 'masters' Kandinsky, Mondrian and Klee.

Greenberg was especially impressed with the development of a post-cubist pictorial space within Miro's Surrealist abstractionism – which, characteristically, he counted as belonging to French painting – in contrast to the degeneration of Kandinsky's work, which he took to reflect a failure to understand the true painterly significance of abstraction. Kandinsky and Leger, he argued in 1941, in anticipation of a problem that would recur later within American abstraction, 'demonstrate how easy it is for the abstract painter to degenerate into a decorator'; although it should be noted that he does add that to be an interior decorator is still more creative than to be an academic painter.[9] Meanwhile, Malevich's work, although taken to be of 'documentary value', is dismissed as 'meagre in aesthetic results'.[10] The fact that Malevich considered his work a frontal attack on the very notion of the 'aesthetic' ('Aestheticism is the garbage of intuitive feeling')[11] is ignored.

Greenberg sets out his disagreement with Kandinsky in his obituary of January 1945. Kandinsky's paintings from the mid-1920s onwards, he argues, 'represent a misconception not only of cubism and its antecedents, but of the very art of putting paint on canvas to make a picture'. They recognise that the cubist revolution freed painting from representation, but they fail to see what for: namely, 'its recapture of the literal realisation of the physical limitations and conditions of the medium'. Instead, they return to the essentially illustrative, albeit 'abstract', material of the *art nouveau* motifs and peasant decoration of Kandinsky's youth, failing to exploit the new pictorial space Kandinsky himself had helped created.[12]

The problem here concerns expression, and it was to dog Greenberg from hereon. Greenberg deplored the 'expressionistic' elements in both German expressionism and surrealism, since they seemed to him to throw away the painterly gains of an abstract, post-cubist pictorial space for meagre and essentially illustrative aesthetic effects. At the same time, however, he was equally uncomfortable with the almost mechanical *lack* of expressive qualities in Suprematism (a critique he would later repeat with regard to minimalism, its heir), and to some extent in Mondrian. He was thus stuck in the unfortunate situation of having to acknowledge the 'indispensibility' of this element to the originality of good abstract art (indeed, ultimately, to its status as art), whilst at the same time treating it as a 'serious handicap'.[13]

His solution was to promote that art which others called 'Abstract Expressionism' (Pollock, de Kooning, Newman, Rothko et al) on the basis of an interpretation which went *against* its expressionist dimension, emphasising instead the way in which it exploited the possibilities of post-cubist pictorial space for the exploration of the emotional content of the *pure physicality* of pictorial means (rather than the artist's psychic state or, as in Rosenberg, the 'event' of painting itself). He thereby opened up the conceptual space for Rosenberg's alternative and equally one-sided existential analysis of Pollock's work as 'action painting', which was able, unlike Greenberg's, to acknowledge the influence of Surrealism. (He also, of course, unwittingly, opened the way for Minimalism. But that's another story.) In this respect, Greenberg and Rosenberg are very much the 'torn halves' of an adequate criticism of American Abstraction to which, however, they do not add up, since they remain in conflict with each other. It is for this reason that, despite its association with Pollock, Greenberg's criticism is actually much more happily associated with the material literality of 'Post-Painterly' Abstraction (Nolan, Louis and Olitski): a movement he not only sponsored but more or less brought into being.[14]

For all his sponsorship of Abstract Expressionism, the basic tendency of Greenberg's work is in accordance with the emergence of an *opposition* between abstraction and any materially significant concept of expression within what I have called the 'spiritual' tradition of the understanding of abstraction in modern art. His humanism dictates the recognition of the necessity of a submerged residue of expressive content, but he is unable to integrate this recognition into his account of the meaning of the work. Thus, although he is formally less dogmatic than the Suprematists in his ban on the reintroduction of representative and expressive material into modern art – in principle, abstraction is viewed as an historical tendency which might be reversed – his position is effectively just as absolutist as the Suprematists', since there is no conceptual space within his account that would allow for anything but a *regressive* 'return'. The tension within this position is clear in the following passage from 'Modernist Painting' (1965):

> It is not in principle that Modernist painting in its latest phase has abandoned the representation of recognisable objects. What it has abandoned in principle is the representation of the kind of space that recognisable, three-dimensional objects can inhabit. Abstractness, or the non-figurative, has in-itself still not proved to be an altogether necessary moment in the self-criticism of pictorial art, even though artists as eminent as Kandinsky and Mondrian have thought so. Representation, or illustration, as such does not abate the uniqueness of pictorial art; what does do so are the associations of the things represented. All recognisable entities (including pictures themselves) exist in three-dimensional space, and the barest suggestion of a recognisable entity suffices to call up associations of that kind of space. ... [It is] two-dimensionality which is the guarantee of painting's independence as an art.[15]

This does nothing to weaken the necessity of abstraction. It merely provides an alternative explanation of it. What is conceded at the outset is soon taken back. Abstraction may not be indispensible to painting 'in-itself', but it is a necessary correlate of something that is. In this respect, it *is* indispensable. The gesture towards the openness of the future is empty; at least insofar as an 'independent' painting is concerned. Yet it is, of course, with this very notion of independence that the problems with Greenberg's account begin. It is because of its ability to deal with these problems through a socialised account of artistic autonomy that Adorno's work recommends itself as a standpoint from which to consider the current return to painting in historical but still immanently artistic terms.[16]

Adorno: abstraction as moment and problem

Greenberg has a dim if dogged recognition of the ineliminability of art's expressive dimension, but he does not deal with it theoretically, and, in the form in which he understands it, it exists in more or less open contradiction to the stress he places upon the artist's exploration of the emotional content of the 'literal physical properties' of traditional artistic media. What is more, he sees it as threatened, in principle, by constructivist techniques, since they eliminate the trace of 'originality' which stems from the subjectivity of the artist. The idea of constructivist techniques as means for the expression of a specific form of social experience is unknown to him; ruled out by the subjectivism of his concept of expression and the self-referential interpretation of autonomy to which it corresponds. For Greenberg, objectivity resides exclusively in the physicality of the medium. It is the medium that 'imposes' a style.

For Adorno, on the other hand, objectivity is embedded within the structure of artistic production at a number of different levels. All art is the product of an historically evolving *dialectic* of expression and construction (mimesis and rationality) within which the subject and means of expression develop as mediations of wider social processes. Expression in works of art is 'the non-subjective in the subject'. Construction is understood not as a corrective of expression, but as 'something that has to emerge in an unplanned way from the mimetic impulse'. Art 'absorbs both the mimetic [expressive] impulse and the [constructive] critique of that impulse by objectifying it'. It is this objectification of mimesis or expression which is for Adorno 'the constitutive act of spiritualisation in art'. ('Spiritualisation' being understood here not in a mystical but in a fully social and strictly Hegelian sense.) And it is the reification of the objectifying subject that tends towards abstraction.[17]

In this respect, Expressionism and Constructivism are to be understood as movements which strategically emphasise opposite sides of an evolving dialectic in which they both partake. Their critical viability and historical meaning are to be judged, not according to some general principle of the 'pictorial', but in terms of the artistic (and extra-artistic) contexts into which they intervene, and the specific forms that they take: the superiority of constructivism as a strategy at a particular time being seen to lie in its rejection of the myth of a spontaneous subjectivity and its *expression* of the reification of the subject and the transformation of its powers through technology. Expressionism, on the other hand, can be decoded materialistically, in relation to the thesis of the progressive elimination of a socially substantive subjectivity, as an alienated protest against alienation which can take either progressive or reactionary forms.[18] Both are inherently connected to the movement towards abstraction insofar as each involves a downgrading of the representational content of the work in favour of an increased self-consciousness of (one aspect of) the process of its production, in response to the development of mechanical forms of reproduction (photography). But there is no necessary elimination of representational content here. The strategic retreat from figurative representation (naturalism) in the face of mechanical reproduction must be distinguished in principle from the more general impulse towards abstraction inherent in the reification of the subject, although the two converge.

The importance of Adorno's approach is that, while it does not foreclose future developments in the way in which absolutist interpretations of abstraction do, it does nonetheless provide a framework for their comprehension, and a set of terms for critical debate. Adorno was well aware of the trap set by history for constructivism once it became an established artistic norm,[19] and his later work is fixated on the implosive artistic consequences of the 'aging of the new' – not simply through the passage of time, but through the neutralisation of forms by their refunctioning in the advertising and culture industries. It is precisely this problem that is addressed by recent painting in its return to the 'old' and its apparent transfiguration as 'new'. This is a structure common to the reactionary avant-gardes of all neo-classicisms, but it is by no means confined to them. The necessity of a reorientation towards past forms is built into the implosive consequences of modernism in minimalism and conceptualism. The issue is: which forms of reorientation, which modes of appropriation of past forms, represent a genuine renewal of artistic creativity, and which a simple repetition that, in merely recycling such forms, enacts the end of art in the victory of the commodity form? And how do they relate to the movement towards abstraction? Everything depends on the registering within the work of a self-consciousness of its historical position, and our understanding of the consequences of this self-consciousness for the ontology of the artwork – issues which cut across the conventional distinction between 'abstract' and 'figurative' painting to pose the question of modernism's critical legacy in a quite different way.[20]

Post-conceptual painting: representation, abstraction, reception

In a recent essay on Andy Warhol, Benjamin Buchloh sets out three paths for art in the aftermath of the critical movements (and art-institutional changes) of the 1960s:

> (1) reinforcement of the erosion of the high art-mass culture dialectic by an affirmative repetition of Warhol's modified Duchampian strategy of mapping the aspirations of high art onto the products and practices of the culture industry;
> (2) reinstitution of traditional artistic role models, object conditions and production procedures in an artificially reconstructed separate realm of high art; and
> (3) transposition of Warhol's (now re-stabilised) destabilisation of the art object onto the framing conditions of representation.[21]

The return to painting, and to figurative and expressive painting in particular, is paradigmatically associated with the second tendency.[22] It is the third option, which 'departs from the assumption that critical intervention *within* the realm of representation is ... the motivating force of aesthetic practice', that Buchloh himself recommends as the critical strategy. What I want to suggest, however, is that what is characteristic of a lot of recent painting is that it spans the second and third options; hence its inherently problematic status. What is at stake is the possibility and possible forms of 'post-conceptual' painting: a painting which is capable of addressing the 'framing conditions of representation' through its interventions within the realm of representation itself.

The reason that certain critics have taken the return to painting to be regressive *in principle* is because it seems to reinstate a traditional notion of artwork as an autonomously meaningful object which it was the historic task of Minimalism, Conceptualism and Pop to deny by drawing attention within the work itself to various conditions upon which it depends for the production of meaning. The problem with this position, however, is that it fails to take account of what might be called 'second order' representational strategies, and their relation to the movements which preceded them. For, whilst it may appear that the current recourse to figurative representation in painting marks a return from 'abstraction' to 'representation' (as well as a return to paint), there is a sense in which, in certain instances, it may also be understood as a *continuation* and *deepening* of the movement towards abstraction (and an increasing instrumentality of artistic means) in a new form. Everything turns on the sense in which conceptual art may be understood as the culmination of the movement towards abstraction (a recognition that the ontology of the artwork is bound up with the social history of its forms), whilst certain recent 'representational' painting, in its self-consciousness of the problem of representation, may be said to be 'post-conceptual' in its incorporation of the insights of conceptualism into its conception of the work.

Debate about the return to painting has tended to focus on Neo-Expressionism, figurative content, and the extent to which traditional forms of representation, spectatorship and artistic identity are celebrated or problematised by the works in question.[23] Yet the issues which are raised apply equally to abstract works. For if the main problem for painting after conceptualism is how to avoid the reinstitution of a traditional notion of the aesthetic object, this would seem to be all the more difficult for a painting which refuses to depict, and is thus apparently denied the representational content in relation to which it can deploy a second-order representational strategy capable of registering the 'conditions of representation' within representation itself. If a return to painting is to be critical, it would seem, it *must* 'represent', at at least two levels, the second of which will involve some kind of *distanciating* depiction of the representational forms of the first level. This does not rule out the possibility of post-conceptual abstraction (it is possible to depict non-figurative representational forms), but it does restrict its scope. It also poses problems of reception which, while they are common to all post-conceptual painting, are especially acute in this instance.

These claims may be illustrated with reference to Buchloh's own reading of Gerhard Richter's large abstract paintings from the late 1970s and '80s as 'a memory of the past of painting' – 'when gesture could still engender the experience of emotional turbulence, when chromatic veils credibly conveyed a sense of transparency and spatial infinity, when impasto could read as immediacy and emphatic material presence, when linear formation read as direction in space, movement through time, as operative force of the will

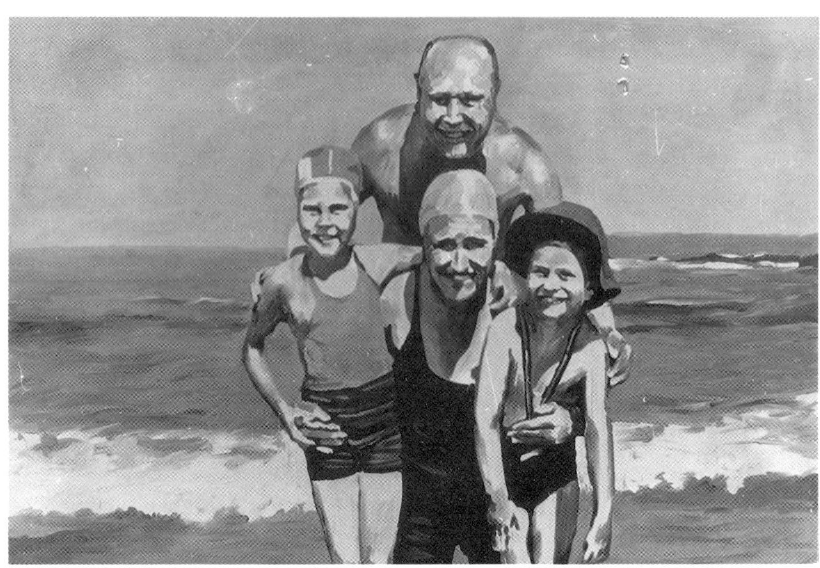

Gerhard Richter. *Family at the Seaside*, 1964. (Courtesy of the artist)

of the subject, and when composition and successful integration of all of these elements into painting constituted the experience of the subject.'[24]

Artists have never been slow to plunder the store of past forms in order to provide reflective commentary on the social or art-historical location of their work. What is peculiar about post-conceptual painting is that it must treat *all* forms of painterly representation 'knowingly', as themselves the object of a variety of second-order (non-painterly) representational strategies, if it is to avoid regression to a traditional concept of the aesthetic object. The difficulty is to register this difference without negating the significance of the painterly elements; to exploit the significance of paint without reinstituting a false immediacy. Buchloh's reading of Richter's abstracts is of interest because of the claim it makes for them in just this regard. At the same time, however, it depends upon an understanding of their position within the development of Richter's work as a whole which, to the extent that it goes beyond anything registered immanently within the works themselves, suggests that ultimately they *fail* to address the framing conditions of their own meaning.

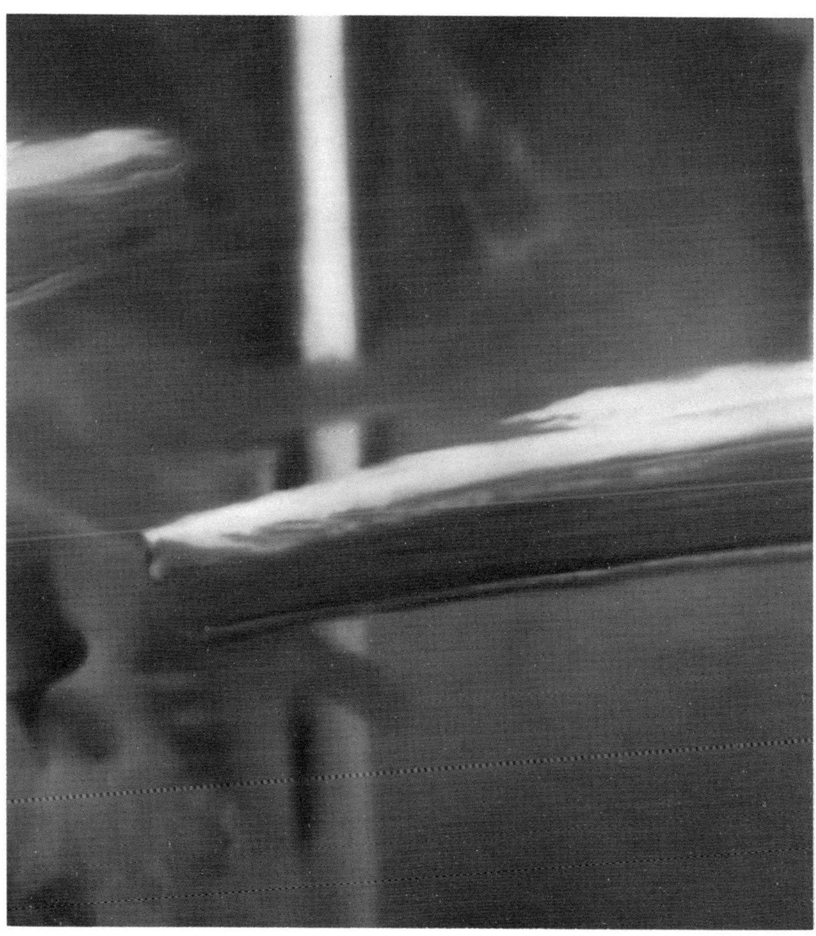

Gerhard Richter. *Abstract Painting*, 1977. Buffalo, Albright-Knox Art Gallery. (Courtesy of the artist)

Buchloh's reading sets out from a recognition of the inadequacy of two alternative interpretive perspectives: Richter's own claim to have resumed 'a traditionalist position with regard to the assignment of meaning to pictorial structures' and a postmodernist position (premised on the idea of the end of painting) from which Richter's large abstracts appear as wholly

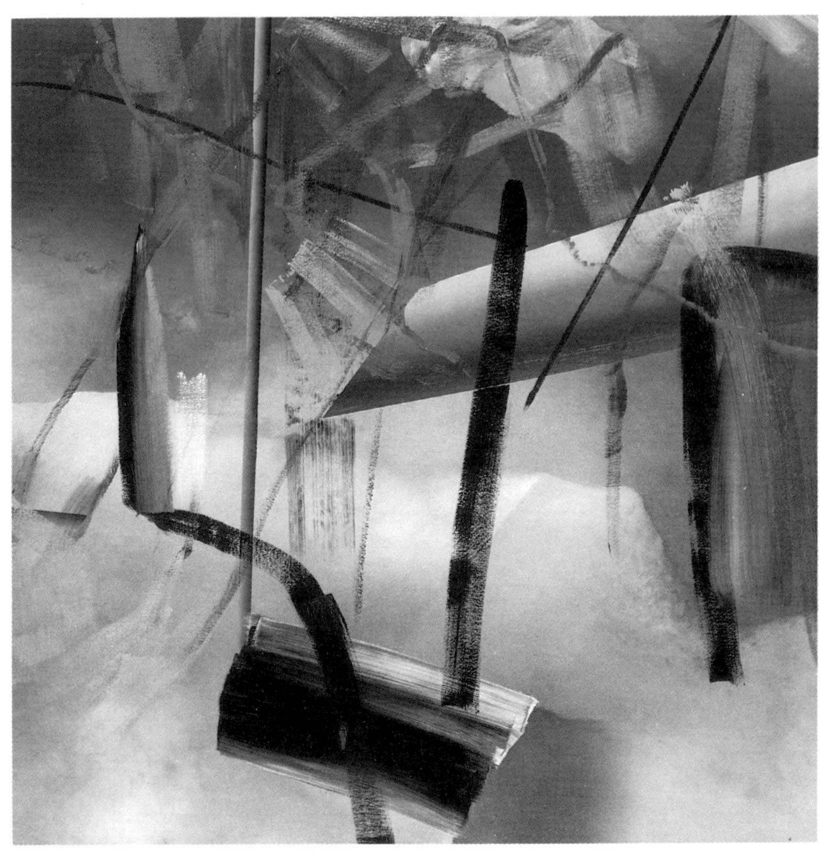

Gerhard Richter. *Abstract Painting (July)*, 1983. Essen, Collection Schwartz. (Courtesy of the artist)

second-order representations of a dead painterly rhetoric. If the problem with the first position is that it takes the pictures' painterly qualities at face value, the problem with the second one is that it fails to take them seriously at all. Buchloh's response to this dilemma is to inquire more deeply into the technical aspects of the pictures' production in the context of the development of Richter's work as a whole. What this reveals is the extent to which the paintings represent a renewal, rather than a repudiation, of Richter's interest in photographic reproduction and its relation to painting. Thus, while his earlier photopaintings had been distorted painterly representations of photographs, in the mid-1970s he began to invert the process and produce large-scale photographic reproductions of small colour-sketches. It is these reproductions which provide the models for the structural form of the later abstract paintings. 'Organic' or painterly gestures are 'mechanically' reproduced and enlarged, and the structure of these reproductions is then itself 'organically' reproduced and varied in large abstract paintings. What this suggests is that the paintings are *about* the mechanical mediation of organic processes. It is, in Buchloh's words, their 'manifest subject'. As such, they are seen to provide us with 'immediate insight into the contemporary conditions of painting: to exist between the irreconcilable demands of the spectacle and the synecdoche'.

The interpretation is convincing, but it stops short of a full analysis. What it lacks is reflection on the significance of the 'organic' or painterly character of the final product. It is at this point that Richter's own remarks become significant. For, while the 'mediation of an original, direct and organic painterly activity ... through the various stages and practices of a mechanical construction of a pictorial sign' may be the subject of the works, their form is unashamedly 'painterly'. As such, they enact an organic *recuperation* of the 'mechanical mediation of the organic', a counter-movement which restores the primacy of the organic over the mechanical at a higher level. In this respect, they continue the appropriative strategy of the photopaintings (on Buchloh's analysis they are themselves a new kind of photopainting), but with one crucial difference: here, *the photographic mediation vanishes in the act of painterly reappropriation*. This is why the paintings lend themselves so easily to traditional interpretation. There are serious problems of reception.

If the return to painting is to involve more than a simple repetition of past practices, it will have to register its difference – a difference of historical time – immanently, within its forms. To the extent to which such differences may nonetheless still fail to be recognised, however, debate about the return to painting is also bound up with a debate about reception, and the responsibility of the work to the conditions of its reception in the art market. It is at this point that the institutional changes to which reference was made at the beginning of this essay become of *critical* significance: conditions of reception are part of the historical conditions of production which must be registered within the work if it is to assert its difference from earlier manifestations of those forms in relation to which it represents a 'return'. It is the difficulty of addressing these conditions within the enclosed form of the picture which is registered in the semantic instability and critical ambivalence of so much recent painting. Critical self-consciousness of the problems of representation is all too often accompanied, and negated, by an affirmative or at best neutral relation to conditions of reception in the art market: the assumption of a traditional conception of the aesthetic object. This problem is particularly acute for abstract painting because of its refusal to depict. Even a self-consciously neutral stance towards reception becomes affirmative once an historically conscious criticism becomes displaced as the mediating agency of the work's circulation in the market: objective indifference to reception mimics the market's indifference to all values except exchange-value – something that was recognised and exploited by Warhol with a single-mindedness, and a higher level ambivalence of its own, that would be hard to match. In this respect at least, it would seem, *both* critics and defenders of recent painting are right: semantic instability and critical ambivalence are constitutive features of the form.

Notes

1. Hal Foster, 'Against Pluralism', *Recodings: Art, Spectacle, Cultural Politics* (Bay Press, Seattle, 1985), p. 13.
2. See, for example, Walter Grasskamp, 'Art Fair Blues', *Art and Design*, Vol. 5, No. 11/12 (1989), pp. 51–57; and Benjamin H. D. Buchloh, 'Periodising Critics', in Hal Foster (ed.), Dia Art Foundation *Discussions in Contemporary Culture*, No. 1 (Bay Press, Seattle, 1987), pp. 65–70.
3. Fredric Jameson, 'Postmodernism, or the Cultural Logic of Late Capitalism', *New Left Review* 146 (July/August 1984), pp. 53–92. See also Andreas Huyssen, *After the Great Divide: Modernism, Mass Culture and Postmodernism* (Macmillan, London, 1988).
4. For a defence of the idea of 'autonomous' art as a distinct cultural space, against the postmodernist thesis of cultural homogenisation and with reference to Adorno, see my 'Torn Halves and Great Divides: The Dialectics of a Cultural Dichotomy', *News From Nowhere* 7 (Winter 1989), Special Issue on 'The Politics of Modernism', pp. 48–63. I take issue with Jameson's recent Adorno interpretation, *Late Marxism: Adorno, or, the Persistence of the Dialectic* (Verso, London, 1990), in 'A Marxism for the Postmodern? – Jameson's Adorno', forthcoming.
5. Hal Foster, *Recodings*, p. 28.
6. I am thinking in particular of the 1985 exhibition at the Los Angeles County Museum, 'The Spiritual in Art: Abstract Painting 1890–1985'. The 1981 Royal Academy exhibition 'A New Spirit in Painting' displayed a similar tendency, but in a less systematic or explicitly mystical way.
7. The work of art, van Doesburg insists in an early statement of Neo-Plasticist principle, 'must be completely conceived and formed by the mind before its execution. It must not receive any formal impressions from nature, nor from the senses, nor from sentiment' (quoted by Harold Rosenberg, 'Mondrian: Meaning in Abstract Art I' (1972), *Art at the Edge: Creators and Situations*, University of Chicago Press, Chicago, 1983, pp. 39–40). There is a similar emphasis on the creation of painterly forms as ends in themselves in Malevich. 'The artist can be a creator,' he writes, 'only when the forms in his picture have nothing in common with nature. ... Intuitive form should *arise out of nothing*' (Kazimir Malevich, 'From Cubism and Futurism to Suprematism: The New Painterly Realism' (1915), in *Russian Art of the Avant-Garde: Theory and Criticism*, 1902–1934, edited and translated by John E. Bowlt, Thames and Hudson, London, 1988, pp. 122, 128; emphasis added). Both Malevich and Mondrian turned to geometry as the sphere of a pure intuitive or creative reason: Malevich to the square as the 'face of the new art ... the first step of pure creation'; Mondrian to his grids of vertical and horizontal lines. Vertical and horizontal lines, Mondrian argued, are 'the expression of two opposing principles: [which] exist everywhere and dominate everything; their reciprocal action constitutes "life" ... the equilibrium of any particular aspect of nature rests on the equivalence of its opposites ... the tragic is created by unequivalence.' He thus arrived at the principle of the equivalence of plastic means ('different in size and colour they

should nevertheless have equal value') as the expression of an overcoming of the tragic and an impulse towards a new society composed of 'balanced relationships'. Plastic art 'must not only move parallel with human progress, but must advance ahead of it' (Mondrian, quoted by Hans L. C. Jaffe, *Mondrian*, Thames and Hudson, London, 1990, p. 106; and by Rosenberg, 'Mondrian', p. 47).

8. El Lissitzky, 'Suprematism in World Construction' (1920), in Bowlt (ed.), *Russian Art of the Avant-Garde*, p. 158.

9. Clement Greenberg, 'Review of Exhibitions Joan Miro, Fernand Leger, and Wassily Kandinsky' (1941), *The Collected Essays and Criticism*, Vol. 1, *Perceptions and Judgements, 1939–1944*, edited by John O'Brian (Chicago University Press, Chicago, 1986), pp. 64–65.

10. Clement Greenberg, 'Review of Four Exhibitions of Abstract Art' (1942), *Collected Essays*, Vol. 1, p. 104.

11. Malevich, 'From Cubism and Futurism to Suprematism', p. 135.

12. Clement Greenberg, 'Obituary and Review of an Exhibition by Kandinsky', *The Collected Essays and Criticism*, Vol. 2, *Arrogant Purpose, 1945–1949*, edited by John O'Brian (Chicago University Press, Chicago, 1986), pp. 3–6.

13. Clement Greenberg, 'Review of an Exhibition of Georgia O'Keefe' (1946), *Collected Essays*, Vol. 2, p. 86.

14. It should be noted that Greenberg was waging an explicitly *nationalist* campaign, not only on behalf of an American hegemony of modern art – hence the running together of what are actually rather different kinds of painting under the label 'American-Type Painting' – but more specifically, on behalf of the American inheritance of a French tradition which he was keen to defend against its 'expressionistic' German counterpart. His judgement on expressionism, like that of the Hungarian Marxist Gyorgy Lukacs, must thus be grasped in the context of an anti-fascist cultural politics which, in this case at least, was perhaps too crude.

15. Clement Greenberg, 'Modernist Painting' (1965), in Francis Frascina and Charles Harrison (eds.), *Modern Art and Modernism: A Critical Anthology* (Harper and Row, London, 1982), pp. 6–7. Cf. the original formulation of the position in 'Towards a Newer Laocoon' (1940), *Collected Essays*, Vol. 1, pp. 23–38.

16. For an account of the differences between Greenberg's and Adorno's ideas on the autonomy of the modernist artwork, and their consequences for the concept of modernism, see my 'Aesthetic Autonomy and the Crisis of Theory: Greenberg, Adorno, and the Problem of Postmodernism in the Visual Arts', *New Formations* 9 (Winter 1989), pp. 31–50.

17. Theodor Adorno, *Aesthetic Theory* (1970), translated by C. Lenhardt, edited by Gretel Adorno and Rolf Tiedemann (Routledge and Kegan Paul, London, 1984), pp. 65, 162, 165. One of the main problems with Jameson's reading of Adorno is his failure to see the way in which the categories of mimesis and expression overlap. His view that they are 'irreconcilable opposites' (*Late Marxism*, p.159) makes nonsense of Adorno's whole ontology. For Adorno, it is expression and illusion (*Schein*) which are 'mostly antithetical to one another' (*Aesthetic Theory*, p. 161), not expression and mimesis.

18. For a revival of the classical dialectical critique of expressionism, see Hal Foster, 'Between Modernism and the Media' and 'The Expressive Fallacy', *Recodings*, pp. 33–78. For a (somewhat overblown) reading of minimalism as a kind of negative expressionism, see Donald Kuspit, 'The Minimalist Line as an Attenuated, Tragic Act of Art', *Art and Design*, Vol. 5, Nos. 11/12 (1989), pp. 64–73.

19. See, for example, Theodor Adorno, 'The Aging of the New Music' (954), *Telos* 77 (Fall 1988), pp. 95–116.

20. It might be objected at this point that I have presupposed the continuing validity or precisely that *modernist* art history of continual formal development which is problematised by the very fact of 'returning' forms. To a certain extent, this is true: to pose the issue in the way that I have does assume the possibility of one version of such a history; albeit a less 'purist', less unilinear, less 'absolutist' one than that propounded by either Greenberg or the spiritualists. But the charge can equally well be thrown back at its prosecutors. To proceed otherwise is simply to presume the opposite: namely, that such a 'return' necessarily marks the end of the dialectic of modernism. But this is precisely what is in dispute. In any case, as has been frequently pointed out, the case for postmodernism as the historical successor to modernism is itself inscribed within the temporal logic of modernism.

21. Benjamin H. D. Buchloh, 'The Andy Warhol Line', in Gary Garrels (ed.), *The Work of Andy Warhol*, Dia Art Foundation, *Discussions in Contemporary Culture*, No. 3 (Bay Press, Seattle, 1989), pp. 52–69, 66–67.

22. See, for example, Buchloh's own 'Figures of Authority, Ciphers of Regression', in Brian Wallis (ed.), *Art After Modernism: Rethinking Representation*, New Museum of Contemporary Art, New York, 1984, pp. 107–36.

23. For a defence of Kiefer along these lines (against Buchloh, amongst others), see Andreas Huyssen, 'Anselm Kiefer: The Terror of History, The Temptation of Myth', *October* 48 (Spring 1989), pp. 25–65.

24. Benjamin H. D. Buchloh, 'Gerhard Richter's Facture: Between Synecdoche and the Spectacle', *Art and Design*, Vol. 5, Nos. 9/10 (1989), pp. 40–45, 45. Colour reproductions of some of Richter's large abstracts can be found in *Gerhard Richter: Paintings*, edited by Terry A. Neff (Thames and Hudson, London, 1988), pp. 113–44.

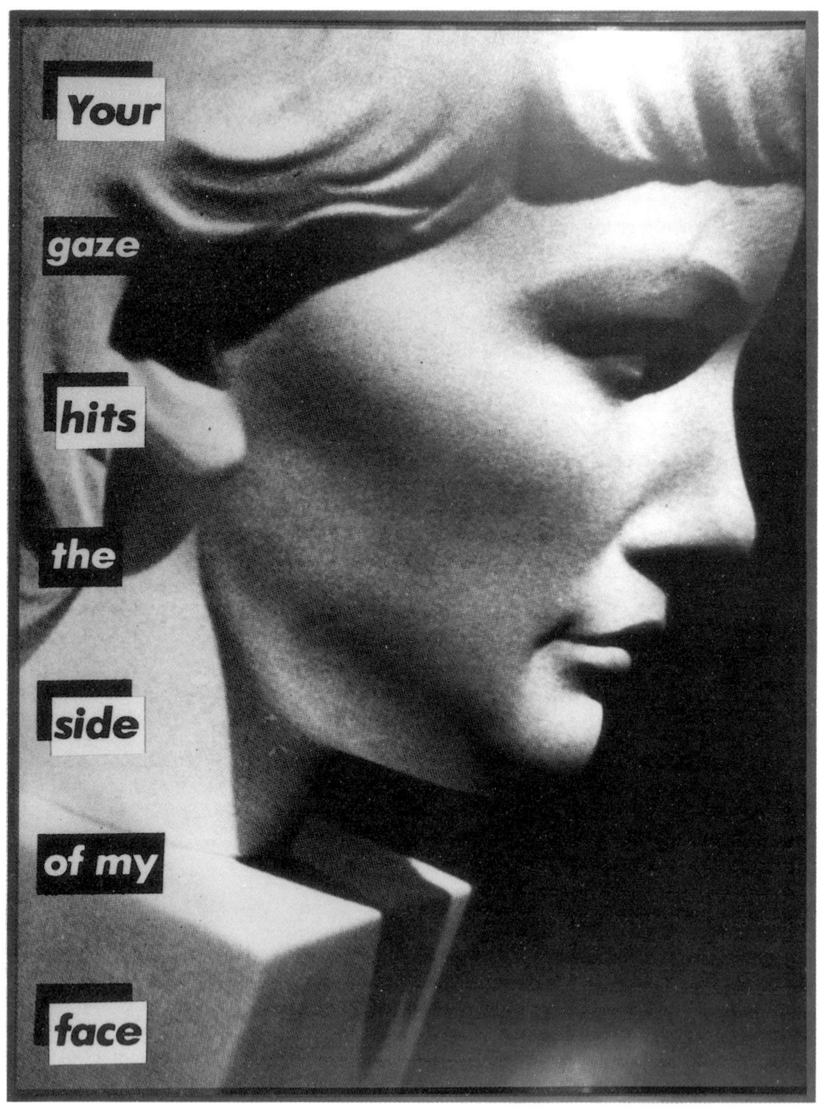

Barbara Kruger. *Unitled (Your gaze hits the side of my face)*, 1981. 55"x 44", photograph.
Collection Vijak Mahdavi and Bernardo Nadal-Ginard, Boston, MA. (Courtesy Mary Boone Gallery, NY)

The Deflationary Impulse: Postmodernism, Feminism and the Anti-Aesthetic

Margaret Iversen

> The idea of transcendence is used to obscure oppression
>
> *(Jenny Holzer)*

> The bourgeoisie has a small but considerable interest, I believe, in preserving a certain myth of the aesthetic consciousness, one where a transcendental ego is given something appropriate to contemplate in a situation essentially detached from the pressures and deformities of history. The interest is considerable because the class in question has few other areas (since the decline of the sacred) in which its account of consciousness and freedom can be at all compellingly phrased. *(T. J. Clark)*[1]

Given the pervasiveness of the aesthetic of the Sublime and the avant-garde posture of alienated outsiderism in the 1940s and '50s New York art scene, the inversion of these values in the '60s comes as no surprise. Instead of the Abstract Expressionist ideal of a transcendent or autonomous art, we find an emphasis on pre-determination of forms or images in Minimalism and Pop. Minimalism, particularly, had a powerful detranscendentalising effect. This effect was decisive for a particular strand of feminist art practice in the late

'70s and '80s which stressed the politics of determination in and through representations. My paper argues for the importance of the minimalist moment in the development of feminist art practices and also indicates some of the limitations imposed by that inheritance.

The Sublime was then

In a review of 1947, Clement Greenberg contrasted the vitality, virility and boldness of the American Jackson Pollock with the charming and technically proficient Frenchman, Jean Dubuffet.

> [Pollock] is American and rougher and more brutal, but he is also completer. In any case he is certainly less conservative, less of an easel-painter than Dubuffet. ... Pollock points a way beyond the easel, beyond the mobile, framed picture, to the mural perhaps.[2]

Dubuffet is here positioned as an artist who stays within the domesticating boundaries of the frame: 'Dubuffet's sophistication enables him to "package" his canvases more skilfully and pleasingly.' No doubt the commodity status of the mobile easel painting is also invoked here. Pollock's art breaks the boundaries of the frame and at the same time replaces the 'ideograph' with sheer abstraction having no assignable meaning. In this review, Dubuffet is made to play the classical Apollonian to Pollock's Dionysiac, the consolingly beautiful to Pollock's unruly sublime. In fact, the rhetoric of the sublime is incompatible with Greenberg's conception of avant-garde art practice as a self-critical activity which progressively eliminates what is inessential to the art of painting. But reference to the sublime always signals a desire to transcend the vulgarity and instrumentality of modern civilization which is also the ultimate aim of Greenbergian renunciation.

The very next year, 1948, a journal called *The Tiger's Eye* published six opinions on the subject of the sublime in art. Barnett Newman's response, 'The Sublime is Now', argued that, while French painters like the Impressionists and the Cubists endeavoured to destroy beauty, they failed to create a new vision because they 'still exist within the reality of sensations'.[3] Artists in America 'free from the weight of European culture' are finding a new sublime vision in the 'concern with our relationship to the absolute emotions'. Although Greenberg and Newman advance quite different notions, the ideal of an art transcending certain given limitations or conventions is constant.

The political motivation behind the Abstract Expressionist recourse to the rhetoric of the Sublime has been well analysed by David Craven who sees their ethos as one of romantic anti-capitalism. He is particularly good on the anarchist sympathies of Newman and Clyfford Still. Holding the view that people are naturally good and society inherently corrupting, alienation from society becomes something to be embraced. In other words, a demand for freedom *from* alienation turns into a feeling of freedom *through* alienation.[4] The fallen social sphere is bound by convention; the artist operates outside history and artistic conventions. In 'The Sublime is Now', Newman declared that:

> the image we produce is the self-evident one of revelation, real and concrete, that can be understood by anyone who will look at it without the nostalgic glasses of history.[5]

The call for spontaneity and immediacy coincided with a very pessimistic view of the 'totalitarian hegemony' and pervasive ideology of post-war United States. This sense of inescapable predetermination engendered a sense of 'sublime autonomy in the face of impossible odds'.[6]

One can perhaps be sympathetic to the advocates of sublime autonomy in the 1950s. However, it is more difficult to understand Lyotard's recent call for a new sublime in art practice and his veneration of Newman. The artist's mission, he says, is to 'represent the unrepresentable'. His writings on the subject, particularly at the end of 'Answering the Question: What is Postmodernism?' sound very much like an 'Avant-garde and Kitsch' for the '80s.[7] Communication and conformism in the commercial sphere are set against the loneliness of the avant-garde artist who breaks the rules and is therefore met with incomprehension. Several writers have pointed to this oddity. Richard Rorty, for example, wonders why one should assume, as Lyotard seems to, that escaping from rules and practices and institutions that have been transmitted to us 'is automatically a good thing'.[8] Feminists have, rightly, been particularly suspicious. Feminist philosopher Jane Flax questions Lyotard's (and Derrida's) stress on individual creative activity which reactivates the high modernist ethos of the hero struggling against the banalities of mass culture. She adds:

> shifting the metaphor from the individual artist-author to 'writing' or the 'sublime' cannot successfully conceal the congruence of this view with the 'high culture' modernist view of the work of art and artist.[9]

Somewhat less diplomatically, Meaghan Morris speaks of Lyotard's aesthetics of the sublime as 'overwhelmingly familiar' and as invoking the 'propulsing force of unresolvably recurrent oedipal seizures'.[10]

Feminist art practice of any persuasion has little use for this revival of '50s sensibility.

Social subjects

Even in the mid-'50s, Robert Rauschenberg and Jasper Johns had seemed to be criticising the pretensions of the Abstract Expressionist Sublime. Max Kozloff was one critic who welcomed the 'deflationary impulse' as regards the grand manner and its assumption of 'spiritual privilege'. He also offers an eloquent account of Rauschenberg's and Johns' concern

> to materialize the slippage of facts from one context to another, the possibility inherent in the blurring of all definitions, the mutually enhancing collision of programmed chance and standard measurement. And all this was understood in the larger mental simulacrum of a game structure in which, not the potentials, but the deceits of form become the main issue. ... They found in the numbness that afflicted any sensitive citizen agog before the disjunctive media stimuli of his world, a source of iconic energy.[11]

The modern condition of the subject within the slipperiness of representations becomes the theme and the artist's job is to explore its effects, assuming an 'anthropological attitude'.

Yet the real challenge to the Expressionist paradigm was Minimalism and the classic article that sounded the alarm was Michael Fried's 'Art and Objecthood' (1967). Fried uses an eccentric critical vocabulary which distinguishes between the purely pictorial 'presentness' of the preceding generation's work and the literal objecthood and theatrical presence of minimalist sculpture. However, his basic point is that the quasi-object of art which had been the occasion for a self-transcending experience had in the work of the minimalists been reduced to an ordinary empirical object. Fried's last sentences are – 'we are all literalists most of our lives. Presentness is grace.'[12]

In 'Reviewing Modernist Criticism', first published in *Screen* (1981), Mary Kelly notes other art practices apart from Minimalism which deflate transcendence.

> Artistic practices employing film and photography as well as those using found objects, processes or systems where creative labour is apparently absent, continue to problematise the transcendental imperatives which predominate in critical and historical literature on art.[13]

What I am suggesting is that it is not so much the absence of labour that is at stake, but the reduction of art to a thing in the world, undifferentiated from other objects or insufficiently differentiated.

This project of narrowing the gap between art and everyday life applies as much to artists as to their work. Artists in the '60s and '70s are inclined to view their practice and their very subjectivity as subject to all kinds of forces beyond their control. Carl Andre, for example, speaks of the way his sculpture submits to gravitational force. The modules he works with are pre-fabricated and his method of arrangement is thoroughly repetitious and methodological. He declares his art to be 'without transcendent form, without spiritual or intellectual quality'.[14]

Minimalism's effect was to make the spectator conscious of him or herself as embodied, as in a room or space with certain contours. As Robert Morris says: 'The better new work takes relationships out of the work and makes them a function of space, light and the viewer's field of vision.'[15] Conceptual artists expanded on this theme, drawing attention to institutional and discursive practices which impinge on the production, display and circulation of art.[16] As Benjamin Buchloh says in his *Artforum* article, 'Allegorical Procedures: Appropriation and Montage in Contemporary Art', the works of Hans Haacke, Danial Buren, or Broodthaers 'draw attention to the repressed element in cultural production'. Consider, for example, Haacke's *Manet Projekt* (1974), a chronology of the owners of Manet's *Bunch of Asparagus.* Buchloh also notes an important paradigmatic shift in the late '70s when

> the precision with which these artists analysed the place and function of aesthetic practice within the institutions of Modernism had to be inverted and attention paid to the ideological discourses outside of that framework which conditioned daily reality.[17]

An extrapolation is made from the art institutions to the wider world and particularly to the discursive determinations affecting the de-centred subject. As Victor Burgin says, the postmodern subject is 'a precipitate of the very symbolic order of which the humanist subject supposed himself to be the master'.[18] This generation of artists engages in a critique of mass media, advertising, photographic practices and the ideology of everyday life.

The subjection of women

This enquiry into the relations between representation, ideology and the subject has proved extremely productive for feminists and for feminist artists who are, of course, particularly concerned with the ways in which femininity and masculinity are produced and reproduced within representations. Barbara Kruger, for example, explores the power of the media and the market to shape our lives and thoughts. In one of the DIA *Discussions in Contemporary Culture* volumes she says that:

> one should become aware of all the machinations of the market. And they are everywhere – in every exchange, every conversation. Every deal we make, every face we kiss, involves a politic – a politic which is constituted within the strictures of the market place.[19]

This statement reminds me of a portion of the 'Inaugural Lecture' delivered by Barthes at the Collège de France in 1977. The passage I'm thinking of, which is inflected by a reading of Foucault, suggests that we should cease thinking about power as unitary and instead conceive of it as plural.

> We discover then that power is present in the most delicate mechanisms of social exchange: not only in the state, in classes, in groups, but even in fashion, public opinion, entertainment, sports, news, family and private relations, and even in the liberating impulses which attempt to counteract it.[20]

The power relations 'present in the most delicate mechanisms of social exchange' are what Kruger explores. With her super-imposed slogans, she forces out into the open the ideological content latent in the media images she appropriates (all of which have a '50s feel to them). The picture of a man kissing someone's hand together with the slogan 'You re-enact the dance of insertion and wounding' (1982) lays bare the power relation embedded in courtly, even tender, gestures. Or, a sculptural profile with 'Your gaze hits the side of my face' (1981) evokes the objectification and violence of the masculine gaze. Laura Mulvey notes that in this instance 'voyeurism slips into sadism'.[21] She refers to two other pieces, 'I am your slice of life' and 'I am your almost nothing', which she says represent a 'retreat into a cliché that ironically restates masochistic self-denial in love'.[22] The 'pain of self-effacement' is a recurrent motif.

Cindy Sherman also re-presents clichés from films, centrefolds, fashion plates and paintings, which she acts out, taking on all the roles like a chameleon. The so-called film stills from the late '70s have a consistent theme – the place of women in classic cinematic narrative. They could easily be used to illustrate Mulvey's 1975 article 'Visual Pleasure and Narrative Cinema'. All of the women respond to something outside the frame. They are not initiators of action but its audience, watching, waiting, listening, reacting. The 'Hitchcock' style still is formally typical in this respect. It makes reference to a whole genre of murder mysteries: the ingenue's eyes are turned back over her shoulder, she is alone in a big city. Is she being pursued? Is that fear marking her brow? The whole baggage of cinematic conventions and scripts that we carry with us are brought into play. Despite the critical stance she assumes with respect to the scenes she stages, Sherman has been criticized by some feminists for confirming the position of women as spectacle and for staging scenes of threat and violence.

Photographs and films of Jackson Pollock at work suggest one possible theory of the genesis of performance art. Instead of the Abstract Expressionist trace of a gesture, one is given the gesture itself, an immediate presence which is in some cases amplified by nudity and the infliction of pain. Laurie Anderson's performance art can be read as a critique of that tradition. Like Sherman, she assumes a variety of personae, but she does so by using a vocoder or harmonizer which distorts and changes the register of her voice. She also uses found language like the motto of the US Postal Service which occurs in her song 'O, Superman' transmuted into a sinister threat of bombers delivering death. In her performance piece 'United States' she represents the country as a technological nightmare, even while she is surrounded by and mediated through the most high-tech equipment. One montage in that piece shows the *Statue of Liberty* in a negative print so that it looks white hot and a film strip of the American flat in a washing machine. This montage effectively taps the close connection in the American unconscious between guilt and obsessive cleanliness, and does so in a way which suggests how the image of woman is used to sustain patriotism and to launder history.

There can be no doubt that a space for feminists was opened up by the breakdown of the high modernist paradigm of art practice. Working with the model of woman as sign caught in a web of discourses and representations is a clear alternative to the transcendental ambitions of the abstract sublime. Yet, in sticking to this model, one is obliged to focus on woman's subjection and to portray how she is forced to live in a world structured by the interests of patriarchy. In so far as this art practice shifts the discussion of gender onto the level of the symbolic or discursive, the historical or political, it serves an important role. Yet I would want to reiterate Mary Kelly's claim: 'You should have a practice in art that actually looks forward to a moment that will be different.'

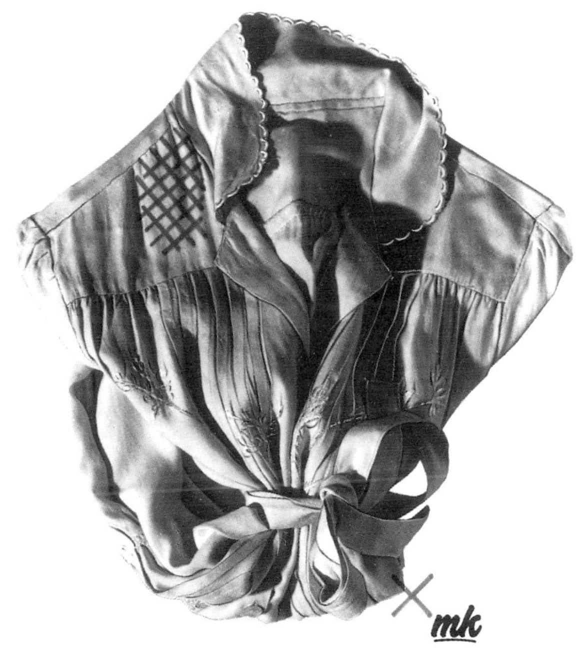

Mary Kelly. *Interim: Part I, Corpus*, 1984–5 (detail: *Extase* section). 30 panels 36" x 48" each, laminated photo positive, silkscreen and acrylic on perspex. (Courtesy of the artist)

Interim

Mary Kelly's large-scale project Interim is about women and middle age, on the face of it an unlikely position from which to look forward to a moment that will be different. Yet Jacqueline Rose has suggested that 'middle age' is metaphorically the position of the women's movement itself 'which pauses, takes stock, and then redefines itself'.[23] That is exactly what Kelly has accomplished in Interim. The work consists of four parts which focus on the Body, Money, History, Power. In an essay about the piece, Laura Mulvey

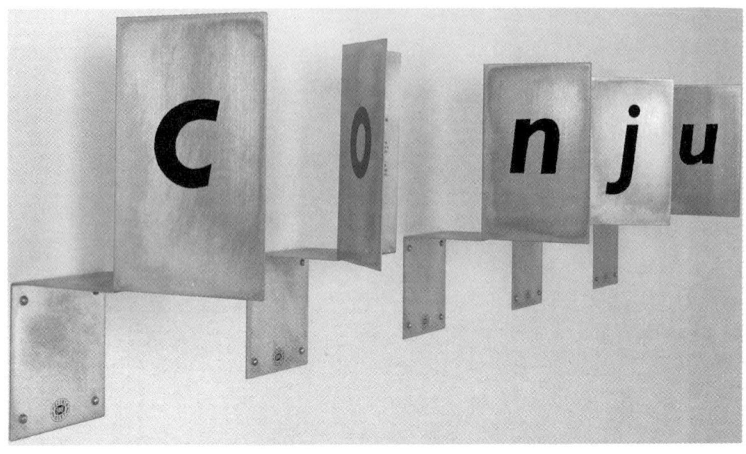

Mary Kelly. *Interim: Part II, Pecunia*, 1989 (detail: *Conju* section). 20 units 16" x $6^1/_2$" x $11^1/_2$" each, silkscreen on galvanised steel. Collection Vancouver Art Gallery. (Courtesy of the artist)

observes that this work 'achieves a fine balance between the iconoclastic repression of the body during the '70s which led to woman becoming unrepresentable and a recognition that such a reaction against the exploitation of women in images could lead to a repression of the discourse of the body and sexuality altogether'.[24] By using articles of clothing to represent the body, Kelly clearly signals that she is dealing with the body imagined or fantasized. The lovely image of a summer dress with its tiny waist was inspired by shop window displays which frequently show impossible anatomies. But she does not stress the aspect of women's relation to their bodies that conforms to male desire nor ('I shop therefore I am') consumer fetishism. Instead she connects this image with the fantasies of romantic fiction which she reads as a symptom of desire for release from normative strictures.

In visual form, Kelly presents an argument similar to the one I have advanced here that Minimalism represented a crucial break in art practice which was to prove fruitful for feminist elaboration and critique. There are very explicit references to minimalist sculpture in her work. In the section called 'Pecunia', for example, a series of projecting metal surfaces, evacuated

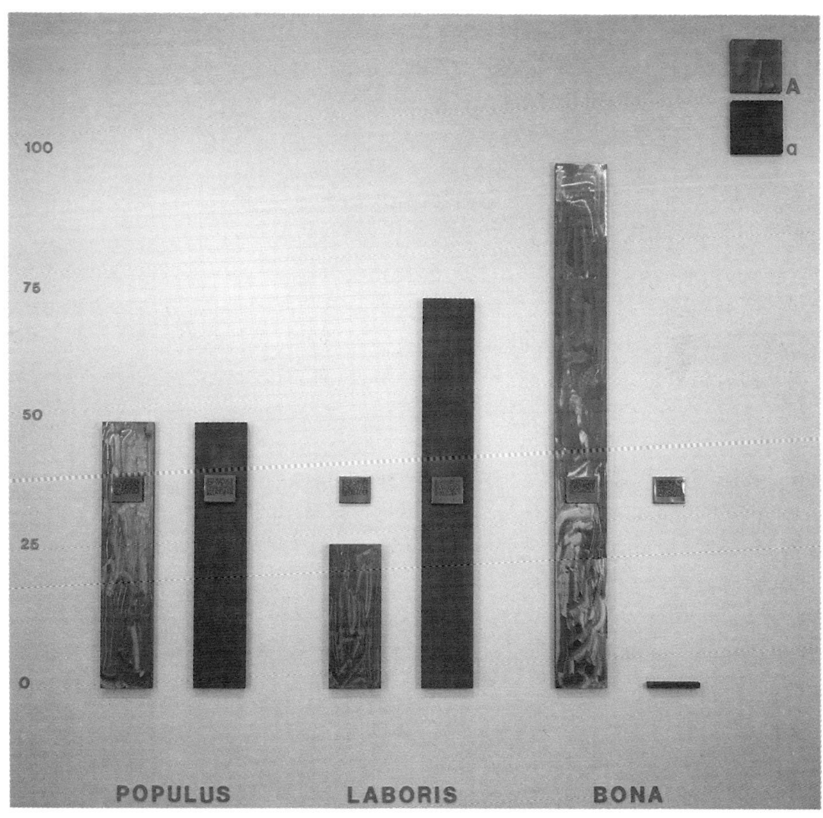

Mary Kelly. *Interim: Part IV, Potestas*, 1989. 100" x 114" x 2", etching, brass and mild steel. (Courtesy of the artist and Postmasters Gallery, NY.)

of any trace of a transcendental subject, is inscribed with the subjects of history, of discourses, of familial networks and complex sets of identifications. The last section, 'Potestas', makes monumental metal bars serve as a graph showing the relative situation of men and women on a global scale. The contrasting bars are of materials that evoke, for men, the work of Abstract Expressionist sculptor David Smith and, for women, the rusted surfaces of Richard Serra's much-maligned minimalist prop pieces.

Kelly's project could well be described as 'representing the unrepresentable' in the sense that the older woman is marginalised and silenced within our culture. But the distance between her approach and that gestured toward by Lyotard is great. Like Lyotard she is sensitive to what he calls the 'fantasies of realism', but she does not on that account abandon figuration. Rather she invents means of indirection, distanciation, invocation, allusion and multiplication. We are presented with the media and pop cultural forms in a sort of *grisaille* so that we can simultaneously engage with them and reflect upon them. She describes her practice as like that of an indigenous ethnographer of a community or, better, communities of women – observing, recording and analysing her data, yet without assuming a privileged position. Although the work is deeply informed by psychoanalytic and Foucauldian theory, it does not rest content with representing the circumstances of women's oppression. Self-transcendence is presented as a possibility within the history of the women's movement.

Notes

1. T. J. Clark, 'Clement Greenberg's Theory of Art', in F. Frascina (ed.), *Pollock and After*, London, 1985, p. 86.
2. C. Greenberg, Review of exhibitions of Jean Dubuffet and Jackson Pollock (*The Nation*, February 1947), reprinted in John O'Brian (ed.), *Clement Greenberg: the Collected Essays and Criticism*, vol. 2 (1945–1949), Chicago, 1986, p. 125.
3. B. Newman, 'The Sublime is Now', *The Tiger's Eye*, New York, vol. 6, December 1948, p.6, partially reprinted in H. B. Chipp, *Theories of Modern Art*, 1958, p. 553.
4. D. Craven, 'Abstract Expressionism, Automatism and the Age of Automation', *Art History*, vol. 13, no. 1, March 1990, p. 95.

5. Newman, *op. cit.*, p. 53, p. 553.
6. Craven, *op. cit.*, p. 95.
7. J.-F. Lyotard, 'Answering the Question: What is Postmodernism?', in *The Postmodern Condition: A Report on Knowledge*, Manchester, 1984, first French pub. 1979. See also several pertinent essays in A. Benjamin (ed.), *The Lyotard Reader*, Oxford, 1989.
8. R. Rorty, 'Habermas and Lyotard on Postmodernity', in R. J. Bernstein (ed.), *Habermas and Modernity*, Cambridge, Mass., 1985, p. 174.
9. J. Flax, *Thinking Fragments: Psychoanalysis, Feminism and Postmodernism in the Contemporary West*, California, 1990, p. 216.
10. M. Morris, 'Postmodernity and Lyotard's Sublime', *The Pirate's Fiancée: Feminism, Reading, Postmodernism*, London, 1988.
11. M. Kozloff, 'American Painting During the Cold War', in F. Frascina (ed.), *Pollock and After*, *op. cit.*, p. 117, first pub. 1973.
12. M. Fried, 'Art and Objecthood', in G. Battcock, *Minimal Art: A Critical Anthology*, New York, 1968, p. 147.
13. M. Kelly, 'Reviewing Modernist Criticism', in B. Wallis (ed.), *Art After Modernism*, New York, 1984, p. 91.
14. C. Andre, cited by David Bourdon, 'The Razed Sites of Carl Andre,' in G. Battock (ed.) *op. cit.*, p. 107.
15. R. Morris, 'Notes on Sculpture', in G. Battcock (ed.), *op. cit.*, p. 232.
16. A more detailed discussion of these issues is found in my paper 'Postmodernist Art Practices: From Minimalism to Feminism', in Francis Barker et al (eds.), *Postmodernism and the Re-reading of Modernity*, forthcoming from Manchester University Press.
17. B. Buchloh, 'Allegorical Procedures: Appropriation and Montage in Contemporary Art', *Artforum*, vol. 21, September 1982, p. 48.
18. V. Burgin, 'The Absence of Presence: Conceptualism and Postmodernism', in *The End of Art Theory*, London, 1986, p. 49.
19. Barbara Kruger, statement in H. Foster (ed.), *Discussions in Contemporary Culture* 1, Seattle, 1987, p. 52.
20. R. Barthes, 'Inaugural Lecture, Collège de France', in S. Sontag (ed.), *Barthes, Selected Writings*, 1983, p. 459.
21. L. Mulvey, 'Dialogue with Spectatorship: Barbara Kruger and Victor Burgin', in *Visual and Other Pleasures*, London, 1989, p. 459.
22. *Ibid.*, p. 129.
23. J. Rose, 'The Man Who Mistook his Wife for a Hat or a Wife is like an Umbrella – Fantasies of the Modern and Post-Modern', in Andrew Ross (ed.), *Universal Abandon? The Politics of Postmodernism*, Minneapolis, 1988, p. 248.
24. L. Mulvey, 'Impending Time: Mary Kelly's Corpus', *op. cit.*, p. 154.

Kiefer's Approaches

Andrew Benjamin

Active forgetting involves a particular stance in relation to history. The content of that history, even if it is yet to be specified, works within the present. It is the nature of that work, and the conception of the present articulated therein, that opens a way towards an understanding not only of the stakes of active forgetting, but of its possible overcoming. The work of history – perhaps work in general – demands a presentation in which the actative rather than the substantive dimension should be emphasised. Within the work of Anselm Kiefer the overcoming of active forgetting is connected to a more general problem. This problem concerns representation: the conception of the event that comes to be represented and thus to be the representation. The event does not form the subject matter to be represented. It has a twofold presence, one which demands its own constitutive doubling or repetition. The occurrence of the event – its constitution as event – always involves an initial determination constructed by the relationship between representation within the frame and the frame as representation. (Both are, of course, always potentially delimited by an internal series of frames.) These frames do not simply mediate presence, they sustain it, and in so doing comprise part of the event's work.

Identified here are a number of preliminary problems and areas of investigation. However, they are only preliminary in terms of their generality. They do not precede Kiefer's work and as such do not form an approach to it. They approach it only insofar as they are already at work within it. The pre-liminary is not to be located 'before', as though it led to the frame. The paintings do not exemplify generality. There is a sense in which general concerns are enacted by them, with the consequence that the generality (and therefore any recourse to it or identification of it) will exist as an after-effect. Generality will have become a trope of the work: the work of Kiefer's approaches.

The temporality of the 'preliminary', of that which is prior to – on but before the edge – will need to be rethought in relation to an envisaged doubling. This doubling is a repositioning of the general in terms of the particularity of content. The paintings, as paintings, can no longer be thought in terms of their being exemplars. The paintings do not exemplify. They are only examples of that which comes to be presented as their content. And yet that content is never simple. As will be suggested, part of the work involves a spacing – an opening – that necessitates judgement; if only because it is spacing – heterology versus homology – that establishes the conditions of possibility for judgement.[1]

Despite the difficulty inherent in the act of interpretation one of the difficulties that is not posed by Kiefer's approaches concerns the approach to be taken to the frame. The arbitrary comes to be restricted in two specific ways. The first concerns the overdetermined historicity of any approach, its figuring within and thus in some sense figuring tradition. The second is the inscription of an ineliminable historical presence – and therefore of a necessary historicity – within the frame. This inscription takes place in the form of sites: mythological figures, named landscapes, historical characters, actual events, etc. However, the inscription of history is not reducible to these sites even though it is present within them. The sites form part of works that are always delimited by the active work of framing both within the painting and of the painting. As is suggested later, both instances are mediated by their presence within the logic of the again and anew. Framing presented in this way has two different types of relationship with

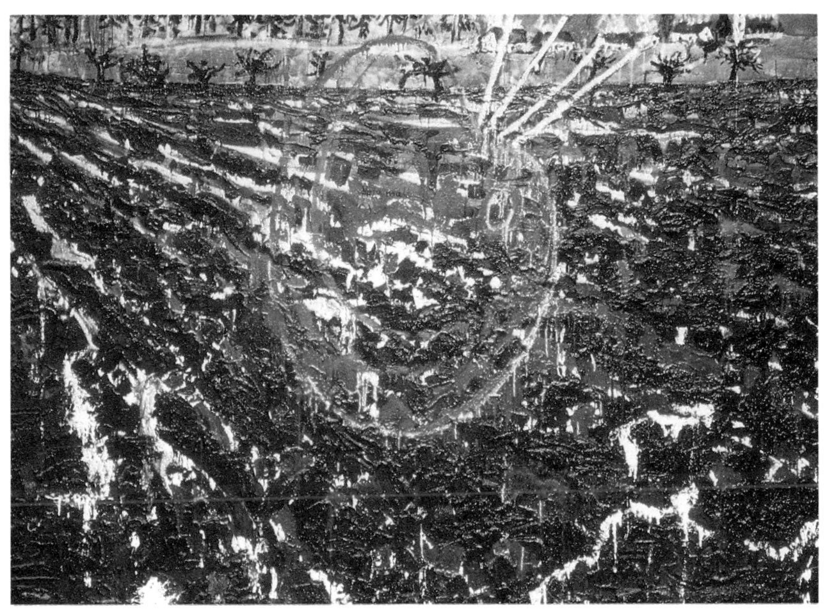

Anselm Kiefer. *Nero Paints*, 1974. Munich, Staatsgalerie Moderne Kunste. (Courtesy of the artist)

representation. On the one hand, there is the setting for representation, and on the other there is the setting of representation. In other words, what comes to be framed is the interplay – though the exact nature of this interplay remains to be determined – between the sites as representations and the standing of representation itself. This interplay is enacted in a number of different ways.

In the case of *Nero Paints*, *Painting=Burning*, and *Icarus, March Sands* an important part of this enactment is the palette; the floating and/or winged palette. These paintings, the first two completed in 1974 and the latter in 1981, have been the subject of different and conflicting interpretations. At this stage the emphasis will be given to the first two paintings. One general interpretation – general since it would have to include both these early works and, for example, the 1987 painting *Die Milchstrasse* (*Milky Way*) – is that the scorched earth and the distant building allude to or evoke a world

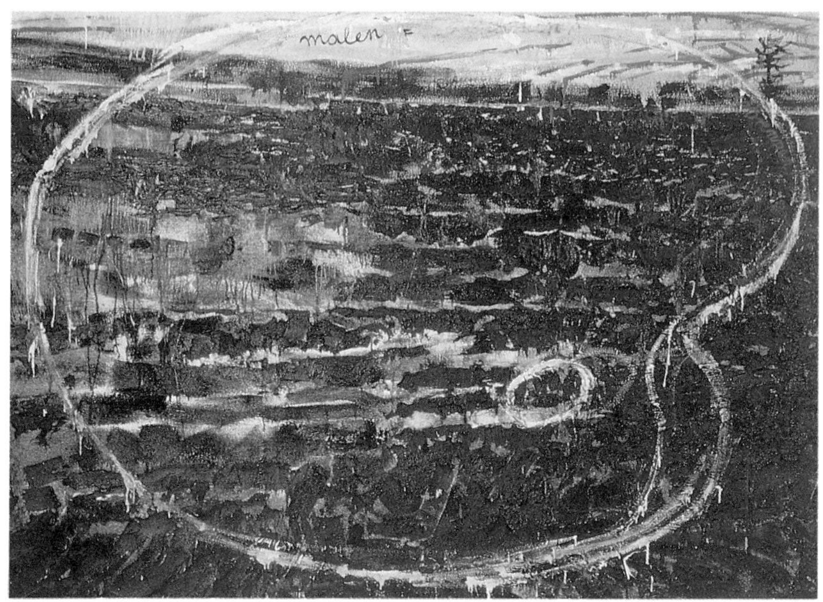

Anselm Kiefer. *Painting=Burning*, 1974. Private collection. (Courtesy of the artist)

that art will come to transcend, and, in transcending it, will redeem the fallen world. Art would emerge therefore as the transcendental source and site of redemption. In the case of *Nero Paints*, it is argued that both emperor and artist have similar aspirations of dominance, to which it should be added that they both destroy, with the consequence that a new order may arise to take the place of the old. While the problem of the secondary representation and thus the possible painterly *mise-en-abyme* is never addressed in interpretations of this kind, what is also overlooked is the content as well as the contact of the palette.

The presence of the palette within works of art already has a long and complex history. The palette as presenting painting necessitates its own representation as holding paint. The palette would in general therefore be painted to contain the paint that would come to be used in painting. The

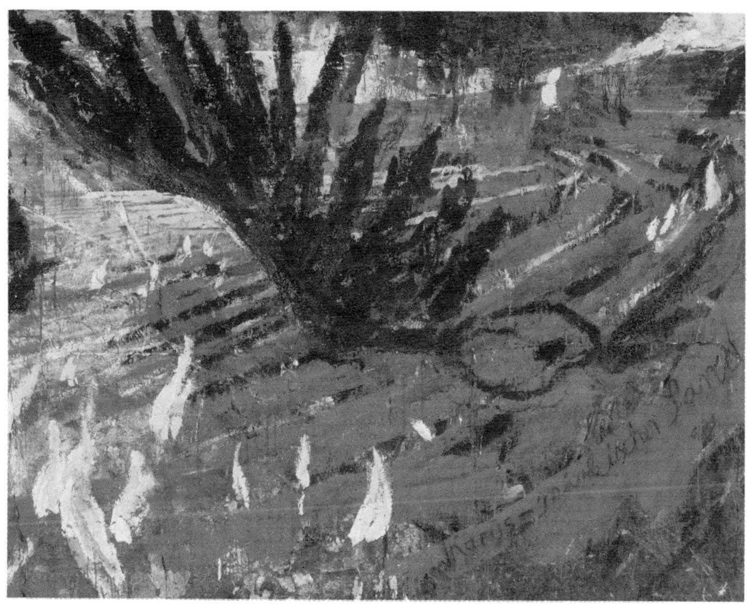

Anselm Kiefer. *Icarus: Märkischer Sand*, 1981. London, Saatchi Collection. (Courtesy Saatchi Collection and the artist)

potential for painting is painted onto the canvas. It is made present. With Kiefer, however, in these works, not only is the palette empty, it also works to frame and, in framing, to gesture towards limits – perhaps the preliminary – and thus to provide a type of border. There is therefore more at stake. The palette is not just the inscription of art – the means of its own production – into and as the work of art. Its presence is in addition, though this is by no means a simple addition, the presence of the problem of frames, limits and borders. The addition becomes the framing of representation; what was outlined before as the setting of representation. This turns the palette such that the absence of held paint becomes the mark of a different presence. A difference that repositions identity by checking any obvious identification of the painting's source and thus the source of painting. There is no origin of the work of art.

What is important is the nature of the absence, the sense of the emptiness. For it goes without saying that the empty palette is, in addition, not empty. Part of what it frames is the burnt field. The framing is not an enclosing. The palette opens up a field of inquiry. In the case of *Nero Paints*, part of what the palette touches are houses either lit by the paint-brush as taper, or painted, as blazing, by the paint-brush as paint-brush. The brushes become the site of a descriptive paradox. The paradox is compounded by the presence of the palette. For the fire that is linked to the brushes/tapers is fuelled by the palette placed over the burnt field. The field as the site is marked and framed – the incomplete nature of this framing will be significant – by the palette. The palette, therefore, while part of the painting, is apart from the represented site, in that it is also present as the site of representation, its setting. The palette constructs an opening within the frame: a spacing. The paint-brush/taper yielding a descriptive paradox and the palette as 'a part yet apart' plot the limit of description, and thereby of any posited formalism. What is, can no longer be described in terms of a synthetic unity; a repetition governed by the Same. Description of the site/sites only attests to paradox and thus to spacing by bringing with it, and thus enacting, a plurality that is not simple diversity. Description reaches its limit in the positing of a spacing that gives rise to judgement. This limit and the subsequent need for judgement figure within the painting, as well as already being figured as the painting.

Spacing and paradox are also at work in the burnt field. The field as the site of renewal will not just be used again, but again and anew. The site therefore becomes one of repetition or, to be more precise, a site for that conception of repetition which only sustains the same by differentiating it from itself. Repetition, in this sense, breaks from the rule of the Same. For it now involves the unruly co-presence of an identity (the again) and difference (the anew). Merely seeing the field as the site of renewal stills the work of repetition, in that the landscape is reduced to the simple presence of landscape. This reduction marks the limit of description – of that which can be described – since it involves another form of repetition. This time one governed by the Same, rather than involving the again and the anew. Repetition governed by the Same posits an intentional trajectory of description. The repetition of genre is constrained to exclude any element that would work against the effectivity of generic repetition. Here that element would be both the presence of the anew and the work of the interplay of the again and anew.

While their detail remains to be clarified, it is the interarticulation or co-presence of the 'again and anew' on the one hand, and the 'apart yet a part' on the other, that provides a frame for an interpretation of *Nero Paints* and *Painting=Burning*. (It should be added of course that their interpretation will have already commenced.) Again, the preliminary is never before the limit, where that limit is the frame of interpretation. This interpretive frame does not contain a grid within which the paintings can come to be placed and thereby mapped. The interarticulation alluded to above is already present, and not just in the frame. It is both subject to the frame and the frame's subject. To which it would be added that paradox as an opening – a spacing – gives rise to the possibility of accounting for the difference between the two above-mentioned forms of repetition. The difference here is, though perhaps with a certain irony, the paradoxical one between Nero and painting.

If it can be assumed that the houses burning in *Nero Paints* can be viewed as the result of Nero's fictions, then this fire needs to be distinguished from the fire marking the burnt fields. The first form of fire is the nihilism of a projected pure destruction. It is not nihilistic because of the destruction but because of the projection. Here the projection involves both pure destruction and absolute renewal. This is the nihilism diagnosed by Nietzsche in *The Will to Power* and countered by his claim in *Ecce Home* that while he was decadent he was also not decadent. This claim of Nietzsche's needs to be seen as the affirmation of 'relation', in that it signals the acceptance of the inevitability of history – the ineliminable presence of the work of tradition – while at the same time resisting the reduction of the present to a moment of historical continuity.[2]

The consequence of the disassociation of fires means that, while painting may equal burning, the painter is not Nero. The title *Nero Paints* identifies, names, a division within the painting. The title as naming division, taken in relation to the palette, the burning houses and the scorched fields, works to differentiate two types of artistic activity, two different intentional logics, and finally two types of fire. Fire is linked to representation. As such it raises both political and ethical questions for, as is known, the fire of destruction cannot touch remembrance. It can destroy, and that which has been destroyed cannot be represented as such. But remembrance is announced from the position of the witness who is vigilant in relation to what defies or precludes its own representation. Vigilance in this sense envisages a responsibility. It opens onto and enjoins present remembrance. The point that must be recognised is that the two types of fire, and all that they bring with them, do not simply inform the painting. On the contrary, they are part of what forms it. While the presence of the two fires will be pursued, as an opening move, what needs to be examined is their relation to active forgetting.

In outline, active forgetting is a conception of history in which relation comes to be suppressed. Relation, however, is not continuity; at least not a simple continuity. By relation what is envisaged is a type of repetition. The fire of destruction aims at elimination, absence without memory: a destructive disavowal in which any renewal is premised upon a complete overcoming of the disavowed object. What is given is given such that its existence can be subjected to that form of negation the operation of which intends to abnegate its repetition. That which is will be no more. Willed repression. The fire of destruction depends upon – because it also articulates – a certain ontology of objects. (Here 'objects' is to be given its largest possible extension: objects in this sense become events). The reference to ontology will allow for the distinction between the fires to be reworked in terms of difference such that the canvas becomes the site of the interplay of differential ontology. What is intended by the term 'differential ontology' is a construal of ontological difference, where difference pertains to differential modes of being rather than, as for Heidegger, taking place between Being and beings. The posited universality or primacy of Being is checked by its having been dispersed within differential modes of being. While the presence of dispersal works against universality, this neither hinders nor weakens the force of ontology. Being is central to a dispersal that turns it into the site of an irreducible plurality. Being names that site and that site, in turn, is Being's content.

The fire of destruction identified in *Nero Paints* posits an object situated within the ontology of delimited stasis. It is structured by and articulated within that mode of being in which the object comes into existence and after which it can cease to exist. Both of these moments exist in chronological time. In other words, existence here involves a temporality of sequential continuity. These moments can be fixed and to that extent dated. The last date – the final point in the sequence – marks the moment at which destruction occurs. Even though dating and fixing are open to a questioning that strikes at their very possibility, it is nonetheless still the case that the intended obliteration of the event is the intention to end presence. However, this end is only possible if obliteration is at the same time marked by active forgetting. Here, forgetting is not simply the denial of both repetition and remembrance. It also involves the refusal of responsibility; where responsibility is understood as involving vigilance. The question posed by active forgetting – the question of how its potential can be maintained while its actuality is overcome – is addressed by the other fire, since within it obliteration is also announced. Here however something else is taking place since henceforth, destruction – the intended obliteration – involves a different logic. Before taking it up, it is essential to note that their difference, and hence their relation, a relation of difference, and the related spacing it involves, form and inform the frame, and thus in part work to comprise the site of judgement. What is at stake here is that as difference emerges all that description can ever accomplish is a re-presentation of that emergence. It is precisely this irresolvability on the level of description (namely, the impossibility of a description that encompasses the totality of that which is framed) that points towards judgement. While the nature and the content of that judgement is a separate problem, the necessity for its occurrence marks the finality of description.

***

Returning to the field of repetition, the first element that must be noted is the presence of landscape. This repetition is true for a large number of Kiefer's paintings. The landscape yields a field of interpretation and yet the field is not a landscape. The generic repetition gives the field. It is given as the site of destruction. It is however a site that only endures when, and if, this endurance is linked to painting. Painting figures as the setting of representation, presented by the palette in its being part of the painting. The repetition of landscape presents a site that is neither a simple landscape nor just the locus of history. Identifying it as such would present it as no more than an historical landscape. This form of presentation would seek to actualise that distancing that begins to broach forgetting. The presentation of the field as the site of history – a site articulated within the logic of the again and anew, here beginning with the repetition of landscape – in this instance gives rise to a reversal of this movement. This reversal arises out of the projected overcoming of the reduction to landscape. The abeyance of genre breaks the hold of the merely historical, and by freeing landscape introduces history as the work of remembrance. In addition, while distancing is maintained, its maintenance is construed or presented in terms of the necessary obligation of a relation to the distanced. Remembrance is enacted within the painting in terms of the logic of the again and the anew. Present remembrance is to be differentiated from simple memory, in which the object loses effectivity and in so doing could never involve the distanced relation of mourning. Remembrance within repetition retains that relation but construes remembrance as present, where that presence and the presence of the event of remembrance – incorporating the remembered event – will always involve a difference that precludes the twin poles of a full or empty present. It is the already present incompleteness that gives rise to vigilance and thus to responsibility. It should be added that there is a fundamental link between this presentation of responsibility and hope. Hope does not end action. On the contrary it becomes the end of action; an end that is present. It is this hope that Celan identifies in Todnauberg about a 'coming word', a hope in the end betrayed. It is of course this betrayal that indicates the absence of a causal relation within the complex constructed by present remembrance, judgement and hope.[3]

Differentiating itself from the logic of obliteration and the ontology of a delimited stasis is the logic of the again and anew. The difference in question is not the simple opposition between being and becoming. It is rather that the again and the anew involves a different construal of becoming: one in which there must be the continual non-excluding presence of the given – the field, the genre of landscape – and its being given again. The again entails the anew. Their co-presence means that it is ontological difference that sustains the logic of the again and anew, since the difference of which it is comprised is irreducible on the level of ontology. The complex that this engenders is a site – a frame – that resists synthesis on at least two levels. The first is the difference between the fires. One is presented – at least on the level of intentional logic – in terms of an ontology of stasis; while the other demands an ontology of becoming.

The title *Painting=Burning*, coupled to the painting itself, brings to the fore the work of remembrance. The title posits an identity. The work of the 'equals' sign would seem to establish an equivalence. However, the identity is complicated by its formality. 'Painting' and 'Burning' remain without content. The use of the term formal and the recognition of an initial absence of content should not be seen as alluding to a division between the transcendental and the practical, as though content could be given to the equation in the move to experience. Were this to be the case, then the practical would in some way hold the truth of the formal proposition.

The title names the difference already identified as the co-presence of the two fires in *Nero Paints*. In the example of that particular painting it was their co-presence that introduced a difference demanding judgement. Present remembrance involved the overcoming of Nero's painting. Here painting does not exist as an end in itself. Transcendent art cannot be privileged or seen to be privileged in Kiefer's work. His approach is different. In the case of *Painting=Burning*, an approach would need to be made in terms, firstly, of the title (and the problems of the equivalence invoked by it), secondly, of the palette as a part yet apart, and thirdly, of the burnt field as the field of repetition.

One conclusion to be drawn here is that the concepts and categories that structure interpretation in terms of either genre or pre-given sites are no longer adequate. The question of what is adequate needs to be re-posed such that any response to it, and subsequent interpretation of it, will not work to eliminate the spacing at work within the frame.

***

In *Icarus – March Sands*, a space is opened by an intriguing reversal. In this painting the palette, while empty, is given a type of content by having a wing. The legend of Icarus would seem to figure in a direct way. It is announced in the title and present in the wing. However, the specificity of the legend introduces a complicating factor. In it Icarus refused to take any notice of the advice offered by his father Dædalus. His flight thus brought him close to the sun. The wax on his wings began to melt and he fell to earth. The problem here is the location of the fire. In the painting it is the March Sands that are on fire. Has Icarus already fallen, falling back to a fiery place? Or does the fire work to remove the possibility of the legend's flight and hence give rise to a fall before the fall?

What is at stake in trying to resolve the problem of fire and its relation to Icarus? In the first place, if the burning sands had robbed him of his flight, such that even if he is only aloft for a moment this takes place beyond or at least distanced from a spatial equivalent to transcendence (understood as the turn to utopia), then what emerges as central is the relationship between art and the burning sands as *topos*. The *topos*, in undoing transcendence, has become the place of politics and therefore of history. However, this could only occur if the March Sands are no longer those March Sands present within and thus reducible to an instance within the genre of landscape, but are repeated such that they become both the March Sands of landscape and the site of history; the again and anew. Furthermore, 'Icarus' in the title must name both Icarus and the setting of representation. Even the proper is not limited by its propriety. It must name 'that' and more. Its limitation lies in the always-to-be-determined relation that takes place between the two.

Presented in this way, there is no need to choose between the questions since the second concerns the impossibility of rising above the site of history; the event of the place. Mythology is not to be opposed to the historical. While the precise nature of their relation is not given within the frame – it is, of course, an open question whether or not the frame could ever contain such an abstraction – what is nonetheless countered is the presentation of mythology as in some sense either prefiguring history or overcome by history's subsequent truth. The questions come to be answered

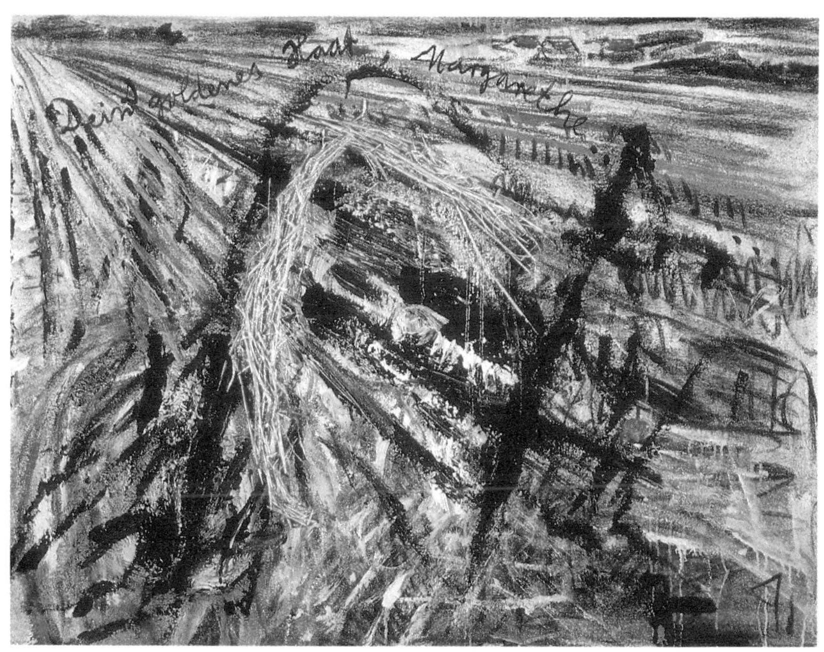

Anselm Kiefer. *Your Golden Hair Margarette*, 1981. Amsterdam, Sanders Collection. (Courtesy of the artist)

by deploying the logic of the again and anew; by grounding them in the presence of a differential ontology. These latter comments only begin an interpretation of *Icarus – March Sands*, but they raise one of Kiefer's major concerns: namely, mythology. I want to conclude by looking, albeit briefly, at two paintings completed in 1981, *Your Golden Hair Margarette* and *Margarette*. They both allude to Paul Celan's poem *Todesfuge* (*Death Fugue*).

***

Celan's poem, while not his only confrontation with the relationship between German history and the Holocaust, is by far his most direct. Indeed, it is precisely this directness that led him to refuse to have it in subsequent anthologies of his work. While the confrontation is uncompromising, it is mediated not simply by the purity of the poetry but by the poem's fugal form. In addition, the relation comes to be played out via the mythical figures of Margarette and Sulamith. The use of repetition within the poem is internal to the lines, as well as involving the repetition, with variation, of whole lines. This is of course the *Abkürzung*. Variation is in some sense already prefigured and yet variety and difference come to be introduced. Within the repetition, perhaps the most violent intrusion is the transformation of the grave into the sky marked by the presence of smoke:

> er ruft streicht dunkler die Geigen dann steight
> ihr als Rauch
> in der Luft
> dann habt ihr ein Grab in den Wolken da leight man nicht eng.[4]

The Margarette named in Kiefer's title is, in the poem, the presence of Germany. Margarette is contrasted with Sulamith whose hair is ashes – *dein aschens Haar Sulamit*. (This line is also the title of another painting). While moving from poem to painting, from one medium to another, is always thwart with difficulties, what is at stake here is the named presence of the poem, not just in the title, but in the case of *Your Golden Hair Margarette*, written onto the canvas. Its presence – enacted both by metonymy and citation – marks the repetition of the poem's concerns. In addition, within the context of the painting, the writing functions as a frame in that it creates a dividing line that intrudes into and forms part of the landscape. While the part in question is, of course, also the apart, the line breaks the symmetry. The vanishing point in the top left hand corner of the painting works by having its work – the construction of a framed finality – undone by the presence of the words just beneath it. The unity, established by finality, that could have been provided by the vanishing point has become impossible. A spacing intrudes. This, taken in conjunction with repetition, will also begin to provide a way of accounting for the presence of mixed media. The spacing, understood in this instance as marking the necessary impossibility of a reunification, a recovery of the lost Jews that would heal the wounds of the holocaust, is once again also the mark of present remembrance.

Marked since it is enjoined, enjoining responsibility, which like alterity resists the abstraction of the absolute because of the work of remembrance.

The confrontation between Germany (figured as the guard and Margarette) and the Holocaust and the Jew (figured as smoke and Sulamith) at work in the poem is rehearsed – rehearsal as repetition – in the frame. This repetition is present both as title and in the presence of mixed media. The straw, the paint and the lead only combine in not combining. The repetition of the poem establishes, in addition, the difference between media while allowing for the continuity of concern. The repetition works therefore within the division already established between representation and the setting of representation.

The approaches taken here to Kiefer, while tentative, open up interpretation. Henceforth, interpretation, rather than involving the banality of an opened pluralism, will be linked to the opening of a plurality in which judgement is constrained to act.

Notes

1. I have tried to develop this conception of spacing and the distinction between the heterological and the homological in *Art, Mimesis and the Avant-Garde* (Routledge, London, 1991). See in particular Chapters 1 and 2.
2. I have provided a more extensive discussion of this aspect of Nietzsche's work in 'Tradition and Repetition: Names as Events', *PLI*, Vol. 4, No. 1 (1991).
3. The relationship between Celan and Kiefer is more complex than mere titles suggest. It is worth noting Celan's own preoccupation with burning and landscape in, for example, *Entwurf einer Landschaft*.
4. 'He calls out more darkly now stroke your strings then
as smoke you will rise into the air
then a grave you will have in the clouds there one lies
unconfined.'

The translation is taken from Paul Celan: *Poems*, translated by Michael Hamburger, Carcanet New Press, Manchester, 1980.

Mimesis and Abjection in Recent Photowork

Michael Newman

Having displaced painting from its mimetic function, thus contributing to the development of non-representational modernist art, photography has assumed a critical role in postmodernist art practice. Influenced by thinkers such as Lacan, Derrida, Deleuze and Baudrillard, recent photowork raises precisely the questions of mimesis, of the good and bad copy, or icon and phantasm, which Plato asks in his late dialogue the *Sophist*. I propose to consider some implications of two different but interconnected aspects of mimesis – *trompe l'oeil*, and the representation of the feminine – through a discussion of photoworks by Olivier Richon and Cindy Sherman.

I

Richon's series *A Devouring Eye* (1990) consists of four pairs of photographs, of which I will consider only one. Both parts are based on models from seventeenth-century painting. The left photograph (over the page) adapts the northern artist Cornelius Norbertus Gijsbrechts' *trompe l'oeil* work *The Back of a Picture*; Richon has added a yellow drape, and changed the number '36' on the peeling label in the Gijsbrechts to an infinity sign.

The drape may recall the curtain in the celebrated classical story of

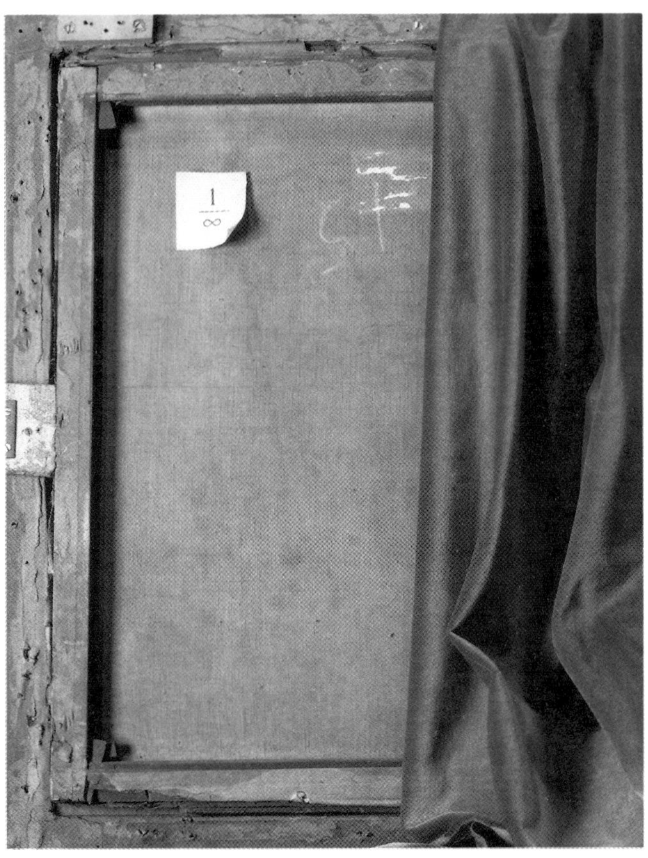

Zeuxis and Parrhasios, where Zeuxis paints grapes so lifelike that they attract the birds, while Parrhasios triumphs over him by painting a veil so deceptive that Zeuxis turned to him and said, 'Well, and now show us what you have painted behind it.' Lacan, in his celebrated discussion of mimesis in *The Four Fundamental Concepts of Psychoanalysis*, sees this allegory of *tromper l'oeil* (deceiving the eye) as '[a] triumph of the gaze over the eye [*Triomphe, sur l'oeil, du regard*]'.[1] The subject is lured and captured by the image which becomes a *vanitas*, 'the figure of a death's head' (p. 92), thus subverting the assurance of the penetrating, knowing, abstracted eye. What mimicry

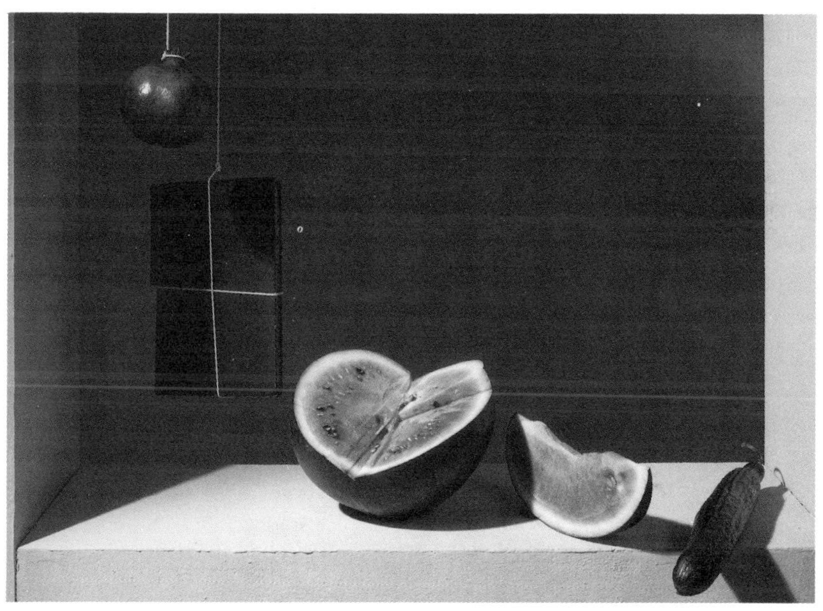

Olivier Richon. *A Devouring Eye* (with canvas and watermelon), 1989.
2 framed colour photographs, 82 x 96cm and 96 x 82cm. (Courtesy Jack Shainman Gallery, New York)

reveals 'is distinct from what might be called an *itself* that is behind' (p. 99): mimicry reveals that the abyss behind the simulacrum, the veil of *trompe l'oeil*, is the abyss, the abyssal or absent origin, of the subject's desire, including – especially – the desire to know. 'To imitate is no doubt to reproduce an image. But at bottom, it is, for the subject, to be inserted in a function which grasps it' (p. 100): the 'lure', the masquerade, has 'a certain sexual finality' but unfixes, for Lacan, any natural grounding of the sexual function.

Trompe l'oeil derives, according to Jean Baudrillard, not from painting but from metaphysics: it is not a genre, not a part of painting, but anti-painting.

Nor is it 'a matter of confusion with the real', as in the tale of Zeuxis and Parrhasios, but rather,

> ... the production of a simulacrum in full consciousness of the game and the artifice by miming the third dimension, throwing doubt on the reality of that third dimension in miming and outdoing the effect of the real, throwing radical doubt on the principle of reality.[2]

This is the Cartesian gesture, but without God to provide the ultimate assurance of the real. *Trompe l'oeil* is the '*ironic simulacrum*': these paintings 'undo the evidence of the world'.

Whereas still life offers objects to the gaze 'in homage to visual incorporation', as Richon puts it in a text written to accompany the series, in the *trompe l'oeil* 'the pleasures of profundity are nullified' – it is the image itself which devours:

> it relies upon a negative use of perspective which absorbs and annihilates representation. The image becomes nothing more – but this is still enormous – than the presence of an absence. The fullness of the image is emptied of its imagined substance; the image becomes nothing and this nothing is to be filled with other images. Like Saturn devouring children, the *trompe l'oeil* swallows everything, repeatedly.[3]

Richon's image takes as its model another representation: the still life painting *Quince, Melon and Cucumber* by the Spaniard Juan Sanchez Cotan. Norman Bryson comments on the Cotan, where the foodstuffs are displayed in a *cantenaro*, a cooling space where for preservation they were often hung on strings,

> ... no one can touch the suspended quince or cabbage without disturbing them and setting them rocking in space: their motionlessness is the mark of human absence, distance from the hand that reaches to eat; and it renders them immaculate.[4]

And Bryson adds, 'What replaces their interest as substances is their interest as mathematical form.' The interest of the Richon is somewhat different. Apart from the substitution of fruit for fruit – pomegranate for quince and watermelon for honeydew – the most striking alteration is that a book has been substituted for the cabbage. This implies that the image which represents the objects is itself to be considered as text, as rhetoric. Photo-graphy, according to its Greek etymology, means 'writing with light': Richon's allegorical, writerly interest in the objects displaces photography from its role as a supposedly 'natural' sign immediately imprinted by its referent; thus, in a sense, inverting photography's initial displacement of realist painting, but in the direction of the pre-realist mode of allegory. The theoretical – indeed, both epistemological and ontological – implication of Richon's approach is that the photographic sign is fundamentally tropological rather than representational: photographic mimetic 'reality' is the effect of a rhetoric, and if this is so of the photographic, commonly taken as indexical, then it may be taken to apply to all signification, into which a fundamental undecidability is thus insinuated. But if sign-value, coupled with the Imaginary desire to incorporate, displaces use-value, this points to an aspect of the Cotan which Bryson neglects: the element of fetishism in the objects displayed for the look yet abstracted against a void and withdrawn from the grasp, as in a shop window or advertisement, to put it anachronistically. To render the relation between signifier and signified arbitrary (the structuralist move) is to raise the question of the condition of possibility of signification as such (the poststructuralist consequence). As a result of the feminist intervention in both theory and art practice, this question can no longer be pursued without taking gender into consideration.

II

In *The Gay Science* Nietzsche writes,

> Finally, women. Reflect on the whole history of women: do they not have to be first of all and above all else actresses? Listen to physicians who have hypnotised women; finally, love them – let yourself be 'hypnotised by them'! What is always the end result? That they 'put on something' even when they take off everything [*dass sie 'sich geben', selbst noch wenn sie – sich geben*].[5]

Hysteric, feminist and the Maenad votary of Dionysius elide in Nietzsche's various statements. In the late nineteenth and early twentieth centuries, feminists, women who did not 'know their place', and whose bodies traced a desire unassimilable within the masculine Symbolic, were often labelled hysterics, and more than once dispatched to the asylum. Nietzsche wrote that 'there are threatening and medically explicit statements of what woman *wants* of man'[6], which Freud echoes in his famous question '*Was will das Weib?, das ewig Weibliche*, [What does woman want, the eternal feminine?].[7] In other words, what is the truth behind woman's mimicry?

Or do we, as Nietzsche seems to hint, need to turn the question around, and ask, what would it mean, when women 'give themselves' in quotation marks? Is mimicry – or more precisely, what has been called a 'double mimesis'[8] – a possible strategy for undoing the question of Woman? To reveal the 'truth' behind the truth of Woman?

Cindy Sherman performs, it could be argued, just such a strategy. Her *Untitled Film Stills* (1977–80)[9] draw on generic images of women from the movies which the artist herself mimics. The 'fine art' gallery context, and the viewer's knowledge that all the photographs are 'of' Cindy Sherman – self-portraits of the self as constructed out of idealised media identities – frames the pictures as 'double mimesis'. In the woman's film, as Mary Ann Doane has shown, femininity is *stylised*, and, she suggests, 'What is needed is a means of making these gestures and poses *fantastic*, literally *in-credible*.'[10] If stylised femininity is a respeaking of socially grounded desires, recuperated in the mass media so as not to threaten the status quo, then a 'double mimesis', 'a "respoken" femininity is subjected to a respeaking in its turn. Double mimesis renders void the initial mime or, at the very least, deprives it of its currency'.

The photographs of Sherman's series of 1981, while still cinematic in their generic allusion, use a horizontal, double-page spread format. The figure, seen closer up, is invariably in a passive pose, and dependency is suggested by the inclusion of a telephone by which the woman waits, or a lonely hearts ad which she holds. This is followed by a series of four vertical format photos in which Sherman appears without make-up – thus apparently without disguise – covering her body with it seems only a pink bathrobe,

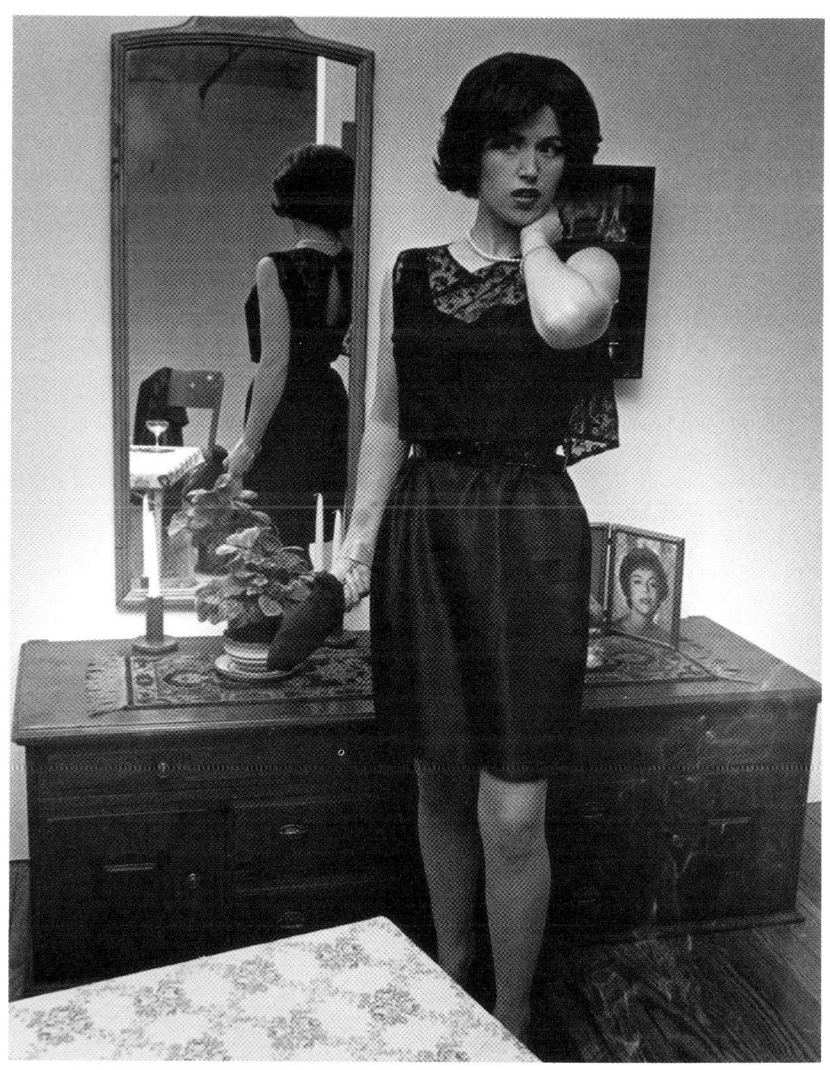

Cindy Sherman. *Untitled Film Still*, 1978. Black & white photograph, 10" x 8". (Courtesy Metro Pictures, N.Y.)

and staring directly, somewhat more assertively, at the viewer. This representation – or rhetoric – of veracity, an apparent zero-degree, is a turning point. Thereafter, the images first become darker and more difficult to read, occasionally androgynous. This is followed by the 'fashion' series of 1983, in which Sherman models clothes while seeming to subvert the idealisation of fashion photography through exaggeration or the grotesque. However, fashion photography had, in the post-punk period, itself become self-subverting and ironic, so this strategy was quickly assimilated.

Apart from its recent recuperation by mass culture, the philosophical problem of ironic or double mimesis was anticipated by Plato in the *Sophist*. Unless there is some standard of truth, there is no way of distinguishing ironic or double mimesis from mimesis pure and simple. Without such a standard – or when, as in Nietzsche and poststructuralism, truth is put in quotation marks – the risk is that the 'double mimesis' collapses back on what it may be taken to ironise. The question I am raising here is: What would permit the distinction to be made between the 'undecidable' and the merely mimetic? And if the allegorical approach renders the mimetic undecidable, what is the status of this undecidability, and the consequence of its application in a material practice?

Rather than answer these questions directly, I want to go on to consider a recent series of works by Sherman in which mimesis itself appears to break down or implode, and the conditions and limits of mimetic representation are momentarily exposed. These works follow a series of 1985, in which the image of woman is de-idealised, threatening the Imaginary structure of narcissistic identification. We find in these pictures the incorporation of skin deformations, grotesquerie, images of a woman who appears to be the victim of an act of violence – in some it is uncertain whether she is alive or dead; she uses a false bottom which recalls Bellmer's dolls, the *Poupées*; and in one a woman's head with the snout of a pig is lying on the ground. The following series of 1986 makes more extensive use of animal masks.

Taking these two series together, it is possible to see that the symbolic oppositions which structure identity are being thrown into question: the inside vs. the outside of the body (in the pictures with skin blemishes); masculine vs. feminine (images in which the artist/subject appears as an androgyne or man); human vs. animal; life vs. death. This development culminates in 1986–87 in a group of works where the body is fragmented and radically decentred, to appear – often in a way suggesting that it is a corpse – at the edge of the image, or reflected in a powder compact or a pair of mirror sunglasses. In one image the woman's presence consists of a suit of businesswomen's clothes on which lies a make-up set, and the dust where there was a skeleton. This is surrounded by the accessories of a computer, the screen radiating a ghostly light. Other images feature worms in place of a meal; large flies and rats; confectionary and chocolate caked together with vomit (below); a Father-Christmas head together with smashed wine-glasses and wine or blood soaked into the snow; and bloodstained women's underwear.

Clearly, like the preceding works, these draw on the stock in trade of horror and fantasy films and thus remain a 'double mimesis' of a mass-cultural genre. But the emphasis on the phobic objects which displace the

Cindy Sherman. *Untitled*, 1987. Colour photograph, 47½" x 71½". (Courtesy Metro Pictures, N.Y.)

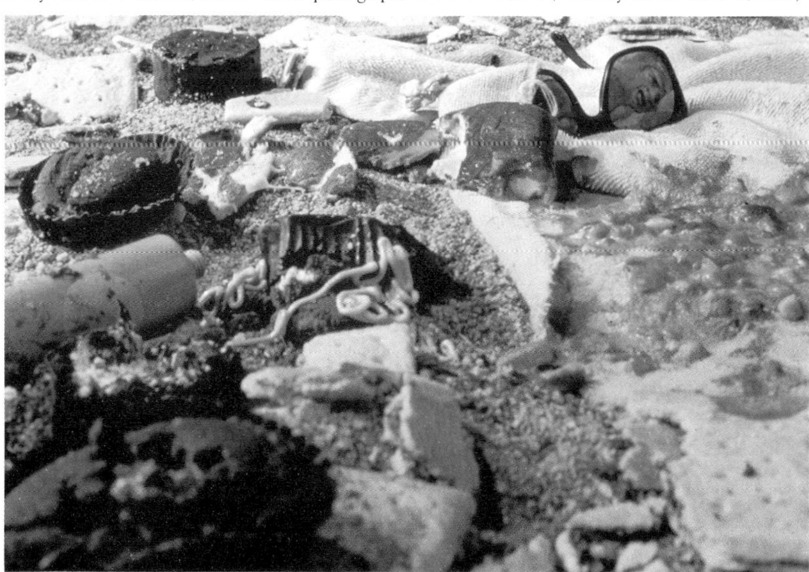

figure, and the almost systematic collection of types of such objects, seems to suggest the exploration of something further: perhaps, we might say, the basis of the effect of such films. We could also see these images as subversions of the genre of still life, better named in the French *nature morte*, dead nature. Bryson draws attention to the way in which the subjects of still life are traditionally associated with the women's domain, the home and the kitchen: for the representatives of academic high art, such as Reynolds, 'even to look at still life, which entails a descent into the sensuous particularity of things, is to put manhood at risk'. Sherman could then be seen as subverting the subordinate status of the furniture of still life by evoking it as rejected, as filth, thus exposing a powerful metaphysical paradigm which identifies Woman with matter. What is also striking is the extent to which Sherman's repertoire of phobemes in these pictures replicate those in Julia Kristeva's book *Powers of Horror: An Essay on Abjection*, published in English translation in 1982, and drawing on *Purity and Danger* (1969) by the anthropologist Mary Douglas: these phobemes pre-eminently involve bodily functions, food loathing, menstrual blood and the corpse.[11]

The abject, according to Kristeva, stands for that which threatens the subject as a 'clean and proper' body which is based on a set of distinctions which condition its constitution as a speaking subject in the Symbolic order. This condition is always tenuous in that it is at once sustained and threatened by the semiotic drives, the energies, rhythms and corporeal residues. The origin of the phobic effect of 'abjects' (neither 'sub-ject' nor 'ob-ject') predates the distinction between ego and object, and the identification with the bounded, reflected body-image in the mirror phase (Lacan). The moment of abjection in infant development is the pre-Symbolic clearing of a space for subjectivity, for the subject-object distinction. As it recurs in adult life, abjection is a reaction to the threat to the Symbolic – a threat which is also the condition for the latter's continual renewal. Kristeva writes,

> We may call it a border: abjection is above all ambiguity. Because, while releasing a hold, it does not radically cut off the subject from what threatens it – on the contrary, abjection acknowledges it to be in perpetual danger. ... Abjection preserves

> what existed in the archaism of pre-objectal relationships, in the immemorial violence with which the body becomes separated from another body in order to be – maintaining that night in which the outline of the signified thing vanishes and where only the imponderable affect is carried out.[12]

We could say that the abject marks the condition of possibility for subjectivity and representation on a psychic level. This gives rise to a problem in applying this theory to Sherman's work: if the abject is the condition for representation, abjection itself should strictly speaking be unrepresentable. Thus it is not surprising to read that 'The abject is edged with the sublime' (p. 11). Just before this, Kristeva writes, '*Sublimation* ... is nothing else than the possibility of naming the pre-nominal, the pre-objectal. ... In the symptom, the abject permeates me, I become abject. Through sublimation, I keep it under control.' The representation – sublimation – of the abject, the abject-sublime in transgression, is a form of control.

What poses the threat, and to whom? This brings me to some further difficulties. As Kristeva shows in the historical section of her study, in the pagan rites of defilement and biblical abomination the representation of the abject can be a way of reinforcing the boundaries and oppositions of a Symbolic, and indeed political, order. Kristeva comments that the ritualisation of defilement, especially that of menstrual blood, is 'accompanied by a strong concern for separating the sexes, and this means giving men rights over women' (p. 70). Abjection could therefore be taken as a symptom of the rejection of the feminine in a particular historical culture. However, Kristeva also argues that the infant's early identification with a pre-Symbolic, pre-Oedipal Imaginary father as the object, other than the infant itself, of the mother's desire and the source of the ego-ideal, and the correlative rejection of the Imaginary phallic mother, establishes the borders and a topography of inside/outside as a necessary phase in the development of subject-hood prior to Lacan's 'mirror stage'. Abjection thus clears the space for and initiates the identificatory structure of the ego. On this level, the stage of abjection would be the condition of possibility for culture (the Symbolic) as such.

It could be argued that Kristeva's attempt to provide a psychoanalytical explanation of the historical involves a confusion of categories, insofar as the theory of abjection remains caught in an antinomy of the transcendental (condition of possibility) and the empirical (explanation of fact). This is a problem which bedevils all attempts to provide a psychoanalytical account of historical phenomena, and clearly recurs in Kristeva's account of avant garde art and literature. *Powers of Horror* culminates in a discussion of the French novelist Céline who reveals, for Kristeva, the fundamental ambivalence of the avant-garde. The irruption of the Semiotic, the level of drive, in the Symbolic as a condition for social renewal ('revolution' in her earlier writings), is now linked to the weakened ego's need to abject the other to prevent its complete disintegration, hence the attraction of fascism and anti-semitism for certain writers of the avant-garde including Céline. While in her earlier writings Kristeva proposed a view of the avant-garde as transgressive in a politically revolutionary sense, from the period of *Powers of Horror* the psychoanalytical account is used to generate an ahistorical norm (including one of heterosexuality) which appears to be taken as the basis for a rejection of politics *per se* as pathological, insofar as attraction to an ideal, as ego-ideal, of whatever persuasion, is taken as symptomatic of a failure of the early phase in ego development.[13] The problem here would seem to originate in the status (transcendental or empirical) of accounts of very early, and consequently unverifiable, phases in infant psychic development.[14] Such an account – of the condition of possibility for the development of the ego – is being used in Kristeva's case to generate a norm which is applied on an empirical-historical level. If this is indeed the case, and the condition has a transcendental status, it would amount to an idealist inversion of the feminist critique of supposedly universal categories having a basis in material oppression, above all in the objectification of women. It is around the question of hysteria that much of the feminist debate has taken place.

III

Insofar as Sherman's photoworks, by their very mode of production, give primacy to the visual in their representation of the feminine, it is, I think, no coincidence that there is a parallel between some of her self-images and the iconography of hysteria, which was primarily a discourse of the visual in which woman, as so often in the *fin de siècle*, was assigned the role of mimic. The question of hysteria, and the question posed by the hysteric to patriarchy, has been a central theme in feminist writing. Hysteria raises the question of mimesis, and woman as mimic, insofar as the bodily symptoms have no biological cause. Although Charcot showed that hysterical symptoms occurred in men, most of his patients were women, and hysteria 'remained symbolically, if not medically, a female malady':[15] the word is derived from the Greek *hustera*, the womb. A painting made famous through its representation as an etching shows a woman swooning half-undressed while Charcot lectures on her before an audience of men.[16]

Photography played a central role in Charcot's investigation of hysteria. In 1875 an album of photographs was assembled, and from the 1880s there was a photographic studio in the hospital, La Salpetrière, and three volumes of photographs were published. The pictures were organised according to phases of the hysterical attack such as the epileptoid phase, in which the women lost consciousness and foamed at the mouth; the phase of clownism, with its physical contortions; and finally the *attitudes passionnelles*, in which incidents from the patient's life were mimed, and which were given subtitles by Charcot such as 'threat', 'amorous supplication', 'ecstasy', 'eroticism', 'appeal' and 'mockery'.[17] One of the most celebrated 'stars' of these photographs was a young woman named Augustine, who displayed the symptom that she began to see everything in black and white, and eventually escaped from La Salpetrière disguised as a man. Showalter comments that 'all of her poses suggest the exaggerated gestures of the French classical acting style, or stills from silent movies'.

Charcot seems in retrospect to have been the paradigm of a fetishistic scopophile, almost a parody of the art connoisseur, a veritable Berenson of hysteria. Freud wrote of him that 'he had an artistically gifted temperament – as he said himself, he was a "*visuel*", a seer ... he was accustomed to look again and again at things that were incomprehensible to him, to deepen his impression of them day by day...'[18] Once again, it was a search for the 'truth' of woman – woman the mimic, pure appearance, the veil –

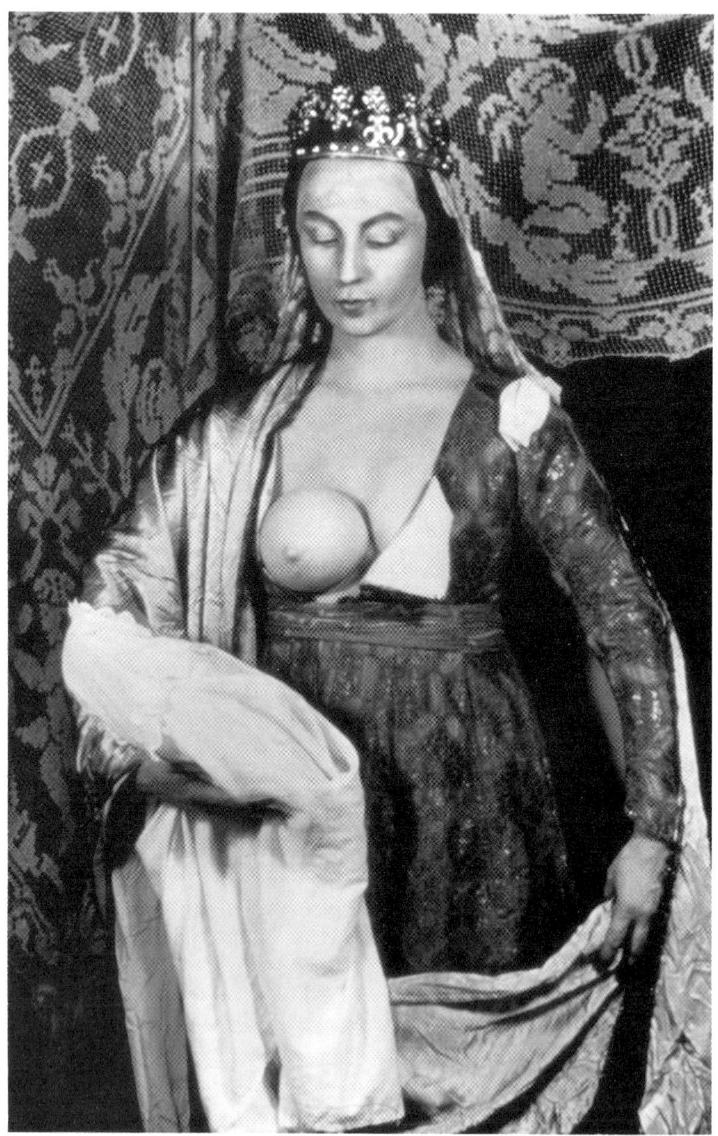

Cindy Sherman. *Untitled*, 1989. Colour photograph, 95" x 64".
(Courtesy Metro Pictures, NY)

conducted on a purely visual level, with women remaining trapped in the Imaginary as an object of the medical gaze. Breuer and Freud, by contrast, turned away from the image to listen to the speech of women – often intellectually brilliant middle-class women frustrated by the routines of domesticity and their role as carers. Developing the 'talking cure' in collaboration with their analysands, Freud and Breuer can be understood as having made the modernist gesture par excellence, the repudiation or overcoming of mimesis, of seduction by the image; or at least, later, its incorporation by Freud into the theory of transference and (although rarely by Freud himself) counter-transference. However, Freud's very concern to establish psychoanalysis as a science shows how tied to sophistry, to the problem of mimicry, it remained. The feminist critique of the patriarchal assumptions of psychoanalysis has involved a reassessment of the discourse of hysteria, and the plight of the women who were its objects.

One of the early women analysands – diagnosed by Ernest Jones as 'a case of typical hysteria'[19] – herself became a distinguished analyst and published, in 1929, a celebrated paper on 'Womanliness as Masquerade'. In it Joan Riviere writes,

> The reader may now ask how I define womanliness or where I draw the line between genuine womanliness and the 'masquerade'. My suggestion is not, however, that there is any such difference; whether radical or superficial, they are the same thing.[20]

In a series of 1989 Sherman masquerades – in one instance explicitly with a mask – as male and female historical types from the Renaissance to the period of the French Revolution (left)[21]: or more precisely, these mime *tableaux*, involving heightened and explicit artificiality and grotesquerie, create the sense of a gap between the historical as signified and historicising representations as signifiers. Sherman's images are 'crossovers' of the genres of high art portraiture and of films such as *Dangerous Liaisons*. While offering a possible critique of the confusion of a signifier with signified, of costume drama with the 'reality' of the past, historical distinctions tend to disappear insofar as all representations of the past are rendered grotesque. The justification for this is that such representations might well be grotesque as signifiers of patriarchy subjected to anti-heroic deflation. The gendering of the gaze avoids the collapse into humanism which would result from a neutral or neuter reading. Again this raises a question of level: of the status – condition or strategy – of masquerade.

According to a certain interpretation, the masquerade of womanliness disguises the woman's self-identification as a man: there is no essential woman because either the woman mimics a man, or masquerades as feminine to disguise this identification. Stephen Heath, following Lacan, comments:

> In the masquerade the woman mimics an authentic – genuine – womanliness but then authentic womanliness is such a mimicry, is the masquerade ('they are the same thing'); to be a woman is to dissimulate a fundamental masculinity, femininity is that dissimulation.[22]

Insofar as woman exists as masquerade, she does not exist. We find here an echo of the problem of the image in the *Sophist*: as masquerade, women do not have real being, as falsity they do not exist.

The alternative responses to this dilemma would seem to be iconoclasm or double mimesis: either 'positive images' which break with the past, in line, perhaps, with a utopian modernism, or postmodernist deconstruction, subverting the discourse from within its own terms. These alternatives are played out in the struggle over the representation of hysteria: is hysteria a feminine language of the body, or a discursive position constituted by patriarchy? It would seem that the trajectory of Cindy Sherman's work, with its emphasis on historically particular genres of representation, shows that as an either/or these alternatives are untenable, in that in both, in the words of Catherine Clément writing on hysteria, 'femininity in revolt is played out along with the historical fetters that enclose it on all sides'.[23] Sherman's 1989 series raises more emphatically precisely the question of history – the relation between ontological condition and the historicity of representation – which a psychoanalytic perspective opens up but has difficulty in articulating, insofar as psychoanalytic theory itself oscillates in its explanations between the transcendental and the empirical-historical.

A further reflection, which would not itself be a mere regress, is required on this problem.

If a 'current disturbance of the old positions' (Heath) is to be a *political* move, it would need to be grounded in some project that exceeds, even if it may involve, the alternatives of utopian modernist iconoclasm or postmodernist ironic, double mimesis. On a temporal-historical level, it could be said that the double mimesis is a moment of negation which intimates a specifically feminine desire which is as-yet unspeakable within the patriarchal Symbolic and is continually appropriated by it. In order to argue this, it would be necessary to loosen the necessity of the Symbolic as determined through the inevitable assumption of castration and positioning vis-à-vis the Phallus, (cf. Derrida's deconstruction of Lacan),[24] for the sake of the utopian, but not constitutively unrealisable, possibility of a Symbolic of the feminine (cf. Irigaray on mimesis, and the morphology of women's bodies).[25]

One of the questions posed by the photoworks of both Sherman and Richon is whether the allegorical deconstruction of the mimetic can avoid becoming trapped in the antinomy of the transcendental and the empirical, the condition and the conditioned, the universal and the historical. If in the socio-historical condition of modernity the cost of freedom is abstraction from the particular, and this manifests itself in aesthetics as irony, can a postmodernism informed by feminism, psychoanalysis and deconstruction, and employing the modes of allegory and 'double mimesis', resist this fate?

Notes

1. Jacques Lacan, *The Four Fundamental Concepts of Psycho-Analysis*, Harmondsworth, Penguin Books, 1979, p. 103. Further page references appear in brackets in the text.

2. Jean Baudrillard, 'The *trompe l'oeil*', in *Calligram: Essays in New Art History from France*, ed. Norman Bryson, Cambridge, Cambridge University Press, 1988, p. 58.

3. Publication forthcoming in *Camera Austria*.

4. Norman Bryson, *Looking at the Overlooked: Four Essays on Still Life Painting*, London, Reaktion Books, 1990, p. 66.

5. Friedrich Nietzsche, *The Gay Science*, trans. Walter Kaufmann, New York, Vintage Books, 1974, aphorism 361, p. 317.

6. Friedrich Nietzsche, *Beyond Good and Evil*, aphorism 232.

7. Quoted, together with the passages from Nietzsche, in Stephen Heath, 'Joan Riviere and the Masquerade', in *Formations of Fantasy*, ed. Victor Burgin, James Donald and Cora Kaplan, London, Methuen, 1986, p. 50.

8. Mary Ann Doane, *The Desire to Desire: the Woman's Film of the 1940s*, Bloomington, Indiana University Press, 1987, p. 181.

9. For illustrations of works by Cindy Sherman up to 1987, see the exhibition catalogue *Cindy Sherman*, New York, Whitney Museum of American Art, 1987.

10. Doane, *op. cit.*, p. 180.

11. For a discussion of the implications of Kristeva's ideas on abjection for aesthetic theory, see Victor Burgin, 'Geometry and Abjection', in *Abjection, Melancholia, and Love: The Work of Julia Kristeva*, ed. John Fletcher and Andrew Benjamin, Warwick Studies in Philosophy and Literature, London, Routledge, 1990, pp. 104–23.

12. Julia Kristeva, *Powers of Horror: An Essay on Abjection*, trans. Leon Roudiez, New York, Columbia University Press, 1982, pp. 9–10. Further page references appear in brackets in the text.

13. 'Under the crossfire of gynaecological surgery rooms and television screens, we have buried love within shame for the benefit of pleasure, desire, if not revolution, evolution, planning, management – hence for the benefit of Politics. Until we discover under the rubble of those ideological structures – which are nevertheless ambitious, often exorbitant, sometimes altruistic – that they were extravagant or why attempts to quench a thirst for love.' Julia Kristeva, *Tales of Love*, trans. Leon Roudiez, New York, Columbia University Press, 1987, p. 5. The first chapter of *Tales of Love*, 'Freud and Love: Treatment and Its Discontents', has a more developed account of the implications of abjection with respect to the formation of the ego than *Powers of Horror*. For a powerful feminist Marxist critique of Kristeva, see Jennifer Stone, 'The Horrors of Power: A Critique of "Kristeva"', in *The Politics of Theory*, Proceedings of the Essex Conference on the Sociology of Literature July 1982, ed. Francis Barker et al., Colchester, University of Essex, 1983, pp. 38–48.

14. This is related to the problem of the status – whether based on trauma or fantasy, primal

event or primal scene – of unconscious mental contents in Freud. For a discussion of this issue, see John Fletcher, 'Poetry, Gender and Primal Fantasy', in *Formations of Fantasy*, pp.109–41, esp. pp. 110–16.

15. Elaine Showalter, *The Female Malady: Women, Madness and English Culture, 1830–1980*, London, Virago, 1987, p. 148.

16. Charcot lecturing on hysteria at the Salpetrière. Etching after André Brouillet, 1887. Illustrated in Showalter, *op. cit.*, p. 149.

17. Cf. Mary Kelly's artwork *Interim*, the first part of which, *Corpus* (1985) draws on Charcot's taxonomy of hysteria: see the discussion with her quoted in Sandy Nairne, *State of the Art: Ideas & Images in the 1980s*, London, Chatto & Windus, 1987, pp. 148–56.

18. Sigmund Freud, 'Charcot' (1893), *Collected Papers: Volume 1*, New York, Basic Books, 1959, p. 10.

19. Ernest Jones, letter to Freud, 21 January 1921, quoted in Stephen Heath, *op. cit.*, p. 45.

20. Joan Riviere, 'Womanliness as a Masquerade', in *Formations of Fantasy*, p. 38.

21. For a brief illustrated discussion of this series, see Kees van der Ploeg, 'Cindy Sherman: Nearly Schizophrenic, Utterly Contemporary', *Flash Art*, Vol. XXIII, No. 153, Summer 1990, p. 142.

22. Stephen Heath, *op. cit.*, p. 49.

23. Catherine Clément, 'Enslaved Enclave', in *New French Feminisms: An Anthology*, ed. Elaine Marks and Isabelle de Courtivron, Brighton, The Harvester Press, 1981, p. 133.

24. Jacques Derrida, 'Le facteur de la verité', in *The Post Card: From Socrates to Freud and Beyond*, trans. Alan Bass, Chicago, The University of Chicago Press, 1987, pp. 413–96.

25. Luce Irigaray, *This Sex Which Is Not One*, New York, Cornell University Press, 1985, e.g. p. 27; and *Speculum of the Other Woman*, New York, Cornell University Press, 1985. Both books include important discussions of mimesis.

Expression and Construction: Adorno and Thomas Mann

Christa Bürger

If one wants to avoid either a simple endorsement of one particular interpretation of the postmodernism debate, or its all-out polemical rejection, and wishes instead to view it as an incentive for further thought, the debate appears as the preconceptual expression of aesthetic modernity's need to rethink itself. It becomes the sign of a changed self-understanding which has not, as yet, found its own concepts.

I would like to introduce the following reflections with a hypothesis, or rather, a question: is Hegel's much cited declaration of the end of art correct after all? Hegel is not, of course, claiming that there can be no more art, but rather that it no longer has the necessity it enjoyed in classical antiquity, and that this is due, in part, to the fact that all artistic forms have become equally available. Aesthetic modernity, as theorised by Adorno, would then be the heroic attempt to retrieve the notion of a necessary form; postmodernism the insight that this is no longer possible. I would like to explore this question using Thomas Mann's *Doctor Faustus* as an example.

That the anti-modernist Lukacs and the modernist Adorno should both be equally justified in claiming Thomas Mann for their respective aesthetics can be explained by the fundamentally ambiguous nature of his work.

In *Doctor Faustus* this ambiguity is elevated to a principle of formal construction. The biography of a fictitious artist which Mann admits to colouring with his own biography, and which is told against the background of Ernst Bertram's Nietzsche myth, weaves the histories of the model (Nietzsche), the fictitious artist (Leverkühn) and the author together under the sign of a pact with the devil. The autobiographical element blurs the border between the work of art and life, moving from the framing device (the figure of the narrator) into the main body of Leverkühn life history, and from the novel back into the actual time of narration. The problem for Leverkühn, or modern art, is the availability of artistic forms from every stage of the historical development of art, in other words, mastering the process of construction. The problem for Thomas Mann is basically an anti- or pre-avant-garde type of phantasmagorical montage; constructing the novel out of fragments of reality and quotations. Both the fictitious composer and the novelist long for the absolute work of art which would succeed in the conversion of rationality into mimesis, of construction into expression. This would simultaneously be the point at which modernity relapsed back into myth, for myth is the realm of the ambiguous. Ambiguity is the historical index of Leverkühn music, as it mixes the ancient with the radically new, forcing upon us the shocking realisation that 'the earliest forms haunt the very latest'.[1] *Doctor Faustus* investigates nothing less than the possibility of the work of art, the question of the relation between construction and expression.

For Adorno, who always argues within the normative framework of bourgeois art or, more simply, idealist aesthetics, the place of the work of art is positioned between mimesis and rationality, or, as we could say, between expression and construction. To understand what he means by this, one must make clear that these are concepts from the philosophy of history.

Mimesis and rationality

The originality of Adorno's aesthetic theory is perhaps due in part to the way he contemplates modern art, enveloping it in an aura of distance, referring very briefly to the mystery of its possibility without dispelling it. However, the work of art, which appears to him as a configuration of mimesis and rationality, remains an enigma because the magic stage in human history, when dreams and images were not merely signs for things, and relations were not those of function but of affinity, belongs irrevocably to the past. 'Art is a refuge for mimetic behaviour. In art the subject, depending on how much autonomy it has, takes up varying positions vis-à-vis its objective other from which it is always different but never entirely separated.'[2] Adorno is absolutely unswerving in his renunciation of unmediated mimesis, and always insists on the separation of history from pre-history. He repeatedly points out that since history began, mimetic practice, even in ritual, has been a part of domination. For him, the bliss of a vanquished prehistory is imaginary. His demand that one give up the delusion of immediacy consequently goes as far as

> a prohibition of everything that the remembrance of nature in art turns to without mediation. Art's separation from nature can be undone but only in virtue of this separation. This reinforces the rational moment of art while at the same time exculpating it, because it stands in opposition to real domination (*AT*, p. 86/79–80).

Art resists existing domination because it is mimetic and therefore holds onto the end of rationality, which capitalism denies; onto 'something other than a means, in other words a non-rational quality' (*AT*, p. 86/79). In Adorno's aesthetics, this irrational moment evades conceptualisation.

Another reason why the dialectic of mimesis and rationality is constitutive of Adorno's *Aesthetic Theory* is that he understands art to be a part of the modernisation process and, simultaneously, just by virtue of its position, its negation. The process of civilisation, which he divides into three phases, is, for him, synonymous with the banishment of mimetic behaviour. During the magic phase 'the organised management of mimesis' takes the place of bodily adaptation to nature.[3] Magic is an instrument of domination, for 'intercourse with spirits [was] assigned to different classes'. What used to be a symbol 'becomes a sign of the established domination of the privileged' (*DA*, p. 33/21). In the historical phase, rational practice, or labour, replaces mimetic behaviour, 'in resistance to which the ego has been formed'

(*DA*, p. 213/181). Civilisation drives 'the archaic schemata of the urge to survive' (*DA*, p. 212/180) out of humanity, drives out the reflexes of stiffening and numbness (mimicry).

Of course, the rationalisation process has not managed to overcome the terror which nature inspired in prehistoric man. Adorno uses the myth of Daphne to demonstrate the archaic scheme of the will to survive: fear transforms developed life back into mere, inanimate nature, in the same way that an animal freezes at the first sign of danger or blends organically with its natural surroundings: 'life pays the toll of its continuing existence by assimilating itself to death' (*DA*, p. 213/180). The permanent constraint of a threatening nature is replaced by that of modern society. One of the most astounding ideas in the *Dialectic of Enlightenment* seems to me to be the way Adorno conceives the modern domination of nature to be a consequence to the process of adjustment which arose out of the original terror. Technology is, for him,

> the most sublimated manifestation of mimicry. Technology no longer completes the approximation to death for the sake of survival by physical imitation of external nature, as was the case with magic, but by automation of the mental processes.

At the same time, however, it pronounces the prohibition of graven images, and thereby 'consigns the indelible mimetic heritage of all practical experience to oblivion' (*DA*, p. 214/181). Unmediated mimesis, whether it be the servile mimicry of the outcast, the victim's lament or the expressive gesture of art, 'arouses anger because, in the face of the new conditions of production, it displays the old fear which, in order to survive those conditions, must be forgotten' (*DA*, p. 215/182).

However, the brandmarks of the civilisation process are legible in art as well. For art is included in modernity's proscription of graven images: 'Art is mimetic adaptation to imagery as well as demystification of imagery by means of forms of control' (*AT*, p. 324/311). Immediacy in art must not be confused with mimetic practice, which disappeared along with prehistory. In a paradoxical formulation, Adorno decrees that aesthetic immediacy is 'tied up with universal mediation', that is, with society as a whole, which bears the impress of rationality. In a world of reification, images would, anyway, be 'those of the dead'. Art's mimetic impulse therefore realises itself not in images but by assimilating itself to technological progress through the development of artistic forms. To the extent that Adorno emphasises the technical moment of art in modernity, he must also affirm its imagelessness, 'the non-representational character of aesthetic images' (*AT*, p. 325/311).

The passages in *Aesthetic Theory* which circumscribe the relation between mimesis and rationality are extraordinarily opaque. On the side of mimesis, one finds image, adaptation and life; on the side of rationality, concept, control and death. One could perhaps summarise what Adorno thinks by saying: art reactualises archaic practice, but always in relation to the process taking place in society as a whole, that is, to reification. This produces the paradox that art assimilates itself to universal reification (mimesis), but, conversely, does so in a mediated way through its control of artistic techniques (construction).

With the concept of artistic technique, it becomes clear that art, too, is bound up with the civilisation process and the guilt associated with it: through form, the artist inflicts violence on the 'material'. The dialectic of mimesis and construction is thus played out in the labour of form. Adorno describes 'the subjective domination through form' by saying that 'the ritual of dominating nature lives on in play', or by referring to 'the cruelty of artistic shaping' (*AT*, p. 80/74). The rationality of art consists in its ability to adapt to technological development, or, to put it another way, to produce expression (mimesis) by technical means. The mimesis of art is thus an aesthetic category which refers to work on the material. Furthermore, Adorno grasps the concept of artistic technique as a paradox, in order to highlight the impossible strain of reconciling mimesis and construction, or, in this more concrete echo of *Baudelairean* formulations, to point out the desire 'to redeem permanently what is fleeting, epiphenomenal and transitory and steel it against the onslaught of the forces of reification' (*AT*, p. 326/312). The desire for permanence, or objectification, in an artwork, betrays art's mimetic impulse. Adorno thus construes the latter as essentially unfulfillable, since this contains both the desire to become a work of art and the knowledge that this cannot be. Art's goal is the work of art, but the work of art is party to the depravity associated with the civilisation process.

Adorno keeps the opposition between mimesis and construction in the balance; he does not, therefore, abandon the category of the work of art. But he does say, too, that art, in as much as it has been made into a work of art, betrays its 'magic heritage'. If it does manage to keep hold of this heritage nonetheless, this is due solely to its position, its autonomy. Adorno grounds art in the opposition between 'pure image' and 'animate existence' (*DA*, p. 30/19). The religious overtones of his view of art are unmistakable in the passage of the *Dialectic of Enlightenment* cited here. It draws its life from echoes of Judaism, which, unlike the Christian notion of grace, knows no mediation between nature and spirit, which means that the terror of the absolute is not mitigated in any way. Earthly life remains strictly separated from the beyond; hope exists only as messianic promise (*DA*, p. 36/23). At a more explicit level, Adorno draws a parallel between the position of art and that of magic: 'The work of art still has something in common with enchantment: it posits its own self-enclosed area, which it withdraws from the context of profane existence' (*DA*, p. 30/19). However, in so far as it renounces any influence on or connection with reality, art steps beyond the magic phase, even though this same renunciation also shores up the 'magic heritage'. For Adorno, the mimetic element in works of art is thus their irreducible reflexivity, 'their resemblance to themselves' (*AT*, p. 159/153). Moreover, mimetic images are distinguished from cultic ones by their autonomy: 'Because of the structural autonomy typical of them, art works are able to ward off the absolute which would otherwise infiltrate them, reducing them to symbols.' Here, too, Adorno stresses aesthetic modernity's prohibition of graven images (*AT*, p. 159/153).

We are now in a position to define Adorno's concept of mimesis with greater accuracy. History has pronounced its verdict on it; the process of civilisation has marched on, leaving it behind as a form of archaic behaviour. Adorno wants art to be rational, tracking down any lapse back into magic and criticising any discussion of art's charm (*AT*, p. 86/80). If art is still supposed to behave mimetically, it is in a very particular way. The dialectic of mimesis and rationality is played out on the side of form. All traces of subjective expression must be eliminated from form. The mimetic impulse may only be put into effect in the form of a construction which leaves no residue behind, in other words, in the form of an ascetic surrender to artistic techniques. Once again one notices the religious moment in Adorno's aesthetics, for instance when he speaks of the effort 'to cleanse [art] of whatever same contingent subject hopes to tell the world through the medium of art' (*AT*, p. 160/153). The aesthetic subject must do violence to itself by disciplining its own mimetic impulses through the process of artistic labour. In so doing, art retraces the painful path of the history of civilisation, in the course of which the modern subject formed itself at the cost of denying the natural part of human beings. Having established the domination of the concept, the subject proscribed mimetic enchantment along with all other forms of non-prescriptive knowledge. 'Its hatred was extended to the image of the vanquished former age and its imaginary happiness' (*DA*, p. 25/14). This other knowledge is alive only in art, and only as long as art presents itself as socially autonomous, and does not intervene. On these conditions, longing can find its imaginary satisfaction in aesthetic illusion (Schein):

> Representing a stance toward reality which is different from the rigid juxtaposition of subject and object, the mimetic mode of behaviour in art has been progressively infiltrated by illusion – the organ of mimesis since the archaic taboo on mimesis (*AT*, p. 169/162).

Adorno actually needs the category of aesthetic illusion in order to control those elements that will not submit to his concept of art, which, even when applied to aesthetic modernity, is tied to the idea of the organic work. As is well known, he gives pride of place to a modernist canon that, just like traditional literary studies, only admits things which bear the characteristics of the organic work, that is, things which are party to aesthetic illusion. Were one to ask what a canon of this kind excludes, one would come across a concept which marks one of the poles of the tension between construction and mimesis that has been explored here: *expression*. Adorno himself uses this term to designate that which rebels against aesthetic illusion, but he tries, in doing so, to control this rebellion with a host of strained formulations:

> The lines of expression which are engraved in a work, assuming they are clear and sharp, simultaneously serve as lines of demarcation to keep out illusion. Even so, works of art continue to be illusory... Non-aesthetic experience affects works of art most deeply through expression, to the point where expression becomes the archetype of the fictitious quality in art, as if at the juncture where art is most permeable to real experience, culture made sure the border is not violated (*AT*, p. 169/162).

Appeals to this border become a leitmotif in Adorno's aesthetic theory, and indicate the degree to which the position he adopts remains within the confines of art as an institution. From this perspective, he can describe expression as resistance to the law of artistic form and try to constrain it with aesthetic illusion, as if he himself were anxious lest undisguised, naked reality – the truth of subjectivity – were to break out of the works of art, both dispelling the aesthetic illusion and unsettling art's autonomy.

The breakthrough beyond construction

The publication of Thomas Mann's post-war diaries has told us that Adorno had a much greater hand in *Doctor Faustus* than had previously been imagined. Indeed, the relation of expression to construction, the 'breakthrough' to expression, the possibility of the (modern) 'work' and, finally, the guilt associated with the process of construction are all central themes in the passages concerning musical theory and the descriptions of compositions to be found in it. Zeitblom, the biographer and humanist who tells the story of his friend, the composer Adrian Leverkühn, sees his later works as a 'reconstruction of expression'.[4] In a passage omitted from the published version of *The Birth of Doctor Faustus* – Mann's novel about writing a novel – Mann tells us that Adorno was particularly taken with the 'idea of the breakthrough beyond construction' (*Tb*, p. 952). This breakthrough is conceived in *Doctor Faustus*, and so also in Adorno's aesthetic theory, as the result of a labour at the level of artistic materials which is in some respects exhaustive, that is, as the conscious command of every technique in the history of music. Furthermore, it is seen as the result of an ascetic technique (the twelve tone scale), that allows no note 'which does not function as a motif in the construction of the whole – there are no longer any 'free' notes (*DF*, p. 658, *Tb*, p. 866). Indeed, music is liberated 'as a language' precisely by a form, such as this, 'which leaves no residue'.

> The creator of "Faustus' Lament" can surrender totally to subjectivity because the material's pre-determination removes all the worries of construction; and so this, his severest work, a work of utmost calculation, is simultaneously purely expressive (*DF*, p. 660).

Guided by Adorno's aesthetic theory, we can read this as the dialectical notion of a second immediacy: the artist's submission (mimesis) to the labour of his material (construction) pushes the 'work' into a region where expression and construction become interchangeable; which brings us back to the enigmatic realm of aesthetic illusion. Ironically, Thomas Mann makes the devil, who bears a remarkable resemblance to Adorno, a critic of aesthetic illusion, which he calls 'expression's subsumption into the conciliatory realm of the general' (*DF*, p. 328). Zeitblom, moreover, interprets Leverkühn's music in the same way. Once again, he takes up an idea of Adorno's but develops it further by suggesting that lament and expression are identical: 'one could be so bold as to suggest that all expression is actually lament' (*DF*, p. 657).

Leverkühn, however, is striving for much more: he wants to find the form which would be absolutely necessary, or, to put it another way, the art which would succeed art. One of the alternatives offered to him by the devil is parody, the play of forms 'whose vitality, as we know, has subsided', but he rejects this as too easy (*DF*, p. 329). Leverkühn's goal, the work beyond the 'work of art', cannot be achieved by losing oneself in the matter at hand, in the labour of artistic material, or by mimesis at the level of technique, but rather by working through this towards the 'breakthrough' or, to quote Nietzsche's *Ecce Homo*, 'inspiration'. Zeitblom, the 'despairing humanist', inadvertently reveals the dangerous regions the composer now inhabits. Leverkühn's 'desire for the breakthrough', and the way he conceives of the decision between 'aesthetic salvation or damnation' as a matter of 'fate', are shown to be 'German through and through, deeply German, the very definition of the Teutonic' (*DF*, p. 420). To the extent that Leverkühn's breakthrough to the new work of art became associated with 'the Germans' breakthrough to the world' (*DF*, p. 418), his necessary form would be immediate expression, and archaic, cultic practice would become identical with modern, cultural ones. Contrary to his naive biographer, Leverkühn knows what this would cost. The work, which he wants to produce nevertheless, would be as ambiguous as life itself. Progressive and regressive at one and the same time, and strangely indifferent to the barbarity of the era that spawned it, Leverkühn's Apocalypse does not have a single note 'in the music of the angels and the spheres which does not have its rigorous counterpart in Hell's laughter' (*DF*, p. 514). This 'explosive old-worldliness', a phrase that Mann borrows from Adorno, is recuperable only because Zeitblom re-reads expression as lament.

Doctor Faustus and its author cast an interestingly oblique light on the historical avant-garde movements. Thomas Mann's use of Adorno's concept of 'the breakthrough beyond construction to expression' (*Tb*, p. 952) involves a subtle displacement, or, to be more precise, a very literal reading of a grammatical category: the preposition 'beyond'. *Doctor Faustus* wants to be more than just a novel or a work of art; it wants, bafflingly, to compete with reality. Even after publication, its author confesses himself to be in the thrall of a book

> such as I have never written before... Though made up entirely of confession and real sacrifice, it seems to be able to contain itself within the strict borders of a work of art, yet it no longer wants to be a work of art. Rather, in the very act of presenting itself as the most rigorous of compositions, it steps beyond art and turns almost uncontrollably into reality (*Tb*, p. 941).

Which brings us back to our starting point and the relation between modernity and postmodernity. The former, we said, involved the will to the work of art and necessary form, the latter the insight that this project was impossible. We hoped to make this clearer with the concrete example of the constellation of Adorno and Thomas Mann. We could perhaps now suggest that Adorno tries to rescue aesthetic modernity by letting expression and construction collapse into one another and making the work of art the place where the tension between mimesis and rationality is resolved. The covert aim of this recuperation is the enclosure of expression; it is betrayed by Adorno's reduction of the concept of form to technique.

Thomas Mann takes Adorno's aesthetics as the raw material for his novel, which allows him to dramatise or stage them at the same time. He is thus able to find concrete images for the artist's complicity with the 'cruelty of artistic shaping' in Leverkühn's cold reserve or the 'symbolic parallels' between the return to barbarity we see in both aesthetics and politics.

However, the novel's construction gives Adorno's ideas a twist which runs badly against the grain of his intentions. The separation of life and art that Adorno makes into the precondition of art is constantly blurred by Thomas Mann: life has a tendency to cross over into the work of art, the work of art into life. And Mann is well aware of this; as early as his *Apolitical Observations* he was playing with the semantic resonance of parallels between concepts like the artist's work and the work of art. The 'irrepressible desire' for quotation that he sees in himself from the Observations onwards leads to a kind of montage which can best be described as phantasmagoric. It grafts unprocessed pieces of life ('the cold portrait of my mother, the surrender of my sister's fate'[5]) onto the work of art with a 'shamelessness' he confesses to be 'worthy of Jean-Jacques' (*The Birth of Doctor Faustus*) and which he feels bears a secret affinity to prostitution. Writing to his son, he declares himself:

> determined to use any type of "montage". For what we both mean by the word is directly related with the curious manner in which the book goes beyond the literary, the way it "shakes off aesthetic illusion", in short its reality.[6]

Although it is hard to conceive of borders quite so permeable before the movements of the historical avant-garde, it is an idea which has little to do with their project of the reintegration of art into everyday practice. In Thomas Mann, the necessity of the work, postulated by Adorno, is presented as the process of turning life-history and the work of art into myth. Life as myth constitutes life as quotation or, as Mann calls it in his Freud essay, 'life as hagiography': formulas and their repetition. Nietzsche, whose life was 'an artistic offering' right up to his fall into insanity, and the self-mythologising of his final moments, is his precursor in this attempt to blur boundaries, for he is someone 'who absorbed much of the past into himself, recollecting and repeating it, making it mysteriously present by a more or less conscious sequence of imitations'.[7] In 'life as hagiography' – in Leverkühn's biography, in *Ecce Homo* and in the autobiographical writings of Thomas Mann – there is no theme or motif that is not related to others in some way; it is, to use a phrase Mann applied to Wagner's music, 'an orgy of interrelations, a whole world of spirited and serious allusions'.[8] And everything is quotation. This is the frame of mind which produces the feeling of *déja vu* that Nietzsche has in the Engadin and Leverkühn has in Pfeiffering. On the level of narrative technique it leads to what I would like to call semantic over-investment (or overdetermination: *Ubersemantisierung*). But that, in turn, makes the necessary work of art radically ambiguous.

For Adorno, the place of the work of art is in the tension between mimesis and rationality. Thomas Mann equates the breakthrough *to* expression with the break *beyond* art. Had Adorno seen to the bottom of this equation, he would have had to reject it out of hand. The necessary work of art, which demonstrates the reversion of construction into mimesis, is, for Thomas Mann, also something which actually goes beyond the work of art and becomes a montage of pieces of reality. While Adorno wants to place the two poles in a dialectical relation to one another, Thomas Mann wants to blend them ambiguously. This then raises the question of whether a reading of *Aesthetic Theory* from the perspective of *Doctor Faustus* would not uncover the ambiguity Adorno had tried so hard to banish with dialectics.

(translated by Ben Morgan)

Notes

1. Thomas Mann, *Tagebucher 28/5/1946 – 31/12/1948*, ed. I Jens, Ffm, 1989, p. 867. Cited hereafter in the text as *Tb*.

2. Theodor W. Adorno, *Aesthetische Theorie*, Ffm, 1970, p. 86; trans. Christian Lenhardt, *Aesthetic Theory*, London, 1984, p. 69. Page numbers to both the German and the English editions will be given parenthetically in the text as *AT*, giving the reference for the German text first, e.g. *AT*, p. 86/79.

3. Max Horkheimer and Theodor W. Adorno, *Dialektik der Aufklarung*, Amsterdam, 1947, p. 212; trans. John Cumming, *Dialectic of Enlightenment*, London, 1979, p. 180. As with Aesthetische Theory, further references will be given parenthetically in the text as *DA*, quoting the German page number first, e.g. *DA*, p. 212/180.

4. Thomas Mann, *Doktor Faustus. Das Leben des Deutschen Tonsetzers Adrian Leverkuhn* in his *Collected Works*, Berlin/Weimar, 1965; Vol. VI, p. 657. Hereinafter cited in the text as *DF*.

5. Letter to Emil Preetorius, 12/12/1947.

6. Letter to Michael Mann, 31/1/1948.

7. Thomas Mann, 'Nietzsche's Philosophy', in his *Collected Works*, Vol. X, p. 6.

8. Thomas Mann, 'Richard Wagner and the Ring', in Vol. X, p. 430.

Mimesis and Construction in the Music of Boulez and Cage

Alastair Williams

The interconnected dialectics of identity and non-identity, mimesis and rationality, operate at the core of Adorno's understanding of modernism. It is through the field of tension etched by these dialectics that I intend to explore the major junctures in the search for an advanced musical language. In an appendix to his *Aesthetic Theory* (469), Adorno cites Boulez as renouncing the separation, upheld by Schoenberg, between compositional technique and aesthetics.[1] To a large extent, Boulez's realisation concurs with Adorno's contention that the contradictions which emerged from the highly rationalised musical systems of the 1950s can be ascribed to a fetish of construction at the expense of aesthetic considerations.

Before examining some of the manifestations this dialectic has taken, I should like to outline the way in which Adorno understands the two poles of mimesis and construction in musical modernism. In a sense, Adorno locates the impulse of modernist music in Beethoven's late style (1814–1827) – roughly synchronous with the establishment of modernity in the larger philosophical frame. For Adorno, Beethoven's late works represent the composer's spiritual isolation from the world and the recognition, in musical terms, of the irreconcilability of direct expression and form, despite the fact that he came close to a genuine reconciliation of these two dimensions in the middle period works (*Eroica, Waldstein*). The austerity and rigour of the late works remain true to the mimetic quality of art; the possibility of reconciliation is kept alive through the tension between sensuous expression and form in the music.

> This illuminates the anomaly, that late Beethoven is referred to at the same time as both subjective and objective. The crumbling (*brüchige*) landscape is objective, the light in which it uniquely glows subjective. (Adorno, *GS*, 17: 17)

To summarise, it is this alienated quality, requiring a seemingly disproportionate emphasis on construction in order to remain true to a genuine untrammelled sensuousness, which becomes the driving force behind Schoenberg's innovations. Adorno describes the construction of the monodrama *Erwartung* – perhaps the quintessential expressionist work – in terms of emerging from the intensity of the mimetic impulse: the emphasis on construction drawing attention to a damaged subjectivity (Adorno, 1985: 65). Certainly, the monodrama creates the impression of an unbridled emotional surge which has a striking immediacy despite the notorious complexity of the score. Yet paradoxically, it was precisely this type of *tour de force*, in which particular compositions were forced to establish their own musical syntax, rather than relying on an external system such as tonality for the context, which allowed Schoenberg to create the potentially stifling system of serialism. In Schoenberg's struggle to create a musical medium which would simultaneously allow for greater freedom and greater discipline, Adorno detects the dialectic which goes right to the heart of Enlightenment rationality. The uncompromising nature of Schoenberg's music embodies, for Adorno, the stance of an autonomous subject in the face of administered society; a protest which was demanded by the state of the musical material with which Schoenberg was composing. Yet on the other hand, the sovereign control over musical resources which serialism allows comes close to epitomising a rationality which can only advance through an increasing domination over nature. Despite the immanent necessity of serialist methods, Schoenberg and Berg at their best succeed despite rather than because of the system. Music is enchained and liberated at the same time.

A significant strand of post-war avant-garde music is normally associated with the innovations arising from the summer courses held at Darmstadt. The experimental phase of the Darmstadt school can be dated from 1951 with the attempt to radicalise the serial procedures of Anton Webern. Webern's aphoristic and terse use of serial techniques aimed to create a totality of integral relationships with no redundant or repeated material, in which the boundary between harmony and melody is blurred. The emphasis moved away from the handling of the series as a whole to distinctive intervallic qualities of the series. The main concern of the early Darmstadt experimental composers was to extend the procedures for organising pitch to the remaining parameters of music, a project which had been partially anticipated by Messiaen's *Mode de Valeurs et d'intensités* (1949) in which the composer employs 'modes' of pitch, duration, intensity and attack. Stockhausen's *Kreuzspiel* (1951) and Boulez's *Structures 1a* (1951) further developed this desire to integrate all the parameters of music into a single organisational logic. Early work in the electro-acoustic studio at Cologne can be seen as a protraction of this impulse to maintain absolute control over the parameters of music, expanded into quasi-scientific explorations of the physical properties of sound. The primary aesthetic is succinctly summed up by Eimert's vision of a 'real musical control of Nature' (1955: 10); a project which suggests, as Adorno feared, the capitulation of musical technique to the closed universe of instrumental reason.

Indeed, this is the line of attack chosen by Adorno in his notorious, scathing article, *The Aging of the New Music*, which he presented as a lecture in the Stuttgart Week of New Music early in 1954. The kernel of Adorno's criticism is that the objectivity of the musical material becomes a fetish or object in itself. Innovation is driven not by a need for subjective expression but by a need to hide behind prefabricated material. The material itself is imbued with a specious meaning rather than the constellations which the composer actually constructs out of the material.

Trenchant though Adorno's arguments are, they are too generalised and fail to take into account differences between individual composers, as well as any self-awareness on the part of musicians of the predicament represented by highly rationalised methods of composition. He also seems to be locked into a theory of advanced musical material which is primarily pitch-oriented. It must be admitted, however, that Adorno's article was written at the height of serialist euphoria. Before examining the dissent from the inside, as it were, which lies behind Boulez's 3rd Piano Sonata, it is worth examining the flagship of integral serialism, his *Structures 1a*, in order to see how the contradictions of an all-embracing rationality manifest themselves.

Structures 1a represents a self-consciously extreme effort, on the part of the composer, to extend serial procedures to all parameters of music. By predetermining his materials and the operations to be performed on them, Boulez relinquishes a large part of the constructional process to automatism. He is then able to make creative decisions with the somewhat crude mass of sound. Boulez predetermines the components of the composition by devising a grid for the 48 permutations of the series – prime, inversion, retrograde and retrograde inversion in each of their transpositions. He then derives other musical parameters from this grid: a duration series, a dynamic series and an attack series. As György Ligeti has pointed out in his searching analysis of this piece, the common derivation of these parameters is essentially arbitrary since there is nothing but an abstract idea uniting the common derivations. There is no particular reason why a 12-note series should yield a meaningful organisation of duration. The contradiction involved in such automated compositional procedures is that much of the actual outcome is unpredictable, though Boulez does make creative decisions with the raw material produced. In the words of Ligeti:

> Interacting decisions lead unavoidably to automatism, determination creates the unpredictable; and vice versa, neither the automatic nor the accidental can be created without decision and determining. (Ligeti, 1960: 61)

The key issue which Ligeti has dredged from *Structures 1a* is the way in which identity and difference fold into each other. The constructional identity of the music exists as an abstract idea, though, even on this level, the methods used by Boulez to try to make the organisation of parameters interlock with the pitch grid are, in essence, arbitrary. Order and disorder map onto each other. In all fairness, Boulez came to recognise these shortcomings, referring to the collection of *Structures* as a 'document' or 'what Barthes might call a reduction of style to the degree zero' (1986: 201; 1976: 55). *Structures 1a* renounces the vestiges of expression which survive in Webern, in favour of a fetish of pure construction as an end in itself. There is a certain austere beauty in the way certain sonorities or constellations of sonorities gleam through the texture, yet this is limited to particular moments which give the slip to the large-scale identity sought by the constructional principles.

Boulez tackled these issues in his article *Alea*, a theoretical correlate to the introduction of mobile form in the 3rd Piano Sonata. The central issue of *Alea*, which can very much be seen as a reaction to the innovations of Cage, is summed up in the following comment:

> ... the less one chooses, the greater is the dependence of the event on the coefficient of hazard implied by the composer's subjectivity. It is the varying degree of interchange between the terms of this antinomy that will arouse interest in a passage of the work so composed (1964: 48).

The 3rd Piano Sonata is undoubtedly a musical entity in its own right, but the complex of ideas in which it is embedded, together with its incomplete state, suggests that it is concerned more with the possibility of an advanced musical language than with its own individual existence. There is a sustained attempt to incorporate the dialectic of control and freedom within the material itself and the whole conglomeration of ideas is enriched by the influence of Joyce and Mallarmé. The Sonata is dubbed – in Joyce's term – 'a work in progress', and is envisaged as being in five movements or *formants*, as the composer calls them. The word *formant* is intended to convey the idea of a form 'understood as a specific fixed structure, which is, however, movable as whole: thus the *formant* in itself is fixed, and as an entity it allows no intrusion into its homogeneous structure, but its place within a work may vary' (1976: 81).

Though Boulez has outlined a plan for the mobility of the *formants* with respect to one another, the Sonata is, so far, incomplete and only two out of the five projected *formants* are complete – *Trope* and *Constellation-Miroir*. The title of the second *formant*, *Trope*, is a reference to the practices of monodic extension in Gregorian chant. It is divided into four fragments which Boulez calls *developments*: Texte, Parenthèse, Commentaire and Glose. The *formant* may begin or end with any of these, but having chosen a starting point, the performer must follow the cyclical order of *developments*, although there are two alternative positions for Commentaire. The *developments* trope one another, but within the *developments* themselves, Boulez introduces tropes either by working them into the 'text' or placing them in parentheses.

Boulez uses a technique of what might be termed late-serialism, whereby the series is divided into four groups, each with characteristic intervals, and it is the groups which are permutated rather than the individual elements. It is the permutations of these groups from which Boulez derives the mobility of the *developments* in *Trope*. As Manfred Stahnke has shown in his exhaustive study of *Trope*, Boulez remains faithful to this scheme by basing each of the *developments* around the appropriate permutations of the basic series, along with the sub-series proliferating from them. The constructional derivations are frequently disguised, but the serial procedures in *Texte* and *Parenthèse* are possible to follow – at least on paper – but in *Commentaire* and especially *Glose*, serious doubts are raised as to whether the music can be called serial at all. Although the relationships between the partitioning of the series and the plasticity of the *formant* are far more subtle than indicated here, the attempt to generate the mobility of the form from the internal qualities of the series, given the recondite nature of the serial derivations, remains something of a chimera.

In *Texte* and *Parenthèse*, not only are the serial procedures relatively clear, the distinction between grace notes or inessential sections and structural notes are also apparent. Similarly, there is a distinction between pulsed time and what Boulez calls time bubbles, 'where only the proportions of the macro-structures are defined. This will give the whole range of durational properties, from the most precise and complex definition to the most summary of statistical phenomena' (1971: 58). *Glose* does not entirely collapse these distinctions, but they become blurred. Despite the fact that *Glose* is meticulously composed, it has an improvisational feel to it, and is the result of having let the material dissolve itself. Stahnke contends that 'the score (*Notentext*), whether liked or not, contains the thesis that a series inside an open logic leads itself to absurdity' (1979: 78). *Structures 1a* provides the corollary that a series inside a confined logic also leads itself to absurdity. The difference is that, in the case of the 3rd Piano Sonata, Boulez has averted absurdity by making compositional decisions in what amounts to an atonal idiom. *Glose*, which is conceived primarily in terms of sonority, is the most coherent *development*, despite obliterating its own structural logic. Pitch organisation, the parameter which drove the quest for a historically advanced musical material forward, has dissolved into sonority and it is this parameter, along with register and intensity, which moves to the fore in *Constellation-Miroir*. If Boulez does achieve a second immediacy through construction it is by dissolving an integrated structural approach rather than emerging the other side of it – unless the two alternatives amount to the same thing.

Boulez divulges that 'literary affiliations played a more important part than purely musical considerations' in the conception of the 3rd Piano Sonata (1986: 143) and acknowledges a debt to Joyce and in particular Mallarmé. It is not difficult to see the overlap between Mallarmé's constellation of words and ideas on the page, his breaking down of sentences into particles, and the use of parentheses which cut right through stable phrases, with the procedures of the 3rd Piano Sonata. By threatening the autonomy of art from the inside, Mallarmé delved into an aporia, and it is this aporia which Boulez resurrects in the 3rd Piano Sonata. Boulez makes a paradoxical double manoeuvre: he recognises the instrumental, fetishistic tendency of high modernism as evinced by integral serialism and tries to soften it, yet he remains devoted to the notion of a sufficiently advanced material solving the problem. He tries to ontologise the paradox, to transcend identity and non-identity by making the interplay an intrinsic quality of the material. He wants to upgrade an over-determined material, which has been brought to the limits of its own feasibility, into a super-material which will engulf its own paradox. The sonata stands on the brink of its own impossibility and even crosses it if we take into account its unfinished state and the composer's inability, so far, to find a practical way of realising the vision of *Sequence*.

Yet Boulez has wrested some victories from the aporia in which the work resides. His extraordinary ear for texture and spacing produces moments of sensuous beauty in this music. The question is whether these moments vindicate Adorno; whether they are a second immediacy which emerges from rigorous construction, or whether they are moments of primary immediacy, composed for their sheer sound qualities which have little to do with the method of construction. If the latter, then the constructive rigour may have facilitated the creation but not enabled it; an Adornian second immediacy is a forlorn hope.[2]

The John Cage of the 1950s is a curious blend of idiosyncratic, homespun high modernist and postmodernist: he combines highly organised methods of construction with an interest in sounds as noise or 'found objects'. In a letter to Boulez, discussing the *Concerto for Prepared Piano* (1950), he talks about using charts as a conceptual tool.

> All this brings me closer to a 'chance' or if you like to an unaesthetic choice. I keep of course, the means of rhythmic structuring feeling that it is the 'espace sonore' in which these sounds may exist and change. Composition becomes throwing sound into silence and rhythm which in my Sonatas has been one of breathing now becomes one of the flow of sound and silence (Campana, 1989: 219)

In the last movement of the Concerto these charts are constructed by chance techniques derived from the *I Ching* (Book of Changes), thereby giving Cage what he considered to be a new freedom, with regard to pitch, by jettisoning creative choice. Furthermore, the charts generated a parity between sound and silence which is evident in the last movement. The next stage, obviously, was to extend the chance procedures to embrace the other parameters of organisation – tempo, texture, rhythm and dynamics – which is what Cage did in the *Music of Changes*, a four-volume piano work.

An extraordinary aspect of the *Music of Changes* is that, despite being a compendium of chance procedures, it is a highly determinate score: little is left to chance on the written page; the only variability in performance results from the sheer difficulties involved in playing the score. The overlaps with *Structures 1a* are remarkable: as in the latter, the organisational procedures of the *Music of Changes* result in contradictory and unplayable markings: Boulez sorts them out, Cage leaves the performer to sort them out. Both scores have comparable extremes of register, texture and dynamics. Cage's music is more fragmented, contains many more silences, and lacks the contrapuntal flow and density of the 12-tone threads in *Structures 1a*. The overall identity of *Structures 1a* is intended to stem from the serial grid, which – though acknowledged as an extreme usage – is meant to carry a degree of truth through its sedimentation as historically advanced material. Cage's chance construction boils down the procedures dictated by the *I Ching*. Though Cage has taken elaborate precautions to eliminate meaning from his music, the fact that he attributes so much significance to chance methods of organisation suggests an underlying meaning or a hypostatisation of *différance*. In any case, the compositional procedure cannot prevent the listener from finding relationships in the music; though the sounding score is irrelevant to Cage. On the local level, Boulez's all-pervasive structure of identity cannot exclude chance, Cage's all-pervasive structure of chance cannot exclude identity. Both scores strive for an anonymity in which the organisational procedures work out their own consequences.

Cage draws the conclusion from his account of the construction of the *Music of Changes* that 'it is thus possible to make a musical composition the continuity of which is free of individual taste and memory (psychology) and also of the literature and "traditions" of the art' (Silence: 59). This statement thus celebrates that which Adorno – as expressed in the 'Aging' – most feared. Cage has striven for exactly that fetish of pure objective construction, which eliminates any subjective impulse, of which Adorno had accused the serialists. The fact that Cage actually tried to achieve this depersonalisation is, of course, difficult for his non-intentionality, and it is hardly without significance that, despite his denial of history and tradition, Cage should have written an automated work at the same time as Boulez did.

Cage makes a strong distinction between compositions constructed by chance procedures yet which are determinate, and those which are indeterminate in performance. He does argue, however, that both situations can occur simultaneously. *The Art of Fugue* is cited as an example of a determinate composition in which, 'timbre and amplitude characteristics of the material, by not being given, are indeterminate' (Cage, 1958: 35). Yet the margin between a determinate composition constructed by chance procedures and a composition indeterminate with respect to performance is not so large. To cross that margin requires only one simple procedure: to hand over the chance procedures to the performer. Coupled with Cage's interest in environmental sound, the obsessive organisation of high modernism quickly becomes the plurality and jettisoning of structure characteristic of postmodernism. Cage continued to refine his chance procedures during the 1950s; it was not until 1958 that indeterminate compositions started to emerge. One such composition is *Variations IV* (1963) 'for any number of players, any sounds or combinations of sounds produced by any means, with or without other activities' (Cage, 1963). The score constitutes little more than a means for determining the spatial distribution of the performers, which can extend beyond the confines of a building. *Variations IV* is thus about the acceptance of environmental noise; the mimetic immediacy of the sound around us, with minimal interference from a constructional principle. This postmodern attempt to merge art and life, to find immediacy in unordered sound, is the antithesis of highly structured music, yet, as we have seen, stems from Cage's own strictly organised music. As an attempt to elude intentional construction, *Variations IV* represents a compositional gesture which cannot be repeated too often.

The procedures in the music of Boulez and Cage discussed above show the interaction of identity and non-identity, mimesis and construction, emerging in a particularly strong manner. This music is very much about its own possibility as music. Boulez's 3rd Piano Sonata is caught up in the contradictions of its own solipsism and Cage's *Variations IV* undercuts its own status as a creative act, whilst evincing a passive acceptance of the surrounding sonic environment, thereby abandoning the possibility of change. Since this bare presentation of the boundaries of modern music, the areas of tension have, in much music, sunk beneath the surface. Thus the composition upon which Boulez is at present engaged, *Répons*, maintains vestiges of serial technique within a mellifluous sound world. Cage's notion of music circus often uses skilled performers, but within an unstructured context. *Roratorio: an Irish Circus on Finnegan's Wake* (1978), for example, uses trained dancers and skilled Irish folk musicians in simultaneous but separate activities. Although it may no longer be appropriate to tackle the dialectic of mimesis and construction head on, the line of tension is still very much there to be met anew in musical creativity.

Notes

1. Adorno is probably referring to the paper *Nécessité d'une orientation esthétique* presented at Darmstadt in 1960. It is translated as 'Putting the Phantoms to Flight' in *Orientations*.
2. For a good account of second immediacy, see C. Bürger's article in the present volume.

References

Theodor Adorno, *Aesthetic Theory*, tr. C. Lenhardt, London, 1984.

Theodor Adorno, 'Spätstil Beethovens', Gesammelte Schriften, vol. 17.

Theodor Adorno, 'The Aging of the New Music', Telos 77, Fall 1988.

Pierre Boulez, 'Alea', *Perspectives of New Music*, Fall–Winter 1964.

Pierre Boulez, *Boulez on Music Today*, tr. Susan Bradshaw and Richard Rodney Bennett, London, 1971.

Pierre Boulez, *Conversations with Célestin Deliège*, London, 1976.

Pierre Boulez, *Orientations*, ed. Jean-Jacques Nattiez, tr. Martin Cooper, London, 1985.

John Cage, 'Composition as Process', *Silence*, London, 1958.

John Cage, *Variations IV*, New York, 1963.

Deborah Campana, 1989, 'A Chance Encounter: the Correspondence between John Cage and Pierre Boulez 1949-1954', *John Cage at Seventy-Five*, ed. Fleming & Duckworth, London, 1989.

Herbert Eimert, 'What is Electronic Music?', die Reihe, 1955.

Gyorgy Ligeti, 'Pierre Boulez: Decision and Autonomism', in *Structures 1a*, die Reihe 4, German edition (1958), 1960.

Manfred Stahnke, 'Struktur und Äesthetik bei Boulez', Hamburger Beitrage zur Musikwissenschaft, XXI, Hamburg, 1979.

Music, Modernism and Signification

Georgina Born

In this paper I will suggest that in order to understand how music produces meaning, it is necessary to develop a framework that engages with it as culture in the widest sense. The analysis of how meaning is produced by music-as-culture poses a broader problematic than that posed by the apparently narrowly textual arts, visual or literary. But rather than being irrelevant to their analysis, this problematic may, in turn, feed back insights into those other arts.

As a preliminary, it seems to me that the development of an aesthetic theory, in the present context of questions around postmodernism, must first depend upon a greater understanding of what has gone before historically; an understanding that encompasses culture in all its fractured forms. It must be able to give insight into musical modernism, but it must also register the character and complexity of 'the other' – that is, popular musics. At the risk of polemic, I think that such an approach will prove more fruitful than a return to the mode of traditional criticism, and the closure involved in focusing too narrowly on specific texts or specific authors – unless one reads out from these to history, as it were.

It seems to me extraordinary if, in a century that has witnessed and heard the debates around Dada, Brecht's epic theatre, Situationism, conceptual and performance art, we can return to or retain a notion of aesthetic experience as centred on the discreet artwork as single object or text; and of the aim of aesthetic speculation as, primarily, to assess values in order to judge – an aim deeply embedded in the dominant institutional forms of modern culture. The social and political dimensions of the movements cited, highlighting and involving critiques of and ironic comments on both the performative and the institutional aspects of art, direct us towards an exploded and constellatory definition of artistic meaning. Any assessment of value must first depend upon expanding our understanding of the multitextuality of this kind of art – and in fact of all media. I want to propose that especially in regard to music, but also the other arts, since meaning inheres in its social, discursive and technological mediations as well as in 'the music as sound', as well as in the notated or visual text, we should consider the aesthetic as subsuming these mediations. The social is, then, in the aesthetic, just as the discursive constructs and yet is distinct from the artwork itself. The terms and the boundaries of art have been redefined. We could go so far as to say that since these movements, art that disdains to be conscious of, or concerned with, its discursive and its social forms – performative and/or institutional – must be seen as negating or refusing that possibility, or as adopting an 'unconsciousness' of it.

In the rest of the paper, I want to sketch a general theory of musical signification. I will suggest that, rather than a representational art, we should think of music as inherently 'mediational' – liable to mediation – and intertextual. Specifically, I will argue that such a framework is necessary in order to analyse the discursive and aesthetic character of musical modernism. Finally, I will make some brief comments on the limits of Adorno's aesthetic and sociology of music.

Meanings around the sound: mediation and multitextuality

It is noticeable that most orthodox aesthetics of music take as their object music-as-sound, or music-as-notated-text, or music-and-lyric.[1] Yet despite this limited conceptualisation, confusions abound. Thus it is common to fail to distinguish between music-as-notated – the ideal, unrealised work, which foregrounds its systemic and structural character, and which is, in fact, music mediated in visual form – and music-as-sound – its aural realisation. Yet especially in the modernist era, some notated musics have resisted aural realisation, have received only inaccurate and approximate performances, and existed (and gained notoriety) primarily as visual or graphic texts; while many electronic and popular musics are non-notated and exist only in aural form, mediated by performance and by electronic technologies.

We have to develop a theory of musical meaning that can account for these distinctive forms, without which, for example, it would be impossible to grasp the specific importance of the visual and notational and conceptual in the modernist aesthetic, or of the aural and electronic in popular music. Just as, in terms of aural realisation, we have to distinguish between live performance – the immediate social realisation of music – and the various forms of technologically-mediated reception, by record, radio, television, film and so on.

The point is not to debate the relative priorities of music as aural or visual text, as live collective event or isolated experience; but to move beyond the currently impoverished and essentialist notions of how music conveys meaning by developing an analysis of the multiple, specific forms in which it is experienced. As a basis for aesthetic understanding, we need to tease out the particular character of the many mediations through which it is experienced: to assess both their distinctiveness, and the effects of their simultaneity and relatedness. A first principle, then, is the *multitextuality* of music-as-culture; and the need to analyse its particular forms – aural, visual, technological, social, discursive – as an ensemble.

Why might this be important? For four reasons.

First, in order to clarify confusion concerning technological mediation. Grasping the inevitable mediation of music allows us to move aesthetically beyond the nostalgia for a pre- or non-electronically mediated music, or for a return to an idealised ambient soundscape: both forms of yearning for the 'authentic' in music. Rather, the mediations can be perceived as inherently part of the aesthetic, and embraced as such. For example, it is still common in the classical music world for musicians and sound engineers, when recording or amplifying instruments, to talk of aiming to reproduce faithfully the instruments' acoustic sound. But this is an impossibility, since recorded or amplified instruments are *inevitably transformed* by that process and cannot be experienced either acoustically or physically as 'the same as before'. It is the same nostalgia (technology as redemptive of an 'original' musical experience) at a second order that feeds the fallacy of the compact disc, the marketing of which claims that it comes closer to 'real' or 'live' sound than previous forms of reproduction. Whereas it is simply *another* form of electronic transformation, perhaps cleaner, less noisy, more acoustically heightened and colourful than the LP. Radio, cassette, LP, CD, video disc: all are aesthetically distinct forms of musical reproduction, all equally 'artificial' or 'authentic', all attesting to the absence of a 'natural' or original sound.

This aesthetic principle has best been grasped, as a practical logic, by the popular music industry, as shown by the common practice when preparing an album of mixing the same tracks differently – or adjusting the aesthetic – for different technological outlets: car radio, cassette, LP, CD. The final mix of pop chart material is tried out, in the midst of high fidelity technologies in the studio, on tiny car radio speakers so as to assess how the sound comes across on that format – so that the voice, rhythm section, treble and bass can be made to reach out musically over the throb of the engine and the street sounds outside. It would be even more appropriate if those 'extraneous' sounds were also reproduced as part of the total soundscape or listening context in the studio.

A second reason for attention to multitextuality is because, as in the movements cited earlier, certain musics have attempted to innovate and to critique previous forms not primarily or only in terms of the aural or the notated, but also in terms of the social relations of music production. Good and related examples are the attempts at a new performance division of labour characteristic of both experimental and improvised musics in the 1960s and '70s, in which the lines between composer, performer and audience were blurred; or the collective musical composition of free jazz and improvised music in the same period. All of these aimed to deconstruct and demystify the role of the composer-author. To look at these musics as aural or notated texts is to miss a major dimension of meaning. Yet it would equally be a mistake to ignore the visual text: while some of these musics had none (free jazz, improvised music), the simplistic scores of post-Cageian experimental music were central to that music's Dada-esque and pointedly 'un-serious' critique of the extreme complexity and abstraction of the scores of the dominant post-serialist avant garde, and of the mystified, directive and pompous role of the 'serious' composer. (Figures 1, 2 and 3 are varied examples of this kind of experimental score by George Brecht, Earle Brown and John Cage. They contrast with figure 4, part of a serialist score by Milton Babbitt.)

Figure 1. George Brecht. *Comb Music (Comb Events)*, 1959–62. (Copyright George Brecht)

COMB MUSIC (COMB EVENT)

For single or multiple performance.

A comb is held by its spine in one hand, either free or resting on an object.

The thumb or a finger of the other hand is held with its tip against an end prong of the comb, with the edge of the nail overlapping the end of the prong.

The finger is now slowly and uniformly moved so that the prong is inevitably released, and the nail engages the next prong.

This action is repeated until each prong has been used.

Second version: Sounding comb-prong.

Third version: Comb-prong.

Fourth version: Comb. Fourth version: Prong.

G. Brecht
(1959-62)

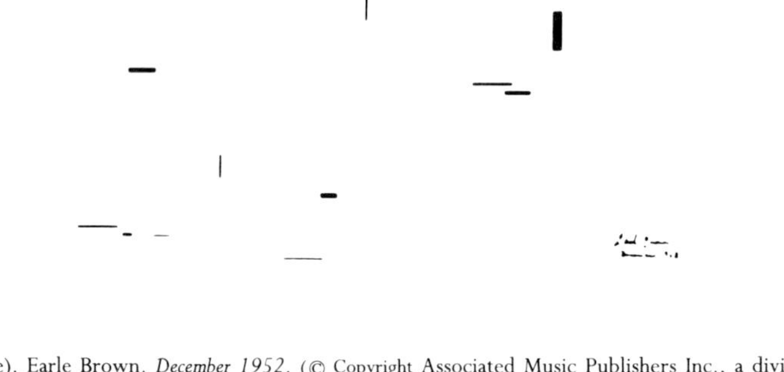

Figure 2 (above). Earle Brown. *December 1952*. (© Copyright Associated Music Publishers Inc., a division of Music Sales Corporation. International copyright secured. All rights reserved. Used by permission.)
Figure 3 (below). John Cage. From *Concert for Piano and Orchestra*, 1957–8.
(Copyright 1960 Henmar Press Inc, NY. Reproduced by permission of Peters Edition Ltd., London)

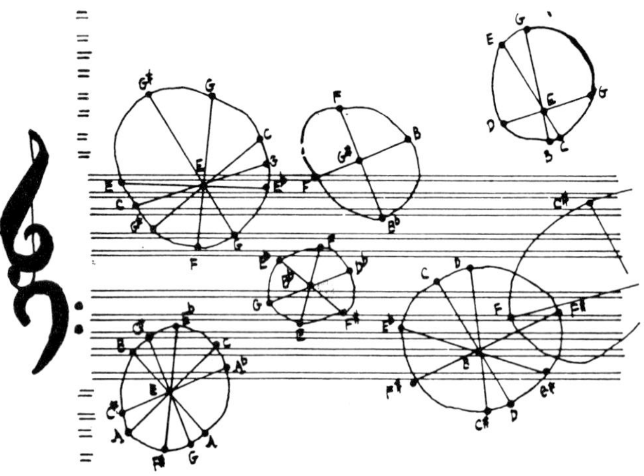

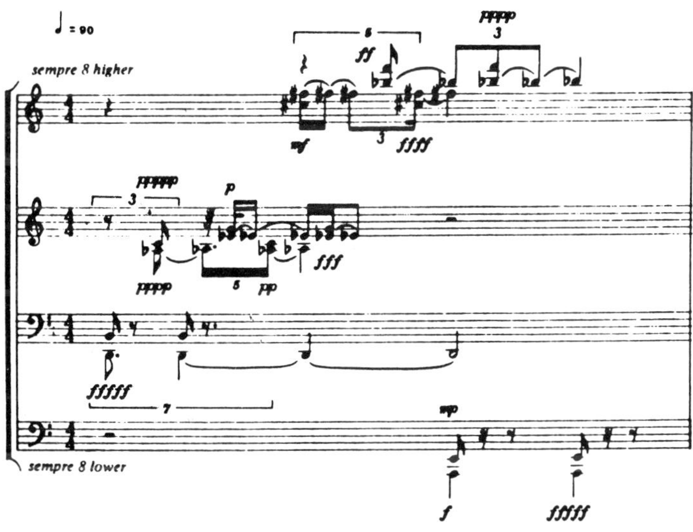

Figure 4. Milton Babbitt. From *Post-Partitions*, 1966. (Copyright 1975 Henmar Press Inc., NY)

A third reason why attention to multitextuality is important is because only with such an analysis of *simultaneous levels* in the production of meaning can one uncover either cumulative and reinforcing effects or, more interestingly, *contradictions and tensions* operating between the levels of the ensemble.

In terms of reception, if pleasure can be derived from the various levels of musical experience, so can displeasure; and the meaning of one level may be in tension with the meaning of another, just as one level may create pleasure while another produces displeasure or invites hostility. This gives us a way of understanding why an audience may be unable to tolerate the experience of a music – for example classical music, or heavy metal rock – not due to the music-as-sound, but due to the associated forms of discourse (respectively, the elitist theories of genius associated with classical music, or the sexist iconography of heavy metal); or the modes and places of performance (inhibited concert hall ritual, or violent and omnipotent mob-behaviour in vast sports stadia) through which particular musics are experienced. On the other hand, it may also be that people are drawn to a music not because of the sound, but because of its social forms or its politicised discourse – which may override an uninterest in the sound. (I've often wondered, for example, if this is not the case for devotees of so-called 'women's music', or for those of the more stolid and worthy folk musics.) This sensitivity to contradictory levels of experience in reception gives us a way of understanding *ambivalence* towards the musical object, and points towards a more complex account of aesthetic experience than hitherto.

Several recent studies provide this kind of reading of musical meaning and pleasure, focusing notably on popular and non-western musical cultures. As yet, orthodox musicology dealing with serious music has evaded these issues, just as it has the social and broader cultural dimensions of music.[2] The studies include those by Barbara Bradby on the Buddy Holly song 'Peggy Sue'[3], and Phillip Tagg's on the Kojak television theme tune and the ABBA song 'Fernando'[4]. Both of these writers focus on the music or music-and-lyric alone, and despite very different approaches, they innovate in two similar ways. First, in focusing on implicit and 'unconscious' factors; and second, in drawing out implicit *contradictions* between levels of the whole – between the musical figures and words, the non-verbal and verbal. Tagg's method also provides an analysis of specifically musical and broader ideological connotations radiating from the aural-musical level alone: a form of intertextuality that he suggests is especially present in the dominant popular musics that he studies.

More interesting are studies by Dave Laing on punk rock[5] and Marina Roseman on the musical culture of the Temiar people of peninsular Malaysia[6] which move beyond the music-and-lyric to embrace the musical culture as a whole, including the discursive, the social and performative.

Laing's study of punk traces every level of meaning – from organisational forms and production practices, to the naming and philosophies of bands, fanzines and record companies, to performance and musical styles (vocal, physical, instrumental), to audience rituals and the punk 'look'. He analyses the way that each level of the whole creates meaning through difference; so that, for example, the organisational and technological forms of punk were not only socio-economic strategies, but also stylised symbolic interventions in, and rejections of, the forms of the mainstream rock industry. Thus punk's experiments in collective and independent (non-) organisation were comments on the entrepreneurial, hierarchical and profit-directed rock business. While at the level of musical style, punk vocalisation – murmured indistinctly or shouted hysterically, usually way off-key or hovering in between pitches – aimed above all to avoid the expressive musicality, the pitch-centredness, the smooth, relaxed and assured communication of most pop and rock vocals. It becomes clear that the movement worked symbolically through the systematic negation of every aspect of mainstream rock. And Laing suggests that the meaning of punk can only be grasped by analysing the simultaneous juxtaposition of these many levels in the bricolage, and by exploring how they work either cumulatively or, more often, against each other in wilful, stylised contradiction.

The kind of contradiction raised by Roseman in her study of a non-western musical culture is equally fascinating. She finds that the beliefs and ritual practices around Temiar musical performance, rather than reflecting the gender differentiation found in Temiar social life at large, systematically invert and negate it. The social character of musical performance exists as a kind of implicit critical commentary on, and questioning of, the dominant social order. Through the myths and feelings associated with their singing, women enjoy a kind of empowerment in fantasy, a utopian premonition. Roseman says, 'Musical and ritual performances do not simply replicate everyday social relations... Symbolic inversions ... [furnish] a framework within which to comment upon or question the accepted order of things.'[7] She thus problematises the relationship between musical culture and social order, indicating that the two may not be continuous but opposed, in tension – and that music may provide an arena for social and symbolic struggle.

A fourth, and final, reason for attention to multitextuality is that this allows an awareness of the distance between the music itself, whether as sound or as visual text, and its theorisation – which can then be seen as but one form of a universal tendency to produce discourse around music, as I discuss shortly. This is to question and dislocate any taken-for-granted synonymy between 'the music' and both those discourses which rationalise and interpret it *post hoc* and, more crucially, those which claim to construct and prescribe it. Rather, we can focus on and interrogate the character of the discourse itself. Such an approach is enhanced by returning at this point to the core of a general analysis of musical signification.

Sounds filled with projection: metaphor, discourse, intertextuality

The core of music-as-culture is its existence as organised and meaningful sound, which is already encultured, and which is perceived as 'music' only by virtue of its difference from 'noise' or 'sound-in-general'. The character of musical sound can best be grasped by contrast with other media and their forms of signification. Musical sound in itself is alogogenic, completely unrelated to language, non-artefact, having no physical existence, and non-representational, referring in the first place to nothing other than the specific musical system or genre to which it is related. That is, musical sound is a self-referential, aural abstraction. This bare core must be the start of any socio-cultural understanding of music, since only then can one build up an analysis of the many mediations around it. And it is this non-representational core of musical sound that makes it especially resistant to decoding as ideology.

We can clarify by extending aspects of Barthes' analysis to music. In terms of denotation, musical sound contrasts with representational media since it denotes nothing other than its musical expressivity as part of a specific musical system. It calls to mind only its difference from other possible musical expressions within the same genre. This peculiar degree of self-referentiality is why music may be considered a relatively empty sign; and at this level, music may be considered pure expressive form, akin to the formal level of other media.

It is at the second, connotative order of signification that music becomes particularly subject to extra-musical meanings through its extraordinary evocative power. The signifieds that music connotes at this level can be of many kinds: visual, sensual, emotional, intellectual – such as theories, domains of knowledge, compositional systems. All are essentially *metaphorical* in relation to musical sound. And they can remain singular metaphors, experienced simultaneously, or they can combine, cohere and extend into fields of discourse – theory, 'knowledge' – surrounding music. But the point is that the relation of these extra-musical connotations to music-as-signifier is cultural, historical, established by convention and in social practice. Yet they are experienced as 'inherent in' or 'immanent to' the music by a process of *projection* of the connotations *into* the musical sound object. It is this process of projection that achieves the 'naturalising' effect: the connotations appear to be natural and universal where they are cultural and historical. It is the forms of talk, text and theory around music – the metaphors and rhetoric explaining and constructing it – that may be liable to analysis as ideological.

Barthes sees denotation as providing an explicit, value-free, 'blameless' alibi for the deeper, implicit levels of ideological connotation. Paradoxically, in music, the lack of a denotative alibi does not have the effect of undermining naturalisation, but rather the opposite effect: the intertextual connotations become even more transparently, 'naturally' and firmly attached to the music. This can be illustrated by two phenomena. First, music is particularly susceptible to a kind of theoretical pre-determination; as shown by W. D. Allen's survey of music historiography[8] and early sociology of music. Thus, it is striking that historical and sociological analyses of music tend to find in it the quintessence of their conceptual approach, while neglecting to attend to the specificity of the music. Second, throughout history there have been two recurring kinds of universalising theory of musical meaning: that music represents the emotions, and that music is, as Dahlhaus puts it, 'sounding mathematics'.[9] In both cases, these properties are read as immanent to music. We can now understand better why, because of music's transparency as a form of signification, it offers little resistance to discursive invasion.

The stress on intertextual connotation accords with recent ethno-musicology which places metaphors around music at the centre of the analysis of both how musical expressivity is translated into verbal and

developed at IRCAM,[12] MIT and similar institutions. (Composers involved in these techniques include York Holler, Kaija Saariaho, Jean-Baptiste Barriere, but there are many others since this is currently an area of great expansion.)

We should note here briefly that some of these discursive strategies are combined in the same composer; and that some are very close, or developments of each other. Thus, the reference to or absorption of folk musics (1) was a principal technique of musical nationalism (2); while the relation between the initial invention of serialism (3), its post-War extension into scientistic total serialism (5), and the later consolidation of music research and psychoacoustics (7) is developmental, yet each discursive era is distinct and autonomous, with some criticism reserved for what went before.

Underlying these seven empirical discursive tendencies, we can analyse four main kinds of strategy at issue, some of which overlap in the same discourse. These four deep structural strategies themselves express a certain symmetry, and take the form of two antinomic pairs. First, there are those appealing to some kind of *representation* (1, 2); and second, by contrast, those operating with some kind of *materialism* (3, 6, 7). Third, there are those which make reference to or propose domains *extrinsic* to music as a basis for legitimation (2, 4, 5); and fourth, by contrast, those appealing to *intrinsic* musical properties as a basis (6, 7).

Although the first analytic couplet may appear to be subsumed within the latter couplet (since music-as-representation appears to depend on extrinsic motivation, and musical materialism on intrinsic properties), the distinction between them is important. Only in this way can we be aware of the specific historical character of, and crucial differences between, strategies of legitimation by appeal to representation and those depending on more abstract extrinsic analogies (with the other arts, or science, or technology); and between the early materialism of serialism – heavily 'constructed', arbitrary, and with a weaker claim to immanence (3) – and the later, sophisticated materialisms that appeal to intrinsic properties of music, both the anti-scientistic, 'naive' materialism of the experimental tradition (6) and the high scientism of music research and psychoacoustics, themselves developed out of post-serialism (7).

Several further observations can now be made. It is noticeable that this shifting discursive spectrum around music resonates with broader, dominant discursive forms characteristic of modern culture: that the various intertextual allusions involve the desire to build alliances with domains of knowledge and practice already highly legitimate or coming in to being as such (the other arts, the sciences, high technology).

The only form of 'representation' at issue in these various strategies is that implicit *social* representation of an idealised people in musical nationalism (2). Or, the representation of the 'other' implicit in modernist reference or allusion to 'other musics' (1). To varying degrees, this *musical* intertextuality was not so much an attempt at a new musical synthesis, so much as a more unabsorbed or one-sided musical borrowing per se. In other words, it seems to have been more a desire to allude to this 'other' music as 'content' or 'element of difference' in the work, so retaining a certain distance from it, rather than aimed at a deeper, dialogical aesthetic syncretism.

Looking over the century, it becomes clear from this analysis that there have been two major developmental paths. One is the move away from discourses of musical representation towards either those which attempt to construct and legitimise a musical system by *analogy* or alliance with another, external domain; or the opposite, those which attempt to discern and delimit *immanent* laws of musical material. The other main development has taken place within the materialist camp: from the arbitrary, constructivist 'musical structuralism' of serialism, towards positions that combine materialism and immanence – as in Cageian experimental materialism, and above all, in psychoacoustically informed composition. It is this last discourse that is currently hegemonic in contemporary serious music, with its unassailable combination of science, high technology and concepts of immanent musical materialism.

Giving up yearning for autonomy

I want finally to make a few comments on Adorno's project, taking this analysis as a starting point.

Adorno rejected inter-media analogies and the attempt to construct musical systems through alliances with the other arts. He commented, 'The bourgeois idea of the pantheon would like to join painting and music in a peaceful relationship. Their relationship, however ... is contradictory to the point of incompatibility'; and, 'The development of a spatial perspective in music is ... a testimony of a pseudomorphism of painting in music. At its innermost core, it is the abdication of music.'[13]

This rejection constitutes a key element of the critique against which Adorno develops his own philosophy of modern music. And it is his appeal, by contrast, to 'autonomy' and 'objectivity', as embodied in serialism and expressionism, that I now want to question. First, as I implied in the previous section, by querying Adorno's view of serialism as an immanent musical necessity. Looking back from the present, serialism strikes us as having tenuous claims to musical immanence, certainly by contrast with later developments.[14] In any case, according to the analysis above, these 'claims to immanence' must themselves be interrogated as discursive motifs rather than accepted faithfully on their own account. Second, and relatedly, one can point to the *retrospective discursive predictability* of serialism as a rational-structural method of composition – how it resonates with broader discursive preoccupations of its time. The same can be said, incidentally, of the concerns of the experimental music of Cage and his followers, which can be detailed as precisely antinomic to serialism.[15]

Adorno's defence of Expressionism is more convincing; and from the contemporary vantage point it can be argued that Expressionism has proven more musically fruitful than either serialism or experimental music. It was also the least programmatic and didactic, the least discursively coherent, and the most confused of all modernist movements. In 'Expressionism as Objectivity' Adorno writes, 'Precisely in its renunciation of communication, the movement insists upon its autonomy, guaranteed only by consistency within works of art.'[16] Perhaps I am suggesting here that there may be an *inverse relation* between the production of discourse surrounding music, and the fertility of specifically *musical* invention, which is neither prescribed nor programmed intertextually. Adorno seems almost to arrive at this view in relation to Expressionism in the remark above.

It may be, then, Adorno's failure to radically separate theory-as-mediation from the compositional process and its musical result that generates his impasse: serialism as at once a (discursive) necessity, commanding, authoritative; and yet as musically hyper-rationalist and determinist and – in relation to many musical parameters – arbitrary. Thus serialism may have been compelling theory, but it derived from the working through of an iron law of negation; and it made poor music.

But the deeper problem with Adorno's project is the unevenness of the attempt to integrate his aesthetics and sociology of music; inasmuch as, although he theorises how the popular music aesthetic relates to its socio-economic forms, he neglects to do the same for his notion of autonomous music. In fact, he defines autonomous music as precisely transcending its sociological base. Adorno's lack of a sociology of art music thus depends upon his desire to retain its aestheticised character as an ontological essence, beyond its sociology. And this is simply assumed in advance. Rather, it seems increasingly urgent to produce an account of the links between the sociology of art music and its aesthetic and discursive forms.[17] Only then will it become possible to analyse the antagonistic interrelations between the two sides – Adorno's 'torn halves' – of contemporary music culture.

In evading this completion of his own project, Adorno's aesthetic theory is opportunistic; since it is only by exempting autonomous music from sociological critique that he can develop the notion of negation as centrally constitutive of that autonomy, and – at the aesthetic level – as part of an immanent development found only in autonomous art music. In other words, if Adorno had addressed the sociology of art music this century – its administered and subsidised character, its base in the major hegemonic nations, the steady growth of its cultural power, the discursive and institutional means by which the principles of serialism became hypostatised into a universal method – this would surely have disrupted the aesthetic-sociological parallels upon which the theory of negation as at once aesthetic and sociological critique depends.

This is compounded by further problems at the level of the aesthetic, because of the inadequacy and the uniformity – despite certain insights – of Adorno's discussions of popular music aesthetics. He fails to specify in what way negation – which he wants always to be tempered by expressivity, by mimesis – can be said to be found only in autonomous art music, and not in popular ('non-autonomous') musics. Although it cannot be pursued here in detail, it could be argued that there *are* negational moments in the aesthetic of those musics; and they could be of several kinds. One form of negation would be a kind found in most art: that is, the negational component in all aesthetic development and change, consisting of the avoidance or transformation of prior or contemporaneous figures or conventions – change that may occur both within extant genres or that may produce new genres. Such change may, however, consist equally in the exploration, the bringing in or synthesis of new influences, and so is not entirely negational in character. Whereas a quite distinct level of negation would be the specific discursive and aesthetic allusions to avant garde music found in a variety of popular musics since the 1950s.

The effect of grasping both the negational and the expressive moments in all musics, and the multitude of 'negations', would be to drastically undermine the one-dimensional character of Adorno's aesthetic, and to pose for him – as it has been posed for contemporary composers – the hard task of theorising that more complex totality. It would dissolve the illusion that negation is a property of modernism alone, and that negation should be privileged as an aesthetic device in any era. It would also raise the possibility that the kind of modernist negation that Adorno emphasises cannot co-exist with, indeed forbids, the 'mimetic'; and it would bring into sharp relief the collusion between his relentless return to negation and the tendency towards a rigidly enforced rationalism that he also wants ultimately to disclaim.

In concluding, to develop these ideas would be to recognise weaknesses in Adorno's aesthetic and sociology of music, while attempting to continue his project – the best start that we have, but one which remains blind to aspects of itself. The method outlined here – which illuminates the simultaneous and yet autonomous existence of the mediations of music, and the meaning that inheres in each element of the constellation – may provide a basis for a creative practice that is more conscious of its many dimensions, of their history, and of their potential critical productivity. Such an approach is founded on the desire to give up yearning for an illusory autonomy.

Notes

1. This can be illustrated by a recent issue of *The Contemporary Music Review* (Vol. 5, 1989) entitled 'Music and Text'. This journal, which began in the early 1980s, sees itself as a radical departure in post-modern music criticism and analysis. Despite the promising title, which might appear to announce a broad consideration of musical meaning, the issue focuses only on the relation between musical 'setting' and words or literary texts.

2. It is significant that the musicologist Joseph Kerman, in a highly influential summary of the field (*Musicology*, Fontana, 1985), calls for musicology to address the social and cultural, while he yet retains a basic analytic split between music and the social. This is shown by his reservations about studies that in his view focus too much on social 'context' at the expense of the 'music as music' (p. 180).

3. Barbara Bradby, 'Pity Peggy Sue', in *Popular Music* 4, Cambridge, Cambridge University Press, 1984; see also her 'Do-talk and don't-talk: the division of the subject in girl-group music', in S. Frith and A. Goodwin (eds.), *On Record: Rock, Pop and the Written Word*, Routledge, 1990.

4. Philip Tagg, *Kojak – 50 Seconds of Television Music*, Gothenburg, 1979; and 'Analysing popular music: theory, method and practice', in *Popular Music* 2, Cambridge, Cambridge University Press, 1982.

5. Dave Laing, *One Chord Wonders: Power and Meaning in Punk Rock*, Open University Press, 1985.

6. Marina Roseman, 'The social structuring of sound: the Temiar of peninsular Malaysia', in *Ethnomusicology* XXVIII, 3, 1984.

7. Roseman, *op. cit.*, p. 432.

8. W. D. Allen, *Philosophies of Music History: a Study of General Histories of Music*, New York, Dover, 1962.

9. Carl Dahlhaus, *Esthetics of Music*, Cambridge University Press, 1982: 'The idea that music's goal was to represent and arouse affections is a commonplace, rooted as deeply in history as the opposing thesis that music is sounding mathematics' (p. 17).

10. See for example Steven Feld, 'Sound structure as social structure', in *Ethnomusicology* XXVIII, 3, 1984; and M. Roseman, *op. cit.* Roseman explains that 'indigenous musical theories are often articulated using terms drawn from "extra-musical" domains' (note 2, p. 438); and she argues that understanding music as culture involves grasping 'primarily the cultural logics informing (the sound) structures... We need to elicit ... the symbolic classifications and metaphors whereby the terms of one domain are layered with meanings drawn from another domain' (pp. 411–12).

11. On this process in modernist architecture, see A. L. Huxtable, 'After modern architecture', *New York Review of Books*, December 8, 1983.

12. IRCAM is the 'Institut de Recherche et Co-ordination Acoustique/Musique', the music department of the Pompidou Centre in Paris. IRCAM is directed by Pierre Boulez and is known internationally as a vanguard centre. It fosters the interrelated development of

scientific research and computer technologies around music, and musical composition informed by both of these.

13. Theodor Adorno, *Philosophy of Modern Music*, London, Sheed and Ward, 1973, p. 191, note 40.

14. This has been the argument of some psychoacoustic research, which set out to question whether the highly complex aural-musical results of serialist techniques are liable to be perceived as musically meaningful by listeners. For a recent example from cognitive music psychology of this critique of serialism as musically incomprehensible, or 'cognitively opaque', see Fred Lerdahl, 'Cognitive constraints on compositional systems', in John Sloboda (ed.), *Generative Processes in Music: the Psychology of Performance, Improvisation, and Composition*, Oxford, 1988. This article is also a good illustration of how after such a critique, a new, more 'musically appropriate', rationalism – i.e. scientific psychoacoustics – is then put forward as providing better guidelines for compositional practice.

15. See Chapter 9 in Georgina Born, *The Ethnography of a Computer Music Research Institute: Modernism, Postmodernism and New Technology in Contemporary Music Culture*, unpublished Ph.D, University of London, 1989.

16. Adorno, *Philosophy of Modern Music*, p. 49.

17. See Born, *op. cit.*: this research is a critical analysis of the social and cultural character of IRCAM (see note 12), a major contemporary centre of the high modernist musical avant garde. See also my 'On modern music culture: shock, pop and synthesis', in *New Formations* 2, 1987.

But What if the Object Began to Speak? The Aesthetics of Dance

Sandra Kemp

> This is it. Not exactly beauty. It is that the thing is in itself enough: satisfactory, achieved... *(Virginia Woolf)*

In 1952, writing 'Of the Modern System of the Arts', Paul Oskar Kristeller lists five as 'major'. These are painting, sculpture, music, architecture and poetry. He adds, reluctantly, that some might want to include 'gardening, engraving and dancing'.[1] The relative lack of scholarship on dance (whether historical or critical) follows from the uncertain status of the art-form itself. If dance is now accepted as art, its vivid reporting, informed technical discussion, and whatever historical research or criticism there might be, are for the most part confined to the newspaper columns. The average reader is more interested in whether a show is worth going to or not than in the state of the art.

In *Dance, Art and Aesthetics*, Betty Redfern asks: 'Is there some difficulty, or set of difficulties, in connection with the dance that is not shared by most of the other arts? Does the fault lie with philosophers, critics, choreographers, dancers, the dance-going public, or with all of these?'[2] There are a number of cumulative historical factors behind the neglect.

Reasons could be multiplied. I mention three briefly, before coming to my proper topic.

Sculpture is physical. But, because of its use as the living body, dance in the past has been treated as a lesser art, its properties considered lesser than those displayed by more metaphysical media. Joshua Reynolds likened dancing masters to hairdressers and tailors, claiming that all three distort and disfigure the human form.[3]

Dance has also conventionally been by-passed because it is a hybrid form, and treated in conjunction with music. (It shares this problem with opera, where the combination of music and drama occasions a similar critical disregard or difficulty.) It is significant how many of the early (and some current) dance reviewers cover dance as an adjunct to their music-reviewing activities, as if dance alone was not generative of its own meanings.[4]

Margot Fonteyn as Juliet in *Romeo and Juliet*. (Photograph: Zoë Dominic)

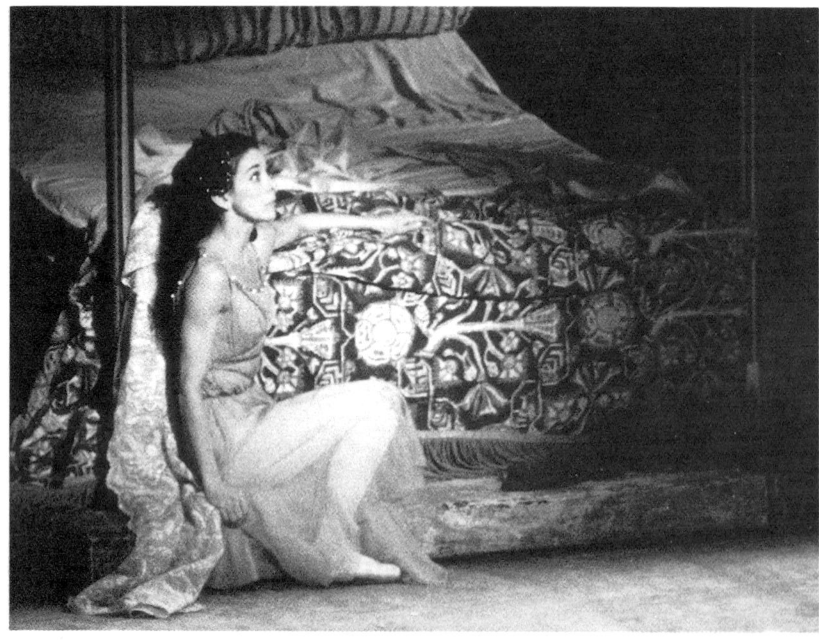

Finally, dance has been treated as a 'minor' form because a satisfactory system of dance-notation was not developed until the twentieth century.[5] Composition and performance were effectively the same. This in turn resulted in a kind of transitoriness. Because one could not study the text or score, there was less opportunity to read or to see a dance than a book or a piece of music. Unlike criticism of the other arts, that of dancing cannot casually refer to a rich variety of well-known great effects, nor can it quote passages as illustrations. It has no specific terminology of description. It is difficult to see great dance effects as they happen, let alone to verbalise them.

Because of the lack of adequate systematic notation it has been commonplace to make analogical reference from dance to language. As Maxine Sheets-Johnstone points out, it is habitual amongst dance critics to believe in its translatability:

> A philosopher who sees the question of expression in dance as a question of language betrays an orientation to movement in dance as a set of counters which function much as words. ... Such views of dance are logocentric ... movement in dance is prejudged to function as, or to be reducible to, a language that mirrors verbal language.[6]

Martha Graham once complained: 'I do not want to be a tree, a flower or a wave.' The 'aleatory' tendency of some modern music writing may be better adapted to dance. Merce Cunningham also writes of *movement* quality made manifest:

> I start with a step. ... This is not beginning with an idea that concerns character or story, a *fait accompli* around which the actions are grouped for reference purposes. I start with a movement ... then possibilities appear as the dance proceeds. New situations present themselves – between the dancers, the dancers and the space, the space and the time. It is not subject to a prearranged idea of how it should go.

He adds: 'Each spectator may interpret the events in his own way.'[7]

1

What then is the nature of meaning in dance? Is it possible to present a conceptual framework for the analysis and interpretation of movement? How can we clarify our understanding of dance through philosophical enquiry? Can we distinguish between the actual experience of dance and the values and preconceptions (however hidden) already surrounding it? It is paradoxical of course that dance is the least generally understood of all the arts, but employs as a medium a material that is closer to life experience than that of the other arts: the movement of the body in its reactions to the environment. And another way of answering these questions of dance meaning would be to look at or isolate the properties of dancer and dance-text. There is a distinction made in literary studies between 'work' and 'text' (the book as an object, and the process of reading the book).[8] Selma Jeanne Cohen's *Next Week, Swan Lake* is a brilliant demonstration of how not only the dance text (in this case *Swan Lake*) is fluid and unstable (a product of the response of the moment, as, say, to a poem), but also (unlike books) how the dance work is constantly subject to change as well – an assortment of interpolations and substitutions from other ballets:

> So next week you are going to see *Swan Lake*. Some facets of your experience may be predicted. You are definitely not going to see the choreography of either Reisinger or the Petipa Ivanov *Swan Lake* as it was done originally. Or even the latter as it was produced by the Diaghilev Ballet Russe in 1911 or by the Vic-Wells Ballet in 1934 or by the New York City Ballet in 1951 or by the National Ballet of Canada in 1966 or by the American Ballet Theatre in 1967. You may, however, see some parts of several of these. You will not see Odette/Odile exactly as she was conceived by Lagnani or by such successors as Galina Ulanova or Margot Fonteyn, though the Ballerina you do see may well incorporate some aspects of those earlier interpretations into her own. You may or may not see Benno. You will probably not hear all of Tchaikovsky's original score, and you may likely hear some music that Tchaikovsky did not write. You will undoubtedly see some period costumes, though of what

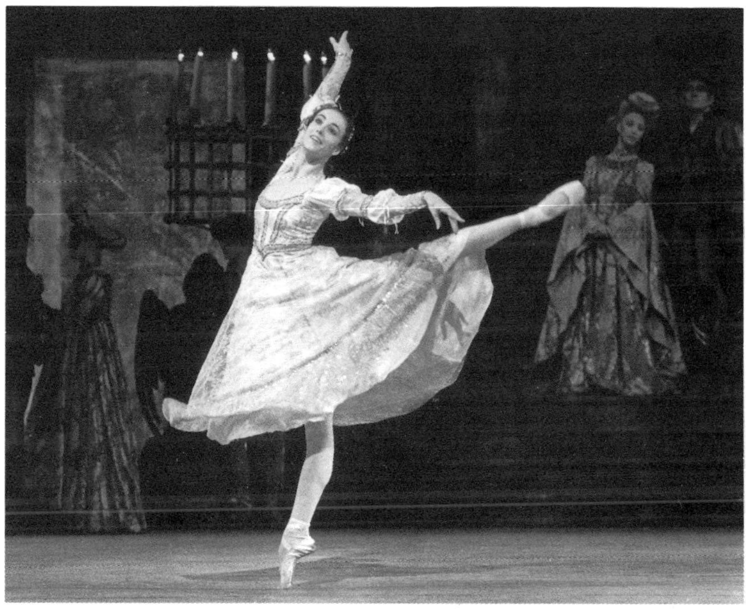

Sylvie Guillem as Juliet in *Romeo and Juliet* at Covent Garden. (Copyright Leslie E Spatt)

> period is uncertain. You may leave the theatre saddened by the tragic ending or gladdened by the death of the evil Rothbart and the union of the virtuous lovers. You may see a true *Swan Lake*.
>
> Through all this can we discern the real Swan Lake?[9]

If plot and characters can change so much, if dances can be moved from one place to another, movements added or omitted, is it possible to identify *Swan Lake*? Cohen also notes that, even if the performers could reproduce exactly that first Maryinsky *Swan Lake*, the audience of the 1980s would not perceive it in the same way as the audiences of 1895.[10]

The changing image of the dancer over the years is also significant here. An aesthetics of dance would have to take into account the historical and cultural 'object' (in this case often the body of a woman), and how its changing manifestations have been produced and evaluated.[11] When Sylvie Guillem danced Juliet at Covent Garden's gala performance (to raise money for Margot Fonteyn) in summer 1990, half a century of dance and its chronicling met. Guillem represents not just a new generation, but a new kind of dancer. Leaving aside the issue of modern dance versus classical ballet, her control, and her urbanity, have nothing of the unstressed balance or the fluency of Fonteyn. Increasingly, writers and reviewers are asking: what do the domains created on the stage, and the characters who inhabit them tell us? Why was an elusive, dark-eyed frail body such a meaningful figure for audiences of the 1940s. And why is a tall, acrobatic body so enticing for the '90s?[12]

The great ballet critics of the past were impressionistic not objective. In reading Noverre or Theophile Gautier or Andre Levinson, what one most enjoys is the illusion of being present at a performance.[13] If the writing is vivid enough, it may reproduce the choreographic spell. This is why films of dance are still not enough. We need to go beyond the account even the film makes possible. In dance, and in fine dance criticism, as in the other arts, the fascination is the discovery of some aspect of our own personality and world, which left to ourselves we might never recognise.

In the end, though, dance reviewers and critics rarely capture either dancer or dance. They may convey something of its conventionality. ('Dancing,' wrote Noverre in 1760, 'is the art of composing steps with grace, precision and facility to the time and bars given in the music.')[14] But they capture none of the self-sufficiency that made Fonteyn, for example, so classical a dancer.

As a critic of both literature and dance, I am particularly interested in the problems involved in capturing the elusive nature of the latter. And I mean elusive, not transitory. What kind of status do we give to the imaginative radiance of certain moments of dancing which remain lodged in the memory for years? If the critics can't answer this, neither can the dancers. During the Gala tribute Roland Petit described Fonteyn's inability to communicate her own art: 'She's irreplaceable. What she had she cannot teach.'[15]

2

History? Dancer and dance-text? Dance criticism? Another possible way of considering an aesthetics of dance would be more synchronic, and could be done, for example, by looking at the kind of philosophic issues self-consciously foregrounded in postmodern dance. For, arguably, postmodern dance is reflexive, and emphasises its own aesthetics. It offers, or presents in itself, philosophical questions of meaning and cognition; things as physical objects, and things as symbols; reality and appearance. Its dislocating techniques, its processes of deconstruction and bricolage, place it in the interventionist mode. It is not a newly defined dance language, but an interrogation of meaning, and of culture itself. Where choreographers had previously turned to past civilisations, postmodern dance is rooted in the present. Postmodern choreographers take their ideas from musical or pictorial structure, mechanisation, mathematics, and abstraction. Emotional motivation is out. There is concern with the movement rather than with the executant.[16] Sally Barnes argues:

> The key postmodern choreographic technique is radical juxtaposition. But also these dances often use ordinary movements and objects; they propose new relationships between performer and spectator; articulate new experiences of space, time and the body; incorporate language and film; [and] employ structures of stillness and repetition... Postmodern dance fits with postmodernist notions (in the other arts) of pastiche, irony, playfulness, historical reference, the use of vernacular materials, the continuity of cultures, an interest in process over product, breakdowns or boundaries between art forms and life, and new relationships between artist and audience.[17]

Yvonne Rainer's title makes the mind a muscle, not a linguistic machine, and her choreography, like most postmodern dance, works against the presumption that movement in dance has a meaning outside itself. Of 'The Mind is a Muscle. Trio A', she writes:

> The limbs are in a fixed, still relationship and they are stretched to the fullest extension only in transit, creating the impression that the body is constantly engaged in transitions. Another factor contributing to the smoothness of the continuity is that no part of the series is made any more important than any other. For

four and a half minutes a great variety of movement shapes occur, but they are of equal weight and equally emphasised.[18]

The point is the refusal of entelechy. Carolyn Brown, one of Cunningham's leading dancers, explains: 'And so goes the afternoon. No talk about meanings or quality. No images given. No attempts to nurture expressivity in any particular dancer. The dances are treated more as puzzles than works of art; the pieces are space and time, shape and rhythm.'

This brings us to the title quotation of my paper: 'But what if the Object began to speak?'. The quotation from Irigaray's *Speculum* enquires whether the body needs language and overtly discursive practices, or whether the body's movement can speak for itself.[19] (I want to leave logocentrism and its relation to dance notation for another occasion. Is there a value in notation beyond the practicality of recording dances? In aesthetics, what is its use for the concept of style?) I want instead to look at two aspects of a possible aesthetics of dance in the light of Kant's *Critique of Judgement*.[20]

In the *Critique* Kant is interested in the nature of beauty and other aesthetic qualities; the distinction between aesthetic and other ways of seeing; the issue of pleasure versus morality, and the necessity of aestheticising within historical and political contexts. But the two of Kant's aesthetic domains that I want to consider are: first, the bringing of the bodily ground of acts of cognition into aesthetics; and secondly, the nature of sensuous surfaces, and their relation, or lack of relation, to a 'metaphysical' world 'behind'.

Martha Graham argues that in dance: 'the body ... must be prepared for the ordeal of expressiveness'.[21] Her comment applies to both dancer *and* audience. In dance, aesthetic appreciation is more than visual, merely 'seeing' is not enough. Response to dance involves sympathy with the mover, rather than 'pure' or 'objective' observation of shapes and patterns from the outside. Watching dance involves a doubling of bodies (audience and dance), a mingling of third and first persons. In watching dance we identify with the *subjectivity* of the dancer. Langer's theory of dance as dynamic image is suggestive. But it is surely not the case, as she argues, that 'in watching a dance, you do not see what is physically before you... The physical realities are given... But in the dance they disappear.'[22] The effect of the dance when it succeeds is that the 'personality' is identified with the 'body', and that the energy projected amounts to more than the visual action occurring in the time and space before us.

Another way of putting this would be to ask the question, as Cohen does: Could someone somatically paralysed from birth respond to dance? The answer would be 'No', because 'the attempt to imagine an aesthetic experience of moving bodies with no prior experience whatsoever of self-movement appears an impossible task. No *dance* emerges'.[23] Thus the visual element in itself is inadequate for the co-creation of an aesthetic object. At the same time, the kind of dance aesthetic that argues that painting is for the eyes, music for the ears, while dance draws on all the senses through the eyes, oversimplifies our responses to the other arts.[24] What distinguishes all art is not clearly anything immediately available to direct visual or auditory inspection. But certainly in dance, the bodily rapport is fundamental. (Perhaps this is one reason why dance seems to strike so many as sexual.) Any aesthetics of dance must start from this process of kinetic transfer for which the dance writer and critic, John Martin, coined the word metakinesis.[25]

If we accept this hypothesis, then the task of dance aesthetics is to record the experience of a live performance, rather than the technicalities of it. In Kant's terms this would be to record the mode in which we commune with the object.[26] We do not usually pay attention to what is actually present, i.e. the nature of the thing being experienced. What generally happens is that description transforms the phenomenon, rather than capturing the properties of the thing *as it is experienced*. What is required is an immediacy of description to reflect the immediacy of the experience.[27] It is what Fry, in *An Essay on Aesthetics*, calls 'removing the automatism of perception.[28] Or, as Floristan says to Perdita in *The Winter's Tale*:

> ... when you do dance, I wish you
> A wave o' th' sea, that you might ever do
> Nothing but that, move still, still so
> And own no other function.[29]

3

I conclude with the problems of symbolisation, and of deep/latent as opposed to 'surface' meaning: the commonly held (unthought) belief that behind the thing is some metaphysical reality, while the ordinary space/time world is illusory. For example, as Maxine Sheets-Johnstone points out, in the immediate and direct experience of movement, movement does not appear as a change of position, it does not appear as a force in time and space; it does not appear as a medium of expression, or as a medium of anything else.[30] Wittgenstein reminds us that most of the time we don't find the business of seeing puzzling enough. Why assume that time and space are *out there*? To assume that time and space are given is to misconstrue the enigma of dance. It is precisely the creation of time and space that dance movement achieves.

If one substitutes 'movement' for 'language', one could paraphrase Merleau-Ponty helpfully here: 'Movement ... does not translate ready-made meanings: it accomplishes them.'[31] In the kinetic transfer there is a positive dynamic of emptying and enclosing; a realignment of inner and outer, subject and object, public and private. This tacit bodily response *is* the thing-in-itself, rather than a substitution which distances or objectifies it. It involves staying close to the surface, or a kind of non-appropriation of the object or of its properties. It represents freedom from inherited meanings and metaphors. It is, in short, what happens when the object itself is allowed to speak: a glimpse of that lost domain where the object holds the subject in its gaze.

For Kant imaginative pleasure is located in the cognitive faculties of imagination and understanding. In watching dance certain mental processes are differently employed in a way resistant to explanation: something less than rational cognition; more than sensory awareness. As Elizabeth Dempster argues:

> Dancing requires its own close watching. It takes time and the 'reading' of dance is an undertaking which may necessitate the development of new critical strategies. Literacy in dance must begin with attention to the body and to the gravity, spatiality and rhythms of its movement.[32]

Aesthetic appreciation of dance does not reside in any of the known categories of understanding – psychological, moral, political, religious, social. Paradoxically the dancer's inability to translate back into the unchoreographed world bespeaks a miraculous weaving that cannot be described, but only transferred from one art form to another. It is what Keats called 'knowledge proved upon the pulses'.

Notes

The title quotation is from Luce Irigaray, *Speculum of the Other Woman*, 1977, p. 22; the epigraph is from Virginia Woolf, *Diary*, Vol. 3, p. 62.

1. Paul Oskar Kristeller, 'The Modern System of the Arts', *Journal of the History of Ideas*, 1951, p. 498.

2. Betty Redfern, *Dance, Art and Aesthetics*, 1983, p. 15.

3. For a more detailed exposition of such historical factors see Selma Jeanne Cohen, *Next Week, Swan Lake. Reflections on Dance and Dancers*, 1982; Maxine Sheets-Johnstone (ed.), *Illuminating Dance: Philosophical Explorations*, 1984; Elizabeth Dempster, 'Women Writing the Body: Let's watch a little how she dances', *Writings on Dance 3: Of Bodies and Power*, 1988. My paper is indebted to the arguments in these three works, and exists in dialogue with them.

4. See John Martin, *The Dance in Theory*, 1965, p. viii.

5. For dance notation see Ann Hutchinson Guest, 'A Brief History of Dance Notation', in *Tracking, Trading, Marking, Pacing*, 1982. See also Nelson Goodman, *Languages of Art*, 1967.

6. See 'Phenomenology as a Way of Illustrating Dance', in Maxine Sheets-Johnstone (ed.), p. 128.

7. Quoted in Selma Jeanne Cohen (ed.), *The Modern Dance. Seven Statements of Belief*, 1965, p.6; *Next Week, Swan Lake*, p. 92.

8. See Roland Barthes, 'From Work to Text', in *Image-Music-Text*, 1977.

9. *Next Week, Swan Lake*, p. 14.

10. *Ibid.*, pp. 10, 7.

11. On the dancing body as a cultural production, see Elizabeth Dempster, pp.21–25; David Michael Levin, 'Postmodernism in Dance: Dance, Discourse, Democracy', in Hugh J. Silverman (ed.), *Postmodernism, Philosophy and the Arts*, 1990, pp. 230–32.

12. See Deborah Jowitt, *Time and the Dancing Image*, 1988, pp. 7–8.

13. See extracts in Anatole Chujuy and P. W. Manchester (eds.), *The Dance Encyclopaedia*, 1949.

14. Jean Georges Noverre, *Letters on Dancing and Ballets* [1760], translated by C. W. Beaumont, 1951, p. 51. See also Theophile Gautier, *The Romantic Ballet as seen by Theophile Gautier*, ed. C. W. Beaumont, 1947, p. 58: 'After all, dancing consists of nothing more than the art of displaying beautiful shapes in graceful positions and the development from them of lines agreeable to the eye; it is mute rhythm, music that is seen. Dancing is little adapted to render metaphysical themes; it only expresses the passions; love, desire with all its attendant coquetry.'

15. See *Saturday Independent*, June 1990, pp. 23–24.

16. See e.g. the interviews with Paul Taylor, Erick Hawkins, Anna Sokolow and Pauline Koner in *The Modern Dance. Seven Statements of Belief.*

17. Sally Barnes, *Terpsichore in Sneakers: Postmodern Dance*, 1986, p. 23.

18. Yvonne Rainer, Work 1961–73, 1974, p. 67.

19. See Elizabeth Dempster, p. 14, on the contrasting choreographic projects of Martha Graham and Yvonne Rainer.

20. Kant, *Critique of Pure Reason*, translated by J. M. D. Meiklejohn, 1924.

21. Martha Graham, *Dance Observer*, April 1963, p. 53.

22. Quoted in *Next Week, Swan Lake*, p. 110.

23. Sibyl S. Cohen, 'Ingarten's Aesthetics and Dance', in Maxine Sheets-Johnstone, pp. 151–52.

24. Quoted in *ibid.*, p. 149.

25. John Martin, p. 23.

26. See Nigel Farndale, 'Against Dance Criticism', *Dance Theatre Journal*, Vol. 8, Autumn 1990, pp. 16–18. See also David Hughes, 'Post-structuralist Dance', *ibid.*, Vol. 8, Late Summer 1990, pp. 28–31.

27. See Maxine Sheets-Johnstone, p. 132.

28. Roger Fry, 'An Essay in Aesthetics', *Vision and Design*, 1931, p. 16:

First, with regard to the greater clearness of perception. The needs of our actual life are so imperative that the sense of vision becomes highly specialised in their service. With an admirable economy we learn to see only so much as is needful for our purposes; but this is in fact very little, just enough to recognise and identify each object or person; that done, they go into an entry in our mental catalogue and are no more really seen. In actual life the normal person really only reads the labels as it were on the objects around him and troubles no further. Almost all the things which are useful in any way put on more or less the cap of invisibility. It is only when an object exists in our lives for no other purpose than to be seen that we really look at it, as for instance at a china ornament or a precious stone, and towards such even the most normal person adopts to some extent the artistic attitude of pure vision abstracted from necessity.

29. *The Winter's Tale*, IV, iv, 140–43.

30. See 'The Phenomenology of Dance', pp. 132–33.

31. Quoted in Sibyl S. Cohen, p. 156.

32. Elizabeth Dempster, p. 24.

Berkeley: Bishop, or Busby? Deleuze on Cinema

Jean-Jacques Lecercle

The lady with the tutti-frutti hat

Let us imagine a singularly pleasing object – a book of philosophy, in which a sentence beginning with the proper noun 'Berkeley' refers not to the author of the dialogues between Hylas and Philonous, but to the director of that celebrated film, *The Lady with the Tutti-Frutti Hat*. If you are looking for such exotic reading matter, you had better read Deleuze's two books on the cinema, *L'image-mouvement* and *L'image-temps*.[1]

There is good reason for the exoticism of the experience. The gap between the two fields of philosophy and the cinema is wide, and any attempt at bridging it is inevitably fraught with danger. The two activities seem to be incompatible, their relationship limited mostly to the fleeting appearance of a philosophy paperback in a Jean-Luc Godard film. *The Extravagant Mr Kant* is not an apt title for a Hollywood film. More seriously, Deleuze's books seem to be threatened by two symmetrical pitfalls. They may be frowned upon by professional philosophers as not serious, or not technical enough (in our distinguished colleague, the film buff has superseded the philosopher), and they may be laughed at by specialists of the cinema. Indeed, it is an empirical fact that many of these did not much like the books, in which they saw an imperialistic attempt by a philosopher at telling them what to think – a case of the philosopher spelling out at great length what is immediately obvious to the specialist, indeed what the specialist has already said on countless occasions.

If we adopt this point of view, Deleuze will appear as a typical continental philosopher, i.e. a busybody. Since the field of literature has already been occupied by others of the same ilk, like Derrida, or indeed by himself, with his books on Proust and Lewis Carroll, his need for patronising intervention in pastures forever new has taken him to the under-theorised field of cinema studies. Or perhaps, since my last proposition is difficult to accept, especially in the French context, we might adopt the opposite point of view and consider Deleuze as a philosophical opportunist, taking advantage of the fashionable interest in film theory to find a place for himself in an over-theorised field, which would explain why he has merely repeated, in obfuscation, what specialists said clearly.

Of course, being a philosopher, and an admirer of Deleuze, I know that repetition is hardly an innocent practice, and that a book on the cinema by a philosopher will be a book of philosophy – not so much a repetition as an exit, not so much a capture as an importation. Even if there is a film buff in Deleuze, as in all Parisian intellectuals of his generation or mine – he has seen an extraordinary number of films, and read an extraordinary number of essays about them – his position lies essentially outside the field of film theory – and there lies its interest. I shall try to draw a map of this movement of invasion and retreat, and to examine the effect it has produced on philosophy, but also on our vision of the cinema. Lastly, and more tentatively, I shall broach the question of the relationship between Deleuze and postmodernism.

A strategy of advance and retreat

The essence of my argument is that I am dealing with philosophical books, not books on the cinema, in spite of their subtitles, *Cinema 1* and *2* (in the English translations title and subtitle are reversed). The cinema here is a particular mode of the image, and the books consequently belong to a long tradition of philosophical thought about imagination and the image. As their title shows, the books' object is to decide what kind of image the cinema is concerned with. The answer is trivial enough – a moving image.

No answer is trivial to a philosopher – behind the triviality, there lies a position. The nature of this position shall appear more clearly if I start off-course by reading the beginning of Chapter 4 of Flann O'Brien's *The Third Policeman*, in which the narrator expounds a rather interesting conception, attributed to the fictional philosopher de Selby, whom I admire even more than I do Deleuze:

> Of all the many striking statements made by de Selby, I do not think that any of them can rival his assertion that 'a journey is an hallucination'. The phrase may be found in the *Country Album*[1] cheek by jowl with the well-known treatise on 'tent-suits', those egregious canvas garments which he designed as a substitute alike for the hated houses and ordinary clothing. His theory, insofar as I can understand it, seems to discount the testimony of human experience and is at variance with everything I have learnt myself on many a country walk. Human existence de Selby has defined as 'a succession of static experiences each infinitely brief', a conception which he is thought to have arrived at from examining some old cinematograph films which belonged probably to his nephew.[2]

The reason why de Selby believed human existence to be 'a succession of static experiences', the consequence of which was his famous thesis that motion is impossible and that 'a journey is an hallucination', is explained in a rather perfidious footnote:

> 1. These are evidently the same films which he mentions in *Golden Hours* (p. 155) as having 'a strong repetitive element' and as being 'tedious'. Apparently he had examined them patiently picture by picture and imagined that they would be screened in the same way, failing at that time to grasp the principle of the cinematograph.

This is the true relationship between philosophy and the cinema. Utter failure to grasp even the most basic principle of the cinema produces the most profound philosophical intuition. I confess to being an enthusiastic de Selbian. Like him, I am a stay-at-home, and undergo as few hallucinations as I can. And of course he and I are not alone in our conception of movement. Beneath Flann O'Brien's text, you have recognised the great Eleatic paradoxes of the impossibility of motion. Those are things of singular beauty, and to me joys for ever, even if common sense might dismiss de Selby's view and approve of the perfidious footnote.

The point of departure of Deleuze's books on the cinema is a similar misunderstanding. They are in fact as much about the philosophy of Bergson as about anything else, and their main thesis is neatly captured by the formula: 'the cinema is a Bergsonian art.'[3] But, paradoxically, Deleuze's contention is that Bergson utterly failed to understand what the cinema is about, so that if it is a Bergsonian art, it is so in spite of Bergson. The most profound philosophical intuitions about the cinema – it is the task of the two books to develop Bergson's intuitions – can coexist with a total incapacity to understand the art and an explicit hostility to it.

Naturally, Bergson's misunderstanding is not quite the same as de Selby's. For obvious reasons, he does not deny the possibility of motion. But this increased philosophical awareness has not entailed significant progress in the understanding of the cinema. What is wrong with the cinema according to Bergson is that de Selby is right – movies appear to move, but they do not really move. This appearance of motion is pure illusion. A film is a sequence of fixed images, following one another in a uniform mechanical time, which has nothing to do with duration, that is with real time, time not interpreted in terms of space through the usual, and illusory, metaphors. The illusion of motion in films is one of those spatial illusions about time that Bergson struggles against in *Matière et mémoire*.

We understand Deleuze's strategy – he shows that Bergson's critique of the illusion of the cinema is itself an illusion, and that those two illusions produce a fundamental insight. Films are the real objects of Bergson's theory of the image, and it is only with him that we can take the idea of a moving picture, or image, seriously: the 'movement-image' is Bergson's concept. And the relationship between the cinema and philosophy is no longer one of patronising officiousness, but of cross-fertilisation. The philosophical account precedes the theory of the art, only unwittingly and blindly; conversely, the practice of the art is the only way of removing the philosophical illusion.

We can even go further. If superiority there is, it may well reside with the cinema. For Deleuze's main discovery, in the light of Bergson's blindness, 'and yet it moves', is utterly trivial, as the very name of the thing shows. It does not only move, it even flickers on the screen. Except that, for a philosopher, this discovery is hardly trivial. First, because it allows Deleuze to rehabilitate an unduly neglected philosopher, to whom he devoted an early book.[4] Second, because it contributes to the rehabilitation of an unduly neglected subject, the image, in a philosophical context where an overwhelming interest in language tends to eclipse other fields. In this, as I will try to show, Deleuze is not only going backwards (towards Bergson) but also forward, into postmodernism perhaps.

Philosophical effects

What I have just described is a philosophical intervention which goes far beyond the question of the cinema. By returning to Bergson, as others have returned to Freud, Deleuze seeks to go against the grain of what he perceives as dominant, and erroneous, trends. And it is true that if Bergson is neglected today, it is because language plays a minor role in his conception of the world, and because his theory of the image is outside the main tradition.

For a competent, if quick, overview of the tradition, the best thing is to go through Richard Kearney's book, *The Wake of Imagination*.[5] It will take you from mimetic to transcendental to phenomenological accounts of the image, culminating in Sartre (for the moment, I leave aside his concluding chapter on the postmodern image). The index lists Walter Benjamin, Bernard of Clervaus and Chuck Berry, but not Bergson, who appears to have no existence within the tradition.

No doubt Kearney would argue that this is right, as he is concerned with the imagination, and there is no specific theory of the imagination in Bergson. Yet this is to a considerable extent unfair. Bergson, even if he is not concerned with the imagination directly, ascribes an essential role to the concept of the image. In *Matière et mémoire*, he claims to defend a commonsensical dualism of objects and consciousness, body and mind, and to provide a solution to the problems such dualism traditionally entails. His solution to the contested problems of a 'harnessing together', to use Gilbert Ryle's phrase,[6] of matter and consciousness is that both are images. Which means that the image is neither a thing nor a representation, but something in between. An object is nothing else but what we see, an image endowed with autonomous existence. And consciousness is an image that reflects all the other images from a single point of view – a centre of images. It is easy to see that we are a long way from Berkeley, since images are not in the mind, but in the world, a long way from Kant as well, as there is nothing 'behind' the image-phenomenon, and even further from Sartre, as this image is certainly not 'nothing'.

Of course, these are strange sorts of images, hardly our commonsensical conception of pictures. Yet they are closer to Busby's images than to the bishop's. What Bergson constructs is a dual image-system. Certain images, objects, act and react on one another, according to laws which physics describes. And one image, my body, a reflector for all the other images. The reason why those two image types are 'harnessed together' is that they relate with each other by transmitting movement. External images transmit movement to my body, which in turn sends back movement to objects. One of the most famous of Bergson's theses is that perception is action rather than representation. And the concept of movement involved here is, contrary to appearances, far from mechanistic. In *L'Evolution créatrice*, it is conceived around three theses, which provide the subject matter for Deleuze's first chapters in *L'Image-mouvement*: (1) movement is different from the space it covers (this confusion is the source of de Selby's mistake); (2) it is an error to construct movement from positions in space and instants in time (this is the source of the illusion of the cinema which Bergson denounces – it is also the practice of modern physics); (3) movement expresses change in duration – in other words, translation in space involves qualitative change.

Here comes Busby. What can a theory which gives pride of place to the image over object and consciousness have to say about the cinema? The answer is, of course, a lot. Bergson's universe of images is best expressed by the equation 'image = movement'. It is easy to see why the art of the cinema lies right at the centre of such a universe. Bergsonism turns out to be a celebration in anticipation of the cinema as the central art form, as the repetition of life. One can distinguish two poles, of equal importance, whereby the cinema embodies Bergson's dualism. On the one hand the best metaphor for the human body, for the body endowed with consciousness is the cine-camera. Bergson's description of the body as the living image, of consciousness as the interval between action and reaction, could be the description of the workings of the camera. And, of course, this goes beyond the trite metaphor of the eye of the camera even if this eye is also trivially taken to be an I. For the two moments of the interaction between the object image and the body-image, receptivity and reaction, can also be expressed in terms of film technique: the reactive activity of montage answers the active receptivity of framing.

If the first pole is the conscious camera, the second is the universe of the film as emblem of the universe in general; or, which amounts to the same, the universe as film, as 'meta-cinema', to use Deleuze's phrase, as a machine-like arrangement of images. We live in a world of films, not only because our physical appearance and behaviour are governed by our attempted imitation of John Travolta, Divine, or, in my case, the late Marty Feldman, but because we live in a space and a time where there is nothing except images. The cinema, as 'movement-image' and 'time-image', is not merely an apt representation of the world, it is a repetition of the world, a repetition heightened, made more acute and more acutely conscious by art. In other words, the cinema is a meta-universe. I shall be content here with one example. In *Matière et mémoire* we find a non-Freudian conception of the unconscious, as the totality of the objects which at any single moment exist beyond the subject's consciousness. Both in space (the objects outside my field of vision) and in time (the objects that my memory may recall). The famous diagram[7] of two perpendicular lines, the vertical line of memory ending on the horizontal line of space at a point which is the point of consciousness, is a representation of this spatio-temporal unconscious, which consists of the whole of the two lines, with the exception of their conscious point of intersection. But this might also be a description of the relationship between the camera and the world that it films. It might even allow us to understand that Bergson's concept of the unconscious is less traditional, and less simple than it seems. The world out of shot, as opposed to the world out of frame, has a virtual presence which may be actualised by a movement of the conscious camera on the horizontal line. But the same applies, through the miracle of cutting, to the world temporally out of shot, or even to the world which lies out of shot as a contingent future or a possible world. The French have an apt phrase: '*c'est du cinéma*', meaning it's not real, it's a fake. The world of the '*c'est du cinéma*' is the world of Bergson's unconscious, the world of potential perception and of the ever widening circles of memory, as the camera pans out to reveal the hitherto hidden out of shot. Deleuze celebrates this falsifying power of the camera as the best means of liberating time from the constraints of spatialisation. In a film, reality is Bergson's natural memory image as described by the first of the diagrams in *Matière et mémoire*.[8]

One brief illustration. The cinema labours painfully when it tries to reproduce the linguistic fantastic of Lovecraft with its plastic monsters and laughable special effects. But there is a type of fantastic in which it goes far beyond literature – in the representation of the epiphany of horror. In Kubrick's *The Shining* the little boy, Danny, is riding his pedal car in the corridors of the Overlook hotel. The corridor is empty. We know this because the camera sees the world from Danny's point of view. Suddenly it turns round to reveal horror on Danny's face. It turns round again, and this time the ghost is there, in the middle of the corridor. In a sense, it was always already there (it has not *entered* the field), as a Bergsonian virtuality. In this sudden leap in consciousness, terror lies – not in the description of similar scenes in the novel by Stephen King, which is the origin of the film.

The film is a universe, the universe is a film. These highly philosophical propositions produce a taxonomy of images and signs in the cinema, as the original 'it moves' is subdivided into 'it sees', 'it acts' and 'it feels', according to the three moments of the interaction between the image-centre and the world of images. In the end, we realise that the cinema is for Deleuze what poetry is for Heidegger: a privileged aesthetic and philosophical mode of access to the essence of things. Deleuze's books are his ontology of the cinema, his *Bild und Zeit*.

Effects on the cinema

There is a strong possibility that all I have said so far is philosophically important, but uninteresting for specialists of the cinema. Do we need all this to understand films? Do we need to be told that one of the modes of the action-image (one of the three types just alluded to) is the duel scene, before we go on to watch Spielberg, or our favourite second-rate Western? My answer is that perhaps we do – partly because of the situation of film theory.

Over the last quarter of a century film theory has developed into a subject, and obtained academic recognition. Where our fathers bored us with Corneille, we now bore our students with Jean-Luc Godard. But the intellectual context in which such recognition was achieved is not innocent. Briefly put, it is the conjuncture of structuralism. As a result, the dominant model in film theory has long been structuralist narratology. Films, like other narratives, are entitled to their specialised discipline, which is a subpart of the general science of signs, semiology. In France, this conjuncture is aptly represented by the school of Christian Metz. The formal analysis of films was conducted in Saussurean, that is essentially in grammatical, terms. The results of the analysis of a film were signs, paradigms and syntagmata. The vocabulary of literary criticism had invaded film criticism: one talked about prolepsis, point of view and punctuation.

The main interest of Deleuze's books is that he goes against this trend. This is where I abandon for good the word 'trivial', which I have used too many times. The return to Bergson allows him to do precisely this, because Bergson, against the current, offers a philosophy where images are far more important than language.

This is the source of Deleuze's interest in the cinema *qua* movies. The negative essence of Bergson's position is that language betrays movement. There is an important passage towards the beginning of the first volume,[9] where Deleuze, following Bergson, describes the transition from pure images, images *per se* that are for nobody, to their inevitable reification by perception and language. Pure movement-images are translated and reduced into bodies, qualities and actions, and this perceptual tripartition is the same as the linguistic tripartition between nouns, adjectives and verbs. What we have so far is the inevitable reduction, which is also a spatialisation, of movement – this is the cost we have to pay for consciousness, for the interaction between object images and the image centre that my body is. But the drift goes further. Language does not only help us perceive, by structuring our perception, it also betrays movement and duration. So that the object of Deleuze's second volume is double. By going back to the prelinguistic origin of the interaction between images, he also aims at reversing a philosophical trend, at taking the cinema, as the expression of pure images, out of reach of language.

What is wrong with language, as far as the cinema is concerned, is that it tries to impose on films the order of narratives. Against this Deleuze defends a conception where a film is essentially *not* a narrative, where its narrative aspects (there is no denying that some films do tell stories) are only superficial effects. Superficial, because moving pictures deal with the prelinguistic matter to which language gives form: prelinguistic images (movements and thoughts), and 'pre-signifying signs' (points of view on those movements and thoughts). This is why the cinema is neither a language, be it universal or 'primitive', nor language in general. The essence of the cinema is something so pre-linguistic as to be entirely extra-linguistic – the primitive *significabile*, that out of which signification is obtained. As a result, the science of the cinema is not a branch of semiology, which deals with constituted signs, but of semiotics, which deals with the matter out of which signs are formed. There is no linguistics of the cinema. (Incidentally, this accounts for Deleuze's obvious nostalgia for silent movies, when films only moved and did not complicate matters by talking as well.)

The movement-image is no utterance. It is not susceptible of analysis in terms of paradigm and syntagma, metaphor and metonymy. And if there is a natural link between the cinema and the unconscious, as we have seen, it is indeed with a non-Freudian, and a non-linguistic, unconscious, the out of shot rather than the repressed signifier. The image is no utterance because the utterance forgets or denies movement, because it is the representation of an absent referent, whereas the movement-image is the object, or rather what Bergson calls a 'modulation' of the object.[10] In other words, where the utterance is digital, the movement-image is analogic. Deleuze's whole enterprise may be understood as a return, very much against the grain, to the analogic.

This is where a return to Bergson, who in such matters is hopelessly out of fashion, is vital. In Bergson, the preeminence of the image is coherent with the absence of a theory of language, or rather with a theory of language as absence. In *Matière et mémoire*, we do find a sketch of a theory of language, but only a sketch – not because Bergson has not sufficiently thought about it, but because the subject is obviously of secondary importance. The sketch is proposed when the question of recognition is broached.[11] How do we recognise what we hear as a sequence of words, that is, how do we associate those sounds with memories that are auditory images? It is clear that if we state the problem in such terms, the question of language, as an autonomous object, will not even arise. Words will be intermediary steps between the perceived image and the reactive idea. Their role will be to fill the interval, i.e. to delay recognition, and the main function of such delay will be to allow generalisation, to gather together a plurality of similar memories and to bring them to consciousness – a necessary replacement for the direct circuit between image and idea. We see that the passage from accepted necessity to accusations of betrayal is easy. In *Matière et mémoire*, one finds a curious conception of the superiority of verbs, which express action, in which a trace of movement is still preserved, over nouns, which sadly reify it.

Deleuze's books, therefore, do not attempt to legislate for a field of study which has no use for philosophy – they are an intervention in that field, on its own terms, an intervention which turns out to be of importance in the intellectual context. Deleuze is no film critic, but he is trying to replace what he sees as the dominant paradigm with another one. And this intervention in the field of film theory is also, of course, an intervention in philosophy, for it appears that, unwittingly or not (and in the case of the structuralist school, wittingly, if I may say so, with a vengeance), the cinema was already, had always already been, the object of a philosophical intervention. What Deleuze does is to turn tables. He makes the cinema his starting point in order to rid it of the unwelcome influence of a philosophy of language, but also to intervene in philosophy, to try and establish a bridgehead on the continent of philosophy for a theory of the image. The centrality of language has long been the dominant thesis in continental philosophy: Deleuze is arguing, after Bergson, for the centrality of the image. This involves serious consequences in the field of philosophy – it might, for instance, enable us at last to understand that curious phenomenon, interior language; it might also provide new insights for a theory of meaning, or of metaphor. And it involves consequences for the cinema. It is the cinema, rather than literature, that provides the wedge with which a dominant metaphysics, not of presence, but of language, is going to be toppled. At the end of the analysis, we discover that not only is there no serious difference between the cinema and the world, but also that there is no serious difference between the cinema and philosophy – they are inextricably mixed, philosophy is a film and the film is meta-philosophy.

Deleuze and postmodernism

I would like to conclude with a few tentative remarks on postmodernism. Deleuze is often associated with philosophers like Derrida and Foucault under the label 'poststructuralist', which is supposed to be the philosophical version of postmodernism. That Deleuze's position is excentric, and the differences with the other two more fundamental than the similarities, we have now realised. However, his theory of the movement-image has been called postmodernist. This seems to be the position of Kearney, who discusses Deleuze briefly in his book.[12]

I dislike periodisations – which is the modern, and which the postmodern period? – and I am wary (and weary) of facile totalisation. If you insist, I shall end up confessing that I haven't the faintest idea what postmodernism is about – a typical postmodernist attitude, of course. Yet I have a feeling that Deleuze's theory of the cinema is less postmodernist than it seems.

If postmodernism is defined as involving the preeminence of discourse, or text, over reality, then Deleuze's theory of the cinema will appear as a return to reality outside language, in the form of the image. Bergson's image, contrary to Sartre's, is not nothing, but the object itself. By this move, Deleuze may be seen to substitute a grand narrative of the image for the dominant grand narrative of language and discourse, which is the specific grand narrative of postmodernism.

But this contradictory subversion of postmodernism, which involves the accusation that postmodernism too constructs a grand narrative, like its predecessors, and that this grand narrative turns out to be the wrong one, is itself a postmodernist stance. After all, the visual arts provide much more convincing instances of postmodernism than literature, in spite of Linda Hutcheon's attempt to invent the genre of historiography metafiction.[13] Deleuze is part of a general movement of substitution of the image for language as the dominant medium, which deeply affects the medium in question. As Kearney points out, there are elements of an analysis of the crisis of the image in the first book, when Deleuze evokes the emergence of a reflexive image out of the ruin of the classic action-image of Hollywood films. I am not, however, entirely convinced by this – I suspect that Deleuze's defence of the cinema is pre-postmodern, expressing deep nostalgia for the images of our childhood, in a world where the dominant form of the image is no longer to be found on the big screen, and where the cinema as a form of art is struggling to survive. Perhaps this is the main contribution philosophy can make to the cinema (and there lies the grandeur of Deleuze's attempt): to help it survive. I am told that, as a species, the grey whale has now been saved.

Notes

1. G. Deleuze, *L'Image-mouvement*, Paris, Minuit, 1983; *L'Image-temps*, Paris, Minuit, 1985; translated as *Cinema 1: The Movement-Image* and *Cinema 2: The Time-Image*, Athlone Press, London, 1989, 1989.
2. F. O'Brien, *The Third Policeman*, London, Granada, 1983, p. 50.
3. G. Deleuze, *L'Image-temps*, *op. cit.*, p. 143.
4. G. Deleuze, *Le Bergsonisme*, Paris, PUF, 1968.
5. R. Kearney, *The Wake of Imagination*, London, Hutchinson, 1988.
6. G. Ryle, *The Concept of Mind*, Harmondsworth, Penguin, 1963.
7. H. Bergson, *Matière et mémoire*, Paris, PUF, 1939, p. 159; 5th French edition (1908) translated as *Matter and Memory*, Allen and Unwin, London, 1911.
8. *Ibid.*, p. 115.
9. G. Deleuze, *L'Image-mouvement*, *op. cit.*, p. 88.
10. G. Deleuze, *L'Image-temps*, *op. cit.*, p. 41.
11. H. Bergson, *Matière et mémoire*, *op. cit.*, pp. 120–40.
12. R. Kearney, *op. cit.*, pp. 329–32.
13. L. Hutcheon, *The Poetics of Postmodernism*, London, Routledge, 1988, Chapter 7.

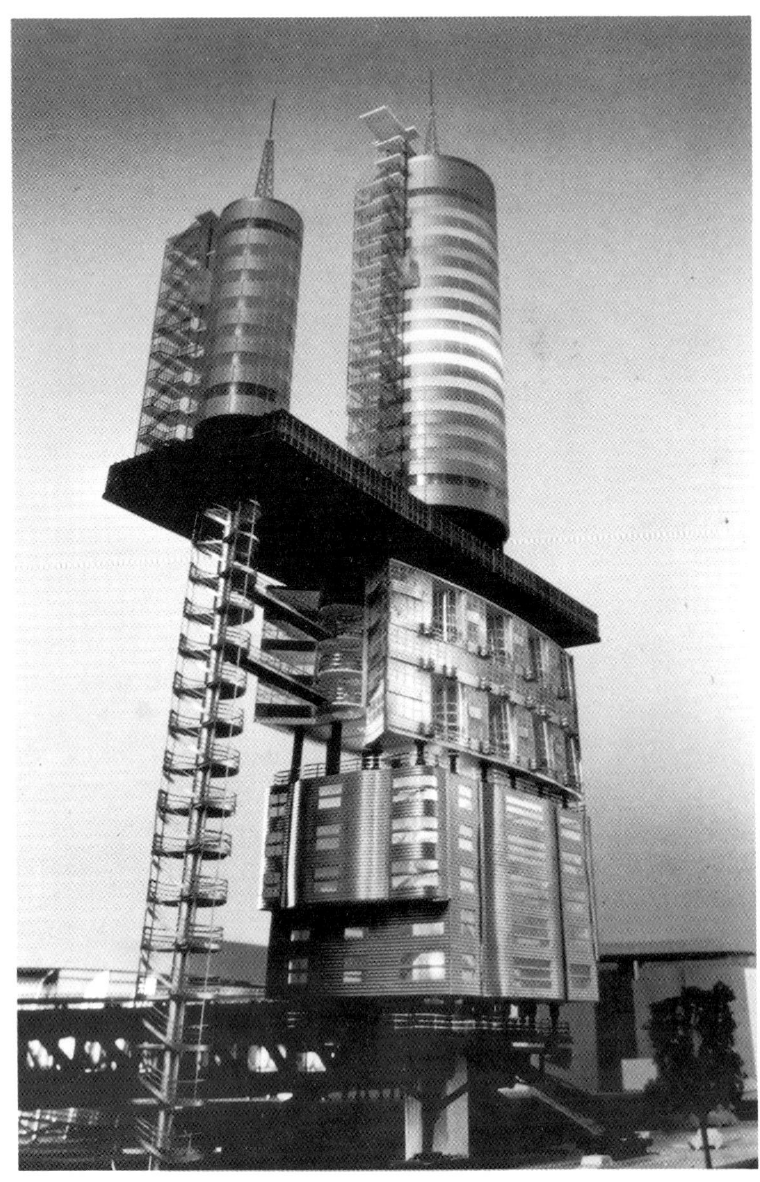

Massimiliano Fuksas. *Hérouville-Saint-Clair* project. (Courtesy of the architect)

Sewing Machine: Building Monumentally

Sylviane Agacinski

As a pretext and only as a pretext, let's take the Hérouville-Saint-Clair project. What can it teach us about art and about the town? I should say straight away that I will neither congratulate nor condemn the project, I leave that judgement to time and the town itself. Instead, I intend to let the project direct me to a set of reflections. These will stray far from the initial pretext and they will introduce a series of themes: astonishment, amazement, memory and forgetting, proper names, technics, matter and what I call the *more than one*. First of all, a comment on the tower's looks. I have to say, when I first set eyes on a photograph of the Hérouville-Saint-Clair project I was rather put out. After a while, the tower, with its columns shaped like reels placed on a plate with a further body of the building beneath it, reminded me of the outline of a modernised and modified old-fashioned sewing machine. Maybe I should say, here, that I like sewing machines, especially old ones, although I do not know how to use one. However, there it is: a sewing machine. To be truthful, this vague resemblance did not come to me immediately. The outlandish character of the model, its totally novel look, made me seek for another shape to which it could be compared, even if this meant pushing things a bit by making approximative comparisons. I do not wish, therefore, to insist on the image of the sewing machine, it is not obvious to all spectators and not even now to myself. I am fully aware of having *sought* for a resemblance and, as you well know, when one looks one finds: this is called *casting*.

Still, this fortuitous meeting of a building and a sewing machine is my starting point. The, albeit trivial, hypothesis that the urban space comes out of needlework is a quite natural one. What is more, when we speak of the urban fabric, we are not only using a simple metaphor, rather, this is a particular metaphor. There is no better word than fabric for the strange urban tissue, more or less closely woven, more or less torn, diversely sewn, cut and patched up. All the metaphor lacks is the notion of relief, the high points and low points, the excavations, the underground and the elevated, tall edifices.

Anyway, notwithstanding the tower's look, it is not absurd to call it a 'sewing machine' given its role as an architectural supplement to the quarters of Hérouville-Saint-Clair. It must be a machine which articulates these quarters into a town. The divided body, made up of independent limbs, requires nothing if not a sewing machine. One of the functions of this machine is distinct from all the others, whether they concern housing, the hotel, offices, shops, etc... And indeed, I am only interested in this separate one: the edifice's symbolic function dependent upon its monumental aspect. By this, I mean its outsized appearance; its slightly monstrous presence. It seems that the architects have quite deliberately avoided discretion and have constructed a grand signifier.

One of the questions, then, that I have to ask is the following: if we disregard any strictly religious aims and all values of remembrance and commemoration, how can such a monumental edifice (it is after all a mega-structure not immediately designed to seduce us) act as a connector? Obviously, it is not celebrating anything, be that a god, a man, a memorable event, and neither is its aim to celebrate anything. And yet, in my opinion, there is a value missing among those that Reigl assigns to monuments (the values of art, use and remembrance, historical and ancient values). I would call this missing element a value or effect of amazement, a value which has little to do with beauty. In a strict sense a monument is supposed to remind us of something, it is dedicated to the memory *of something*, it makes us think *back to something*. Generally, we believe that the essential functions of monuments can be determined in the light of remembrance. However, we rarely see things in reverse, we do not question memory itself from the point of view of the monumental. Do not ask: What does this monument commemorate? Ask: What does the monument teach us about memory? In answer to this, I would claim that the monument tells us that memory is a giving gesture and not a preserving gesture. Memory is something that gives, that we give, in which we give ourselves, and we make traces that will stay. It is a way of bringing together a remainder, the fate of which must be unpredictable and cannot be programmed. By this, I mean the monument puts into place a memory which always gives more than it preserves. The monument is less a memory of something than a thing to be remembered, a memory of itself (in French we say that something '*fait date*'). The edifice goes beyond the event it celebrates, it infinitely exceeds any link back to that initial event and it becomes an event in itself. So, ultimately, the edifice takes on the value of event. The pretext-event cannot be all that it is without this later event that celebrates it and renders it illustrious.

The paradox within the edifice's amazing, impressive, surprising, even provocative aspects is: what was first conceived as a supplementary brilliance then overthrows the thing it was meant to supplement. A supplementary brilliance given to something (an event, a place, a person, etc.) is seen to topple and evict it. There is no more eloquent example of this than the Eiffel tower. Granted, it has little to do with Hérouville-Saint-Clair, but here I'm interested only in a given effect, a given value. It makes no difference that we know the tower was meant to *render illustrious* the universal exhibition of 1889: it was meant to *commemorate* the centenary of the revolution, *elevate* the nation as high as possible with the industrial power to make such a thing. Despite this knowledge, the Eiffel tower has literally wiped out everything it celebrates – even Gustave Eiffel. Here the edifice seems to have points in common with proper names, with their function and nature. First of all, the tower ensures the fame of its builder and of those who commissioned it, etc. A bit like writing, the edifice survives all of these men, like their names. Thus we recall the words of the builders of Babel: 'Let us build a tower and make a name for ourselves.' The name's everlastingness and permanence are tributaries of the same qualities in the work, but we have to ask whether, like the name, the work wipes out the name's holder. The work supplants even the person it renders illustrious because, for example, the name belongs more to the work than to the author. Maybe even Gustave Eiffel was dispossessed of his name when he gave it to the tower. As proof, take the remark of this filing clerk who, while looking for photos of the tower and probably a bit distracted, asked me point blank: 'Come to think of it, who was the architect of the Eiffel Tower?' However, we would be wrong to laugh at the lady's ignorance or distractedness. Eiffel's name is henceforth the name of the tower and it is the engineer's fate to be wiped out by his name and his work. In addition, Roland Barthes says of the tower, and I quote, it was 'the modern gesture whereby the present said no to the past'. For Barthes, the tower 'subjugated old symbols in the same way as it dominated their cupolas and needles'. The tower's destiny is a lesson to all conservatives and apologists for the past – like the signatories of the artists' protest against the construction of the tower. They are all well known: Gounod, Garmier, Maupassant, Dumas the younger, the Comte de l'Isle, Sully Prud'homme and others. At least, there would be a lesson, if it was possible to learn how to recognise art and especially town art, the art that remains the most obscure and mysterious of all. What is interesting is that the artists protested qua artists, in the name of art and taste, *French* taste, and in the name of the beauty of Paris on the verge of desecration. They said: Are we going to let all this be desecrated? Their protest was not simply called 'The Artists' Protest', a protest signed by artists; art incarnate is supposed to be speaking. Therefore, of importance here is that those eminent men thought they were able to speak with an authority invested in them through their works and their notoriety. The letter was much more than a petition, it was art's protest, art's indignation and defence. What was it indignant about? I quote: 'How much longer is the town of Paris going to dishonour and uglify itself irreparably by association with the baroque and mercantilist imaginations of a machine builder?' The voice of art is raised against ugliness, the modern ugliness of the tower, that is, of course, the technics that will disfigure the beautiful face of Paris and humiliate Notre-Dame and the Arc de Triomphe. (By way of parenthesis, I wonder whether it is easy to judge Notre-Dame and the Arc de Triomphe according to the same test. It's far from sure, but at least for the authors it was one and the same thing.) What was absolutely certain then was that the tower is ugly, vertiginously ridiculous, a barbaric mass, a factory's black and gigantic chimney (again the artists damn industry), an ink stain, an odious column of metal sheets. The tower is of almost obsessing ugliness. When François Coppée says (while on the Eiffel Tower's second level), 'Your obsession is pursuing me' with 'the colossal colours of night', he is unaware that he is in some sense eulogising its power while damning it. Those scandalised poets do not notice that in writing to vilify the 'ridiculous mast', they are also singing its praises and in basically the same way as Centrars, Apollinaire or Aragon, those who loved the Tower. This is like the work of the paradoxographs in the Hellenistic epoch, that is, writers who described prodigies. These prodigies, the wonders of the world, made them write. And one of the effects of the tower as great architectural paradox, and perhaps the effect of all astounding edifices, is to make us write. The effect exceeds the writer to the point of forcing him to write *around*, *on* or *about* the edifice. Maybe, here, there is a possible criterion of architecture in seeing how or what it makes us write. But, there again, on the topic of the protest's signatories, let us not laugh too soon at the expense of those who laugh. It is no doubt as easy to do justice to the tower today as it was difficult to like and judge the project yesterday. Was it beautiful? Is it beautiful today? Is it a work of art? In my opinion, these are not the right questions. The artists of the past, those who called themselves artists, did not ask any other questions than these. What is more, they also judged the work through its author, not an architect but an engineer and (shamefully) a builder of machines! Fine-arts, as they wanted to say, have nothing to do with bolts and factory chimneys. So artists, real artists, undo those bolts in the name of nobility. Eiffel is industry, technics, the technics of bridges and viaducts; this precise man cannot fail to be irritated, quite justly, by the disdainful tone adopted by those great, and less great, artists when they talk of bolted steel.

What is at stake here is not, as the artists claim, a conflict opposing the beautiful and the ugly, it is a conflict opposing two possible aesthetics: an aesthetic of representation, that is of pure form, of expressive form; and an aesthetic (if we have to keep this word) that implies putting matter to the test. Classical aesthetics, the aesthetics of representation, are always limited by two constraints: on the one hand, the distinction of the beautiful and the useful, which leads to the disjunction of the functional and the 'soulful' ('*supplément d'âme*'), and on the other hand, the bracketing off of materiality, of the ground, and of matter in general. But when did we decide that technics, in its widest sense, must be *essentially* and *solely* useful, that it must answer and correspond to needs? In what is the invention of a technical dispostive more enslaved to necessity than the so-called, supposedly free, artistic expression? Technical performance is not dependent upon a vital necessity or a bellicose instinct (Spengler). In all technics there is always a play with the possibilities of matter. It seems to me that the question for technics and technician (in the widest sense) could be the following: What is matter capable of?

Therefore, in its widest sense, technics would be a way of experimenting with the possibilities of matter. This is of course very dangerous, but an artist is not someone who produces according to established rules, the artist is an *experimenter*. This is true of the poet, the writer and the architect, who experiments on himself as much as on his foundations or materials. For example, the architect asks what architecture can do, the painter asks what paint can do, or even, what painting is; these are not people assured of the answers to these questions. Thus, the Eiffel Tower is a machine for resisting and defying wind. Georges Simondon spoke of this kind of beauty in his book *Du mode d'existence des objets techniques*. In line with this other aesthetic we must take account of the gesture that works with matter, with what painting calls the resistance of the subjectile; this seems fundamental to me.

Finally, a word on sewing and the four-fold collaboration involved in the Hérouville-Saint-Clair project. When four architects build together (Fuksas, Alsop, Steidle, Nouvel) each one must test his project on those of the others, each architect must build *with* the others, collaborate with them. For too long we have thought, in philosophy and politics, as in art, that the work of one man was worth more than the work of many. Recall this quote from

Descartes' *Discourse on Method*: 'The buildings built by a man alone are worth more than those built by many men,' 'ancient cities, that have evolved through time to become what they are today, are less well drawn than those regular places traced according to an engineer's fantasy in a plain.' But a plain where an engineer *traces according to his fancy* is equivalent to the architect's and the town-planner's blank sheet of paper: they are pure myths, pure illusions, extremely dangerous illusions through which all that already stands can be razed to the ground, which is also to erase the past. In our century, certain régimes tried to do just that when they attempted absolute reinvention and reconstruction, right up to trying to reinvent a fictional history.

When we work with more than one person, there is already a need for patching up, darning and sewing. There is a need for an interminable joining up. When a work is done by more than one artist, then there is no work capable of gathering itself up into a whole and, in this sense, the town always 'undoes' architecture, that is, it stops it from becoming work. So long as what has to be built must encroach on what is already there, the town will infinitely undo architecture. Therefore, the presence of something, and not only the town but also matter, a community, a relief, vegetation, the sky, the earth, forces the architect into encroaching, into taking pieces off and adding new ones, never making anything from one piece of cloth and in one go. To do this, time is needed, and one person's work is insufficient.

Maybe this is also true in philosophy, as Bergson said in 1911: 'Philosophy will no longer be a construction, the systematic work of a single thinker. It will evolve, it will ceaselessly demand additions, corrections, alterations... Philosophy, too, will be written in collaboration.' Thereby, the authority of unique principles and of solitary thinkers is brought into question. In ceasing to pretend to dominate and transcend the urban fabric or the philosophical text, architects and philosophers will have to remake endlessly the experience of writing.

(translated by James Williams)

Notes on Contributors

Sylviane Agacinski is associated with the College International de Philosophie. She is author of *Aparté: Conceptions of Deaths in Soren Kierkegaard* (Florida State University Press). She is currently preparing a book on Philosophy and Architecture.

David Batchelor is an artist and freelance writer on contemporary and twentieth-century art.

Christine Battersby is Lecturer in Philosophy at the University of Warwick. She is the author of *Gender and Genius: Towards a Feminist Aesthetic* (Women's Press). She has also published articles on the history of philosophy and feminist philosophy.

Andrew Benjamin teaches at the University of Warwick. He is editor of the *Journal of Philosophy and the Visual Arts*, and author of *Translation and the Nature of Philosophy*, and *Art, Mimesis and the Avant-Garde* (both Routledge).

Georgina Born is an anthropologist and a musician, and Lecturer in Communication and Media at Goldsmiths College, University of London. Previous work as a musician included playing for composers Mike Westbrook and Lindsay Cooper, and in the groups Henry Cow, the Feminist Improvising Group, The Flying Lizards, and the Michael Nyman Band. Her study of IRCAM will be published by Routledge in 1992.

Christa Bürger is Professor of German Literature at the University of Frankfurt. Her publications include *Tradition und Subjectivität* and *Textanalyse als Ideologiekritik* (2 vols.).

Peter Bürger is Professor of French and Comparative Literature at the University of Bremen. His publications include *Theory of the Avant-Garde* (Manchester University Press) and *Prosa der Moderne* (Frankfurt).

Howard Caygill is Lecturer in Social Studies at the University of East Anglia. He is the author of *Art of Judgement* (Blackwell).

Margaret Iversen lectures in the Department of Art History and Theory at the University of Essex. She has published articles on feminism, psychoanalysis, and contemporary art practice and on theories of the visual sign. Her book on the art historian Alois Reigl is forthcoming.

Sandra Kemp is Lecturer in English at Glasgow University. She is the author of *Kipling's Hidden Narratives*. She also reviews literary criticism, children's books and dance for a variety of publications, and is a 'Shelf Life' columnist for the *Times Higher Education Supplement*. She trained previously in both ballet and in Graham technique.

Jean-Jacques Lecercle is Professor of English at the University of Paris, Nanterre. He is the author of *Philosophy Through the Looking-Glass* (Hutchinson), *Frankenstein: mythe et philosophie* (PUF) and *The Violence of Language* (Routledge).

Michael Newman is an art critic and teaches philosophy part time at the University of Essex, where he is working on a study of Nietzsche and Benjamin. He has curated a number of exhibitions, including *The Mirror and the Lamp* at the Fruitmarket Gallery, Edinburgh and the ICA, London, 1986. His publications include contributions to *Postmodernism*, ICA Documents 4 & 5, ed. Lisa Appignanesi (Free Association Books); *Nietzsche and Modern German Thought*, ed. Keith Ansell-Pearson (Routledge); and *Interpreting Contemporary Art*, ed. William Allen and Stephen Bann (Reaktion Books).

Peter Osborne teaches philosophy at Middlesex Polytechnic. He is the editor of *Socialism and the Limits of Liberalism* (Verso) and, with Sean Sayers, *Socialism, Feminism and Philosophy: A Radical Philosophy Reader* (Routledge), and author of a number of articles on Adorno's aesthetic and cultural theory. He is an editor of the journal *Radical Philosophy*.

Alastair Williams has worked as an orchestral musician and now teaches music at Keele University. He is pursuing research on contemporary music and cultural theory.

Index